Outposts of the Faith

Michael Yelton is the author of *Anglican Papalism: An Illustrated History 1900–1960* (Canterbury Press, 2005), *Alfred Hope Patten and the Shrine of Our Lady of Walsingham* (Canterbury Press, 2006), and, with Rodney Warrener, of a biography of Martin Travers, the leading twentieth-century ecclesiastical artist. He has written extensively on ecclesiological and architectural subjects and on transport history.

He is a County Court Judge and lives in Cambridge.

Also by the same author and available from Canterbury Press

Anglican Papalism: An Illustrated History 1900–1960
'Here is a wealth of material which deserves further detailed exploration.'
New Directions

Alfred Hope Patten and the Shrine of Our Lady of Walsingham

Outposts of the Faith

Anglo-Catholicism in
Some Rural Parishes

Michael Yelton

CANTERBURY
PRESS
Norwich

First published in 2009 by the Canterbury Press Norwich
Editorial office
13–17 Long Lane,
London, EC1A 9PN, UK

Canterbury Press is an imprint of Hymns Ancient and Modern Ltd
(a registered charity)
St Mary's Works, St Mary's Plain,
Norwich, NR3 3BH, UK

www.scm-canterburypress.co.uk

British Library Cataloguing in Publication data

A catalogue record for this book is available
from the British Library

ISBN 978 1 85311 985 9

Typeset by Regent Typesetting, London
Printed and bound in Great Britain by
CPI Antony Rowe, Chippenham SN14 6LH

Contents

Acknowledgements

A book such as this cannot be written without the assistance of many others who are prepared to answer often obscure questions and to allow the author to forage for material. I am deeply grateful to all those who have helped me, although of course all the opinions expressed are my own. A particular mention is, however, due in relation to some people.

For Chapter 1, Michael Paget, the editor of the Throwleigh Archive's model book on the village not only allowed me to use information from the book but provided further documentation and answered questions: he and his late wife Sarah generously entertained me when I went to the village.

For Chapter 2, I am most grateful to the staff of the Devon Record Office at Exeter who keep the Kingdon diaries and other documents relating to the family.

For Chapter 3, I am particularly indebted to Michael Farrer, the former Secretary of the Anglo-Catholic History Society and a mine of knowledge in relation to Athelstan Riley, and to Noel Owen, Riley's granddaughter, for much help with family affairs.

For Chapter 5, I am very grateful to Father Luke Irvine-Capel, the former rector of Cranford, who shortly before he left the parish assisted me with further information and allowed me to see Father Child's own collection of press cuttings and the parish magazines of the time. I am also grateful to St Mary, Bourne Street, for providing a copy of the long obituary of Father Child by Canon Hood from the Parish Quarterly of the time.

For Chapter 7, I was able to interview Rose Dunn, a great devotee of

Father Beresford still living in the village and my thanks are also due to Viv Booty of Peterborough County Court for her help with regard to Newborough. Father P. Etchells assisted with his own reminiscences of Father Beresford, and Father Philip Gray, a great source of knowledge on all recent Anglo-Catholic history, had clear recollections of his own visits to Newborough in the 1960s. Canon Frank Pickard, Father Beresford's successor, was also a great source of information and he and his wife again kindly offered me hospitality while I listened to his reminiscences.

I could not have written Chapter 8 without help from Brian Payne, the biographer of Canon Mowbray Smith, who knows the area around Wisbech St Mary intimately. I am also grateful to Kate Perry, the archivist of Girton College, Cambridge, for giving me access to the Aelfrida Tillyard papers.

Chapter 10 benefited much from the input of Father Gray (again) and I thank him and his wife Anne for their welcome and hospitality; the Revd Canon Dr Brian Findlay, the present rector of Kettlebaston, was also helpful as ever with his time and information. Any writer on Suffolk churches is always grateful for the work of Roy Tricker.

I am also grateful to all the members of the Anglo-Catholic History Society for their encouragement and to SCM-Canterbury Press for showing that even in these difficult times there remains a market for work describing the impact of the Oxford Movement over the years.

Last but certainly not least, I thank my tolerant wife Judith for putting up with the production of yet another book.

Preface

The intention behind this book is to set out the effect of Anglo-Catholicism on a number of rural parishes and to combine with that information about a number of the personalities involved, some of whom, such as Athelstan Riley, Samuel Gurney, and Father Maurice Child, were well known in their time but have been allowed to fall somewhat out of view. Others are less well known, such as Father Leslie Drew and Father Clive Beresford, or scarcely known at all, such as Father Charles Roe of Buxted. There are connections between a number of the parishes and people who are mentioned, which is inevitable bearing in mind the relatively constricted circles in which Anglo-Catholics operated.

It has not on the other hand been my intention to write a history of Anglo-Catholicism in country churches: to do so would have necessitated mention of many more places, some of which, such as Thaxted in Essex and St Hilary in Cornwall, have already been extensively discussed.

Nor has it been my intention to draw profound, or indeed any, conclusions from what is an unrepresentative selection of parishes. I am aware that the places discussed show, for various reasons relating to my own knowledge and interest, a bias towards the West and the East of England and that there is no study of any parish in the North.

I leave it therefore to the reader to draw such conclusions as he or she may from what is set out, and perhaps to reflect on the effort which was put in by some for little lasting result.

Michael Yelton
Feast of St Silvester
31 December 2008

1

St Mary and the Holy Spirit, Throwleigh, Devon, and Fathers Lowe and Drew

The small village of Throwleigh (properly pronounced as if the 'ow' were a cry of pain) in West Devon, on the edge of Dartmoor, has particular interest for the historian of Anglo-Catholicism, because it had a long period in which two successive incumbents attempted to lead the villagers into a way of worshipping which was unlike most other local parishes, and certainly in the case of the second of those priests, was out on a limb so far as most of the Church of England was concerned.

Throwleigh is also unusual in that this period has been very well documented. In about 1911 two maiden ladies, Emma ('Emmie') Varwell (1867–1952) and her younger sister Elizabeth, who for some reason adopted the forename of Michael (1873–1973: she died a few weeks before her hundredth birthday), came to Throwleigh from Brixham in South Devon, where they had been born. In the 1930s Emmie Varwell carried out early researches by way of what is now called oral history, interviewing local residents, many of whose families had lived in the village for many generations, and who were nearly all involved in agriculture, the practice of which had changed less in this remote corner of England than in most other places. The result of these investigations was the publication in 1938 of a well-received volume entitled *Throwleigh: The Story of a Dartmoor Village.*

Miss Varwell was, however, also a devotee of the Revd G.L. Gambier

Lowe, rector of the village from 1895 until his death in 1933, and of his successor, the Revd H. Leslie Drew, who succeeded Father Lowe in 1934 and was to resign in 1969. Her book contains a great deal of information about Father Lowe's incumbency and a considerable amount about the commencement of Father Drew's time in the village which would otherwise have been unrecorded.

In 1943 further light was cast on ecclesiastical events in the village when it was the subject of a short article in the *Fiery Cross* magazine written by Horace Keast. Horace Edwin Keast (1908–92) was a senior officer with Cornwall County Council who wrote a number of pamphlets on Anglo-Catholicism locally and also contributed to the Church Union inserts which produced the article on Throwleigh.

More recently, the Local Heritage Initiative has assisted in the funding of a most informative collection of material known as the Throwleigh Archive, the members of which published in 2006 a well-illustrated book, *Throwleigh: Pictures and Memories from a Dartmoor Parish*,[1] which contains many pictures and reminiscences of the two priests concerned, some of which, in the case of Father Drew, were less than complimentary. That book in particular has been most helpful in illuminating developments in the village and much of the information below comes from that source.

In the late nineteenth century, when Father Lowe came to the parish, Throwleigh, which was spread over a considerable area at the base of the moor, had a population of fewer than 300, and only a small percentage of those lived in the centre of the village, around the church. Most of the dwellings in the parish were either farmhouses or small farm cottages and were scattered about with narrow lanes joining them. The most substantial of these farmhouses was Throwleigh Barton, a rare survival of a sixteenth-century house in vernacular style. In effect, the village consisted of a number of hamlets, only one of which was around the church and others of which were nearer the adjoining parish church of Gidleigh: some parts were near to the larger village of Chagford. The hamlet of

---

1 M. Paget, ed., published by the Archive, 2006. Information from that source has not been separately noted save where direct quotations are taken, but is much appreciated.

Murchington had its own chapel of ease, which had been completed in 1890.

The village also had a Nonconformist meeting house, the Bible Christian Chapel, in the hamlet of Providence, dating from about 1839. The Bible Christians were a West Country sect who had splintered from the Methodists in 1815 but in 1907 rejoined them.

George Lincoln Gambier Lowe (1865–1933) was not only the rector of the parish for almost 40 years, but was also, and most unusually, responsible for much of the expansion of the housing stock which took place over that period. Thus his mark on the village was not only in ecclesiastical matters, but in far wider spheres and he is the dominant figure in the recent history of Throwleigh.

Gambier Lowe, as he was usually known, was born in 1865 in Herringfleet (St Olaves), near Lowestoft, just in Suffolk but very near the Norfolk border. His father was Edward Jackson Lowe (1825–93) who was himself ordained and was serving in that parish at the time: his mother was Mary Lowe (née Wainright) (1841–80).

Edward Jackson Lowe was born in Gloucester, took his degree at St Edmund Hall, Oxford, in 1852 and was ordained priest the following year. He held a number of curacies in London, East Anglia and then Buckinghamshire before in 1873 being appointed as parish priest of Great Gonerby in Lincolnshire and then in 1880 moving to Stallingborough in the same county, where he died in office. It would appear that his own churchmanship was Evangelical, and indeed one of his curacies was at St Bartholomew, New North Road, in Islington, an area which then as now had a strong Protestant tradition. However, his wife Mary was the older sister of the saintly Revd Lincoln Stanhope Wainright (1847–1929), for many years parish priest of St Peter, London Docks: he was thus Father Gambier Lowe's uncle and the latter took his second forename from him. One of Father Lowe's brothers was called Wainright Edward Lowe, again preserving the connection by name.

Edward Jackson Lowe had a number of children by his wife Mary, whom he had married in 1860 when she was very young. The year after her death in 1880 he remarried Elizabeth Sutcliffe, who was nearly 30 years younger than him, and fathered more children by her when he was already in his sixties. Another of his sons, Willoughby Prescott Lowe, who was about seven years younger than Gambier, was also to play a considerable part in life at Throwleigh in years to come.

It certainly appears that, whatever the views of his father, Gambier Lowe embraced wholeheartedly the ideals of the Oxford Movement. As with many of his generation, those ideals were displayed to the outside world in the form of vestments, lights and the like which were not commonly used among the early Tractarians. A consistent pattern can be seen among those born between 1860 and 1880, who were then ordained between 1885 and 1905, of ritual and other advances. In Gambier Lowe's case he had the example of his uncle before him to act as an exemplar.

Gambier Lowe attended Grantham Grammar School. He was certainly a boarder there at the time of the 1881 census, but he may have remained at the school after his mother's death and his father's move from nearby Great Gonerby, both of which occurred in the previous year. He then proceeded, not to Oxford as had his father, but to Sidney Sussex College, Cambridge, which despite its Cromwellian associations was by then associated with the Catholic Movement in the Church of England, and took his degree in 1886. He was ordained in the Diocese of Worcester as a deacon in 1889 and as a priest the following year and served his first curacy at St Edmund, Dudley. In 1891 he moved to be curate of Powderham, South Devon, and combined this for the first two years with the chaplaincy of a local mental asylum.[2]

On 17 June 1890 at the Church of St Maddern, Madron, near Penzance in Cornwall, Father Lowe married Eleanor Trelawny, who was born in about 1857 and was thus some years older than him. She came from a large Cornish family, although her own place of birth was in County Donegal. She became profoundly deaf at the age of about 12 after a bout of scarlet fever, and so had to teach herself to lip read, which she did with considerable facility. However, she retained the style of pronunciation commonplace in the 1860s, which made her appear to later generations as older than she actually was.

---

2 Powderham was the seat of the Earls of Devon, but the Chairman of the English Church Union, Lord Halifax, had a house nearby, through his connections by marriage with the Earls of Devon, and he may have influenced the churchmanship.

Gambier and Eleanor had four daughters and one son, all of whom received their mother's maiden surname as one of their Christian names: the son was actually known as Trelawny. The children in order were Mary Eleanor Trelawny Lowe, born in 1891, Edward Gambier Trelawny Lowe, born in1894, Patience Monica Trelawny Lowe, born in 1896, the splendidly named Florence Faith Loetitia Trelawny Lowe (known as Faith), born in 1898, and Cicely Juliana Trelawny Lowe, born in 1900. The youngest three were born after the family moved to Throwleigh, so the parishioners had from the start a picture of the new priest as a family man.

The place of the church in the life of the village before Gambier Lowe's appearance is not entirely clear. Emmie Varwell, with the overt partisanship often displayed by those who have adopted the cause of the Catholic Movement in the Church of England, particularly those who like her have taken it up in middle age,[3] said that when Father Lowe arrived in 1895 he 'of course found things very elementary indeed'.

She continued, however:

> In a comparatively short time the change he effected in the services and in the beautifying of the church was wonderful. From the first he went forward on a straight course: his path was not always easy and only those who knew him well were able to realise what his ministry meant to himself and to others.[4]

She also wrote of Gambier Lowe, with an element of hero worship:

> he kept the ideal of that great man [i.e. Lincoln Stanhope Wainright] always before him. Indeed, Father Wainwright (sic) may be said to have been the inspiration that began to lift Throwleigh into the wonderful atmosphere of the present day. To his nephew descended the spirit which makes nothing of favour or disfavour. No one appreciated more keenly the kindness and the good opinion of friends, but equally nothing could move him when he believed himself to be doing what was right; he was a brave man.[5]

---

3 The sisters were baptized only in 1913.

4 E. Varwell, *Throwleigh: The Story of a Dartmoor Village* (Sydney Lee Ltd, Exeter, 1938), p. 18.

5 Varwell, *Throwleigh*, p. 18.

The church at Throwleigh is all granite and ashlar in the local fashion in the perpendicular style, with a three-stage tower and a remarkably ornate priest's doorway on the south of the chancel, next to which is an octagonal turret of the rood loft stairs. The interior has wagon roofs to the chancel and to the only aisle, to its north. A rood screen had been erected as late as 1544, which perhaps indicates the religious conservatism of the region, but had subsequently been removed. It would appear, however, that it had not been neglected by the previous rectors, as there had been restorations, all described by the editors of *Pevsner's Buildings of England* as 'discreet' in 1859–60, 1884 and 1890.[6]

Gambier Lowe's incumbency had been preceded by those of two priests who had stayed only for a few years each, but earlier in the century the Revd Samuel H. Archer had been rector from 1852 for some 30 years. Certainly it appears that some work had taken place in 1884, immediately after his death, as a new altar was installed at that time, during the incumbency of the Revd John W. Hanson.

The parish priests of Throwleigh had been somewhat itinerant over the years. When Father Lowe and his family arrived, there was an Old Rectory, which was let out privately. Parson Archer, as he was known, had had built on the glebe land a very substantial property with extensive gardens for his own use, and certainly one of his successors, the Revd Edward C. Spicer (1889–95), also lived there. Another rector of Throwleigh, the Revd John Baddeley, who held the incumbency from 1745 to 1787, had purchased a fifteenth-century house called Wooda, quite near to the church, but it had burned down in about 1880.

Soon after Father Lowe's arrival in Throwleigh there were a number of significant changes which were to mark the course of his ministry in the village.

The first was the acquisition of the advowson, previously held by the Lord Chancellor, by Edmund Sutton QC (after 1901 KC) (1845–1922), who had first practised in Lancashire but then acquired property in the village, known as St Olave's, at Murchington, a hamlet within the parish,

---

6 See B. Cherry and N. Pevsner, *The Buildings of England: Devon* (Yale, 2002), p. 804.

which he used as a retreat from work after he moved his professional base to London. He was sympathetic to Father Lowe and after his death the right of patronage passed to his widow and then in turn to his son Ralph Sutton QC (1881–1960), who was the Editor of the Law Reports from 1941 to 1953 and was made an honorary silk because of that.

The second was the purchase by a Mrs Charlotte Aikenhead, a widowed and childless aunt of Father Lowe's on the paternal side, of the glebe land, including the two rectories, which she then gave to him, followed by the purchase by the rector himself of the site of the old Wooda house and then of the fields around it.

The third important change in the village was that the substantial house constructed by Archer was sold, together with some of the glebe land, to Dr J.C.S. Rashleigh, who lived there from about 1902 or 1903. He initially converted it into a sanatorium for tubercular patients but that lasted only until 1907: the house was then called Rashleighs (it is now Throwleigh House). Dr Rashleigh's main family house was at Menabilly near Fowey and formed the basis for Daphne du Maurier's 'Manderley' in *Rebecca*: she leased the property from him for many years.

Father Lowe lived in Parson Archer's house for a time, but upon its sale the Church Commissioners had built for him the so-called New Rectory, a substantial, long house, originally thatched, in Shilstone Lane, at the corner of the lane to Wooda, which is now out of ecclesiastical use, has been extended, and is known as Summerhayes. Shilstone Lane, which was to be of considerable significance in the ecclesiastical history of the next 60 years, was a narrow way which led up steeply from the centre of the village.

Having moved in to the New Rectory, Father Lowe decided he did not like the house and in about 1911 built himself a new house at Hollow Park, next to Wooda, where he and the family lived. He then developed the garden with ponds and trees and in about 1924 bought further land beyond it, ironically to prevent development on it. The New Rectory was let out in its turn.

The building of Hollow Park was only one of Father Lowe's building activities, which centred on Shilstone Lane. The fact that it was the parish priest who was almost entirely responsible for the expansion of the village over the next years is rightly the subject of a comment in the recent

Throwleigh Conservation Area Appraisal[7] that it was 'a highly unusual turn of events'.

Father Lowe, aided to some extent by his brother Willoughby, who in 1901 purchased a substantial portion of land off Shilstone Lane on his own account, carried out a form of ribbon development along the lane, which resulted in the construction of a number of houses of different sizes, mostly in a somewhat Arts and Crafts style. One of the first, The Hey, a substantial property, was built largely with the stones from the burned-out Wooda house, a course which Father Lowe later regretted. He also had renovated the Church House, a building near the church, with a new roof and a comfortable first-floor flat, rebuilt the Old Rectory, and had converted the old tithe barn with a small flat above and room beneath for village meetings and the like. His foible was that he saw no use for cupboards, and did not include them in the houses he had built.

In the 1920s Father Lowe bought an isolated farmhouse near Chagford, on the road to Princetown (where the prison is situated). He renovated it and lotted out the land, but few parcels were purchased. He then carried out some imaginative conversions of the farm buildings to create more accommodation.

Another contribution which the rector made to the village was the erection of a replica of the village cross, which had disappeared many years before. This was done in 1897 to mark Queen Victoria's Golden Jubilee and it was placed in the old base, which had been found in the wall of the garden of the Old Rectory.

It is not clear from where the rector's enthusiasm for building came, but it is apparent that it began almost immediately upon his arrival in Throwleigh. His friend Guy Whipham, who was the squire of Gidleigh, the neighbouring parish, is said to have remarked of Father Lowe: 'Bless me, what a fellow that is for bricks and mortar.'[8] It was also apparent that the rector was a practical man, and that perhaps was one of his characteristics which endeared him most to the locals. He had installed a private water supply worked by a ram in Hollow Park: although this was a great improvement on the facilities available to the remainder of the village,

7 Published by the Dartmoor National Park Authority, March 2005.
8 Varwell, *Throwleigh*, p. 34.

it was temperamental and liable to stop working. It was not uncommon to find the rector after Sunday mass with his cassock tied up around his waist attempting to get the pump to work again.[9]

What is clear is that the houses which were built along the lane were generally not lived in by the villagers: their cost was far beyond those dependent on agricultural wages. Thus a precedent was established early on in Father Lowe's time in the parish that 'outsiders', attracted not only by the picturesque situation of the village and the walking available on the moor but also by what were then often termed 'Full Catholic Privileges' available at the church, moved in. This meant that there was a ready congregation, attracted rather than repelled by what was offered at the parish church.

There can be no doubt but that for its time Throwleigh was a very 'advanced' parish under Father Lowe's leadership. In later years the parishioners looked back and regarded the churchmanship as somewhat moderate, perhaps by comparison with Father Drew's overt Anglican Papalism, but in fact Father Lowe had moved far ahead of most country parishes very early on. In 1911 he moved the vestry from the north aisle to the ground floor of the tower as part of a number of changes to the interior which he was carrying out at that time. The sexton, Thomas Hill, who was also the village blacksmith and captain of the bell ringers, was deeply conservative in his views about services and had a particular aversion to incense. Emmie Varwell recorded his comments, in the local dialect, to the rector on this innovation:

> 'I knaw what you'me doin that fir: tis so's you'll be able to walk up dru church, with 'em all, swinging thick smokky lantern.'[10]

Incense was very rare outside of the London strongholds of Anglo-Catholicism before the First World War and almost unknown in the country: it appears from the comments that it had been introduced well before the time of the move of the vestry. Once the aisle was free of it an altar was placed there and a chapel formed.

---

9 Varwell, *Throwleigh*, pp. 34–5 and M. Paget, ed., *Throwleigh: Pictures and Memories from a Dartmoor Parish*, p. 94, where the rector's grandson reminisces about this procedure.

10 Varwell, *Throwleigh*, p. 71.

In 1911 Comper designed a new east window and the following year he provided lancet windows, which were a memorial to the rector's youngest child Cicely, who died of appendicitis at that time: one of them shows St Cecilia. Comper's instruction then was a mark of the churchmanship of the parish as he was still regarded as partisan in his furnishings and decorations.

The rood screen in the church was not only constructed at an unusually late date, but it remained in place much later than in many churches. Miss Varwell notes that in 1849 it was recorded that the rood screen had been removed 'within the memory of the Parish Clerk'.[11] Father Lowe was anxious that it be replaced and had a beam re-erected and adapted by Herbert Read of Exeter, who was an acquaintance of his, with two tall candleholders on it on either side of a crucifix and figures which had been carved in Oberammergau. He also had a wooden image of Our Lady set up in the chapel: this too was carved by Herbert Read and was an anonymous gift. It was an extremely unusual addition to the furnishings of a country church at that date. Read was an accomplished artist who had originally been employed by Harry Hems, who in the late nineteenth century was the leading church furnisher in the South West.

In about 1909 a new high altar was installed made of Dartmoor granite and again designed by Read. The altar was provided with a tabernacle and six tall candlesticks, as was the practice in all churches following the Western Use at that time, but it was also given riddle curtains in approved Comper style. The stone floor of the chancel had been replaced before Father Lowe's time by what Miss Varwell terms 'a hideous pavement of red and yellow tiles',[12] but he removed that and put down granite slabs.

One of the most unusual features of the church was an Easter Sepulchre, which well prior to Father Lowe arriving had been placed in the south wall of the chancel, although apparently it had originally been on the north side, which was the more usual position. The Easter Sepulchre was used in the mediaeval Sarum Use to hold the crucifix and a consecrated host from Good Friday until Easter Sunday, when the host was restored

---

11 Varwell, *Throwleigh*, p. 14.
12 Varwell, *Throwleigh*, p. 13.

to the high altar to signify the resurrection. Candles were lit around the Sepulchre and a watch kept over it.

Father Lowe was anxious to move the Easter Sepulchre back to its original position, but was not able to accomplish that during his incumbency. His other great wish was to replace the fifteenth-century lych gate, which one of the nineteenth-century incumbents had had razed to the ground because it was used as a meeting place by the young men and girls of the parish.

Another embellishment to the church was a sundial dated 1663, a memorial to a parishioner, which was put up in about 1914 over the porch: it was purchased in a second-hand shop in Exeter.

The general effect which Father Lowe and others of his point of view sought to produce was that the Reformation had never happened, and in some ways that was easier in a country church than in a Gothic Revival building in a busy inner-city street, where most Anglo-Catholic churches were to be found. He also sought to revive half-forgotten events such as the beating of the bounds of the parish, which restarted in 1923 and was accompanied by merriment and later a dance at Rashleighs.

The ritual in the church was an uncompromising exposition of Anglo-Catholic doctrine. In the First World War, while Trelawny was away in the army, Patience and Faith were working locally in the Women's Land Army. Faith kept a diary which recorded her attendance at mass and the congregation. Because of the very strict discipline of fasting which was maintained at that time, there were of course no evening masses and so all celebrations in the week were very early so as to allow the congregation to go on to work. Her records for January 1918 show that on occasion there was sung mass at 6.30 a.m. in the week, but on Sunday it was at 8.30 a.m. She indicates that during the week the congregation was usually between six and ten, which is a substantial number given the size of the village. However, bearing in mind that that number included members of the rector's family, and that many of the incomers who had been attracted by the religious privileges did not work, it may be that few of the indigenous locals attended. It is also apparent from the diary that on occasion Father Lowe said mass at Murchington, where there was a chapel, instead of in the parish church. The domestic staff on the Suttons' estate of St

Olaves, who numbered about 12, were required to attend: it appears that the chapel, certainly in later years, was generally used only for weekday services although there was a Sunday school there.

The conclusion about local attendance is supported by some remaining testimony which was made available to the Throwleigh Archive. In 1990 a tape was made of conversations with Jack Lewis (1909–2000) and his wife Dorothea (1920–92), both of whom had lived in the village all their lives. They made it clear that they liked Father Gambier Lowe and that he was very friendly with everyone in the village, whether or not they attended his church. However, they were clear that 'not many [local] people used to go to church': more went to chapel and some to the nearby parishes of Gidleigh or even Chagford.

The canard was often put about of Anglo-Catholic clergy that on Palm Sunday they would ride around the church on a donkey: the Lowe family actually had a pet donkey, named Jessie, which Cicely often rode before her untimely death, and which took part in the Rogation Day walk and prayers around the village. This was of particular moment to the rector, as in addition to his clerical and building activities he was a working farmer.

Even with the extra services required by a priest who was promoting the Catholic Faith, the duties of rector of a parish with the small population of Throwleigh were not exacting. Father Lowe was often seen walking round about the village with his faithful dogs, often black and tan terriers, the particular favourite among which was Ripple, known as 'Rip'. The dog died at Candlemas 1919 and was afforded his own memorial stone just outside the graveyard: whether the irony of having RIP on an animal's memorial was noted by others is not clear. Candlemas was a festival of some importance in the church, not least because Father Lowe would not allow the Christmas decorations to be removed until that day.

The rector usually wore grey tweeds for his walks around and sported hats of the same material which Miss Varwell termed his 'mitres': their shape had been distended to resemble a bishop's headgear by being hung to dry by their tops on a line across his study. On some days he then put on a hooded tweed outer cloak which he called his 'Franciscan cape'. However, for all his duties in and around the church he was scrupulous to wear a cassock and the regulation biretta.

As well as ritual advances, Father Lowe's teachings on marriage discipline were entirely unbending. His eldest daughter Mary was completely cut off from the family after she eloped with a married man. The Rashleighs and the Lowes had become the two leading families socially in the village and were frequently in and out of each others' houses. The Rashleighs' house was used for many years to host village, particularly church, events. This intimacy continued for many years, but was sundered shortly after the First World War.

Dr Rashleigh's wife had an affair during the war with an officer, so he turned her out and divorced her. However, he almost immediately remarried one of the senior nurses from St Mary's Hospital in London where he practised. It is easy now to forget how strict were the teachings of most churchmen, and Anglo-Catholics in particular, on remarriage after divorce. The village was divided and scandalized when Dr Rashleigh went to mass for the first time after his second wedding and Father Lowe passed him over at the altar rail. He did not come to the church again, although the house continued to be used for church events. It may have been the discovery of his first wife's infidelity which caused Dr Rashleigh effectively to abandon Menabilly.

Further, and again in accordance with the prevailing view among many of those of his inclination, Father Lowe had little time for the Roman Church, despite the fact that many of the devotions he was introducing came from that source. His brother Willoughby had built himself a house called Gorsemoor in about 1903 and lived there with his wife, although he was very often away for months on end. He was a crack shot and used his skills to collect specimens for the British Museum – over 10,000 birds for example, mainly from the tropics and the Far East, were killed and mounted by him for the Bird Room.

However, in the 1920s Willoughby went over to Rome: shortly after that, and following a fire in 1927 in which his house was badly damaged, he left the village and moved to Exmouth. His brother Gambier, and later his nephew Trelawny, thereafter acted as if he did not exist and he was never mentioned in conversation.

Father Lowe was clearly a man of attractive personality who was welcoming to all and therefore respected by all. He was very committed to the village and to the maintenance of local events, for example throwing open his house and garden to welcome back his son and others who had survived the war: he appeared also not to discriminate socially against those who chose to worship elsewhere or nowhere. However, it also appears that his own particular brand of Anglo-Catholicism was not embraced with any great fervour by the villagers themselves, although they tolerated what were regarded as his ecclesiastical eccentricities because of his pleasant nature. There seems little doubt either that he was acute so far as money was concerned, and Shilstone Lane was often referred to as 'Golden Hill', both to reflect the wealth of those who moved in and the profits which the rector made.[13]

In 1933 Father Lowe fell ill and for some months was too unwell to celebrate. Miss Varwell tells us that the rector had said that he would be carried into the church on a litter rather than be absent from Sunday mass, and so he continued to attend until two weeks before his death, which occurred in the spring of the year.

Eleanor Lowe moved after her husband's death to live with her daughter Faith, who had married the Revd Sylvanus Luke Landon, a Devon man who served his entire ministry in the Diocese of Exeter. He had trained at St Stephen's House, Oxford, which by then had emerged as the leading Anglo-Catholic theological college, and then after curacies in the Torquay area he became rector of Mary Tavy, on the far side of Dartmoor from Throwleigh, in 1929. Father Luke (as he was known) and Faith Landon looked after Eleanor Lowe there until she died only a few years later: he moved on to other livings in 1940 and subsequently. He too was a committed Anglo-Catholic.

Father Lowe was buried in the churchyard at Throwleigh, near the church he loved. His grave was surmounted by a crucifix and other members of his family, including his daughter Faith and her husband, were later buried near it.

The foundations of Anglo-Catholic practice had been well laid in Throwleigh by Father Lowe: his successor did not have to start from scratch as did many of the increasing number of keen young priests who

---

13 See Paget, *Throwleigh*, p. 27.

took on parishes at that time. The new rector was, however, not young, and had a very different background to his predecessor, who had revelled in the countryside.

Father Lowe's eventual successor did not arrive until 1934, because there was an illuminating interlude. The first nomination for the vacancy was the Revd Percy Lemprière Hesketh, who had had permission to officiate as a curate of nearby St John, Bovey Tracey,[14] since 1929 although he had trained for the priesthood as a mature student at Dorchester Missionary College and had then worked for four years in the Diocese of Nassau in the Bahamas, which was almost uniformly Anglo-Catholic in tone. However, the Bishop of Exeter at that time, the Rt Revd Lord William Gascoyne-Cecil, told him that he would not institute him unless he was prepared to discontinue the practice of reservation of the Blessed Sacrament. The Bishop was quoted as saying that he 'never allowed reservation in small parishes, except for some known fixed cause'. Father Hesketh saw the Bishop and told him that he had no power to forbid reservation and that in any event he had no power to require conditions upon him.[15] The offer was withdrawn and Father Hesketh then became a regular curate at Bovey Tracey before moving to be curate of Wrington, Somerset (1934–36) and then retiring to Truro.

The ironic consequence of this episode was that the eventual successor to Father Lowe was far more committed to Anglican Papalism, and cannot conceivably, given his views, have given any such assurance to the Bishop.

Herbert Leslie Drew was born in Brixton, then a more salubrious area than it is now, in 1885. His father was also named Herbert, but the son was always known by his second Christian name. Father Drew's family were, by the class-ridden standards of the time, marked apart from most of those who produced clergy for the Church of England. His paternal grandfather, George Drew, was a tinker from Islington. His father Herbert Drew (born 1860), however, served an apprenticeship as an ironmonger, for which purpose he went to live in Earley, just outside Reading, where

---

14 This is still a firmly Anglo-Catholic church, affiliated to Forward in Faith.
15 See the *Western Morning News,* 14 November 1933, kindly supplied by Michael Paget.

he met his future wife, Julia Annie Golder (born 1863), the daughter of a bookseller and stationer, whom he married in 1884. They then lived in London and rapidly had three children, Herbert Leslie being followed by Annie Maud (born 1887) and Daisy Harriet (born 1898). By the time of the 1891 census the family had clearly achieved a modest degree of prosperity: they were living at 121 Endlesham Road, Balham, and Herbert Drew was described as an ironmonger and gas fitter. Ten years later, they had moved to 68 Ramsden Road, also in Balham and very near their earlier address. By this time they had clearly established a degree of financial stability: they had a living-in servant and Herbert Drew is described as an 'employer'.

By 1901 the young Leslie Drew had left school and was working as a commercial clerk. It is not now clear how and in what circumstances he became taken up with Anglo-Catholicism, or whether his parents introduced him. Certainly his sister Annie seems to have shared his ecclesiastical enthusiasms, because she later moved to Throwleigh with him and kept house.

It is also not clear which church Leslie Drew attended as a young man. He lived in the parish of St Mary, Balham High Road, although near the church of St Luke, Throwleigh Road, but the former was not Catholic in its teaching and the latter only moderately so. The more definite teaching in the area would have come from St John the Divine, Bedford Hill, which was not far away.

What is clear is that, unlike almost all of his contemporaries who were ordained, he had no higher education when he was accepted. Although most of the theological colleges which were being established at this time required a degree to accept candidates, there were some who did not and one of these was Lichfield, which he entered in 1911. A pre-entry examination was required of non-graduates before acceptance on to a two-year course, as opposed to the one year which was standard for graduates. Although Lichfield did not have a particularly Anglo-Catholic ethos, there were clearly others of a similar turn of mind in the College, including the future parish priest of Walsingham, Alfred Hope Patten, who commenced there in the same year as Leslie Drew.

It would appear that, whatever the deficiencies in his earlier education, Drew mastered the academic requirements and indeed was granted a Licentiate in Theology by the University of Durham in 1914. Unlike Hope Patten, whose knowledge of Latin was always rudimentary despite his devotion to Roman customs, Drew was able in years to come to translate sections of the Missal for publication.

Leslie Drew was ordained deacon in 1913 and priest in 1914 in his home diocese of Southwark, then quite recently established. His first curacy was at St Laurence, Catford, in south east London, a moderate church where he stayed only two years (1913–15). He then moved to St Peter, Vauxhall, in a much more densely populated area of the inner city where there was a great deal of work required of young priests. The church had been built by J.L. Pearson in 1864 and was designed from the outset for worship on Catholic principles. In 1916 he joined the Sodality of the Precious Blood, an inner clerical circle of the Catholic League, whose members were bound to celibacy and to the recitation of the Latin Breviary. In due course he became the senior member of the organization.

Father Drew stayed in Vauxhall until 1921, when he moved to his third curacy, at St Augustine, Victoria Park Road, in South Hackney. This church, which was demolished after being bombed in the Second World War, was at that time a prominent Anglo-Catholic centre in the northern area of the East End.

More importantly perhaps for Father Drew's future was that the parish priest of the adjoining parish of Christ Church, Gore Road, South Hackney, was the able and inspiring Revd C.R. Deakin, who in 1923 moved to be parish priest of St Augustine, Queen's Gate, South Kensington, where he was to remain until 1949: he is commemorated by the statue of St Augustine in that church, whose face was modelled on his. He took Father Drew with him as one of his curates and it was from there that the latter moved to Throwleigh, the only parish of which he was ever incumbent. Christ Church, South Hackney is another church which has disappeared.

The parish church of St Augustine, Queen's Gate, was built by William Butterfield in 1871 in characteristic polychromatic brick. Under Father Deakin's leadership it flourished and became very well known as one of the centres of the Anglo-Catholic Congress Movement with which he was intimately associated, not least because it was from a casual wartime remark of his at a meeting that the idea for such gatherings developed. After Deakin moved to South Kensington, the proximity of the church to the Royal Albert Hall, where many of the Congress events took place, meant that it was itself used as a venue for services and as a starting point for processions. During Father Drew's time at Queen's Gate, Congresses were held in 1927, 1930 and 1933, the last being the largest of all and marking the Oxford Movement Centenary. The earlier meetings were in 1920 and 1923.

Carrick Ransome Deakin was born in Cartmel in North Lancashire in 1872: his father was a non-practising barrister and the family grew up in the South Lakeland area. Deakin began his priesthood in the North of England, a far step from the well-known centres of Anglo-Catholicism in the South East. He was ordained in 1898 for the Diocese of Carlisle after taking his degree at Corpus Christi College, Oxford, and initially was a curate in the unattractive and heavily industrialized town of Workington, later moving to the more salubrious surroundings of Penrith and then in 1904 to be parish priest of Christ Church in Carlisle itself. From there he came south to Hackney in 1908 and thus to South Kensington. It was not only this North Country background which was unusual in the circles in which he moved, for, unlike many of his outlook, he married (also in 1898) and had a number of children. His wife Winifred (née Walker), the daughter of a Durham industrialist, played an important part in his parochial ministry at Queen's Gate. In 1935 he was elected a Guardian of the Shrine of Our Lady of Walsingham: as he was already married, he was not disqualified from that position.

It is clear that by at least the time he moved to St Augustine, Father Deakin had become a strong advocate of Anglican Papalism: in other words he asserted that the Church of England should adopt Roman standards of discipline and worship with a view to the eventual reunion of Canterbury and Rome. It was within this framework of belief that Father Drew lived until his move to Throwleigh in 1934.

The parish at that time was active and there were generally two or three curates. Mass was said three times on each weekday and more frequently on Sundays and there were services of benediction of the Blessed Sacrament and vespers on occasion as well. Father Drew found himself for that period in the centre of Anglo-Catholic advance, with many well-known figures in the Movement visiting the church.

In addition, the church was refurnished over that period and beyond in accordance with the precepts of the 'Back to Baroque' tendency: in other words that the Church of England should adopt and adapt the Counter-Reformation spirituality of the Church of Rome. The main exponent of this was the designer Martin Travers, who carried out some of his best work for Father Deakin.[16] It is not clear whether Father Drew had any great input into what was introduced to the church, but in 1926 another curate, the Revd G.L. Tuckermann, joined the staff and he had a background in architecture. He later moved to Borough Green, Kent, and then became parish priest of another small West Country outpost, the church of St Pancras and the Holy Cross at West Bagborough in the Quantock Hills of Somerset, where he succeeded a long-serving and well-known priest, the Revd J.F. Briscoe. Father George Tuckermann was undoubtedly influential in certain respects in relation to the new furnishings.

In 1926 Travers provided a calvary war memorial to the departed of the parish, consisting of a large gilded triptych with blue, dark green, gold and ivory colouring in a mahogany frame, the colouring being intended to harmonize with Butterfield's brickwork. Father Deakin's name and that of others have been added subsequently. On 16 February 1926 Dr Francis Eeles, the then Secretary of what is now the Council for the Care of Churches, and an opponent of ultramontane devotions, wrote to the Chancellor of the Diocese: 'It is a brilliantly clever piece of work, but to my mind it is overpowering in size and is of the ghastly realistic character which is characteristic of the crucifix as used in the period of the Counter Reformation abroad . . . In confidence I may add that the present vicar of St Augustine's Queen's Gate is an out and out Romanist . . . The tract case near the door contained literature of a thoroughly Roman and disloyal type. The Roman priest in cotta and beretta (sic) which Mr Travers has so cleverly suggested in the sketch is quite typical of the church.'

Father Tuckermann then apparently managed to persuade Father Deakin and Martin Travers to whitewash the interior as the backdrop to

---

16 See R. Warrener and M. Yelton, *Martin Travers (1886–1948): An Appreciation* (Unicorn Press, 2003).

the new furnishings, the most startling of which is a huge reredos, measuring 37 feet by 23 feet 6 inches, with a rood as the central feature set below an integral tester with its own wooden tassels, installed in 1927. On either side are large panels, which resemble at a distance pleated material and caused some to refer to St Augustine as 'The Essoldo, Queen's Gate', for they do appear like cinema curtain drapes. The cost was £1200, which was an enormous sum of money at that time, and well out of the financial reach of most parishes.

It was followed in 1928 by a tabernacle and six Italian Baroque candlesticks on the altar and in 1929 by alterations to the pulpit, including a crucifix and sounding board, then by wooden communion rails with pierced knot designs and a double-sided wooden frontal for the high altar. Travers also designed the stations of the cross for St Augustine at about the same time. In 1932 a memorial to a parishioner in the form of a backing to the shrine of Our Lady appeared, and the kneeling desk at this shrine was also included. More work was carried out after Father Drew left, but the atmosphere of the church was most significantly altered by the introduction of the reredos, which at first sight looked as if it had been designed in South America in the seventeenth century, but on second glance revealed many subtleties from 1920s England.

Another important episode during Father Drew's time at South Kensington was the rebellion by some London incumbents against Bishop Winnington-Ingram's attempts to regulate devotion to the Blessed Sacrament after the rejection of the Revised Prayer Books in 1927 and 1928, known because of their number as the Twenty One. One of them was Father Deakin, and the interwoven paths of Anglo-Catholic priests at the time are well illustrated by the fact that two of the others were the Revd C.E. Story, who became vicar of St Augustine, Victoria Park Road in 1923, the year when Father Drew left that church, and the Revd F.G.S. Nicolle, who had been a curate with him at Vauxhall (1917–19) and was at the material time vicar of St Thomas, Bethnal Green. Yet another was the Revd J.E. Watson, a prominent Anglican Papalist, who was then vicar of St Alban, Fulham, but had been Deakin's curate in South Hackney from 1913 to 1916.

While Father Drew was not himself one of the Twenty One (he was ineligible as he did not hold a living) there is no doubt that he and the other curates at South Kensington supported their priest. It was another example of his involvement in a high-octane period of Anglo-Catholicism.

In addition to these matters, Father Drew became involved with the thorny question of which altar book should be used by priests of his way of thinking. By the time that he was at Queen's Gate, there were two main competing missals which were used by Anglicans.[17]

One was *Missale Anglicanum: The English Missal,* which was first published in 1912. Its compiler was the Revd H.W.G. Kenrick, vicar of Holy Trinity, Hoxton from 1905 to 1937 and it was published by W.H. Knott & Sons, the best-known Anglo-Catholic firm in the field. It combined the texts of the 1662 Prayer Book and the Roman Missal, leaving the celebrant to choose which parts he used and was clearly designed for the altar rather than for the congregation. This was a personal venture by Father Kenrick and Knotts sold the missals on commission.

In 1921 the Society of St Peter and St Paul, a vigorous and original pressure group of which there is more detail in subsequent chapters, but which advocated primarily the use of the 1549 Prayer Book but with the liturgy overlain and disguised by Roman ceremonial, published the first version of *The Anglican Missal,* which had versions both for the priest and for the laity, although they differed little. It set out a single rite drawn from both Anglican and Roman sources, but with seven canons so that the celebrant could decide which form to use.

In 1923 the *English Missal,* as the first book was generally known, was republished in a slightly revised edition which drew on some of the better translations which had been used in its rival, and also included the Gelasian canon in Latin as well as English, in parallel text. There were many Anglican priests at this time who used that canon, said silently, in either language, in saying mass. The practice at that time at St Augustine was to use the English Missal and to say the Gelasian canon silently in Latin.

After the failure of the 1927 and 1928 Prayer Books to gain Parliamentary approval, a group of more moderate Anglo-Catholics attempted to gather support for what was termed the 'interim rite', the main proponent of

---

17 See M. Dalby, *Anglican Missals and their Canons: 1549, Interim Rite and Roman* (Grove Books, 1998) for a masterly summary of these matters.

which was Bishop A.C. Chandler, who had retired from his Diocese of Bloemfontein to become rector of Bentley in Hampshire. The more Roman minded among the clergy were not happy with this and in response attempted to produce a missal which they could all use.

It was at this point that Father Drew became involved. He was asked, with the now aged Father Kenrick, to represent the *English Missal* side on a joint committee with the Revd F.E.P.S. Langton, then vicar of the Holy Redeemer, Clerkenwell and later of St Mary, Bourne Street, Pimlico and the Revd C.H. Scott, then vicar of St Michael, Folkestone and later of St Michael, Edinburgh, who supported the *Anglican Missal*. The committee began meeting in about 1932 but were unable to agree, although a prospectus for a new volume, retaining the title *English Missal,* which was Father Kenrick's copyright, was published in 1933. The result was that Knotts published in 1934 (this time on their own account rather than on behalf of the compiler) what was simply a new edition of the *English Missal* with some improvements to the translations: it was still just an altar book.

However, in 1933 Knotts also published the first edition of a new book, *The English Missal for the Laity,* which was Father Drew's own compilation and was sold by the publishers on commission as had been Father Kenrick's original volume. It is a mark of his considerable linguistic ability that he was able to produce acceptable translations, although it was to say the least odd that although they were similar to the 1934 altar edition, on occasion there were marked differences between the two versions. This discrepancy continued as a further edition of Father Drew's book was produced in 1943, which was reprinted with alterations in 1949: another, the last, new version followed in 1958. All of these obviously appeared while he was at Throwleigh and meant that to some extent he remained on the wider Anglo-Catholic scene, although the volumes contained no acknowledgement or mention of his contribution.

It is not clear why Father Drew decided to move to Throwleigh. It is apparent that if he wanted a parish of his own, the options were limited, as they were for any priest with his strongly held views, for he would have been unacceptable to many patrons. On the other hand, there were always livings available in slum areas of London where his Papalism would not have been an obstacle, as it was not to others in those districts. It may be that at almost 50 he felt tired of life in London, where he had been born and had resided throughout save for his periods of study: what is clear is that he had had no experience at all of living in the country, still less an area as remote as West Devon, and no expertise in dealing with a small rural parish.

Father Lowe was obviously not an easy man to follow. His dynamism, affability and wealth were all attributes not often combined in a priest. The villagers and the incomers awaited the arrival of the new rector with interest.

Miss Varwell indicates tactfully that it was 'a bit of a blow' for Father Drew to leave London and his circle, but she says 'many of his friends came to him here, bringing too a shower of gifts to the church'.[18] One generous but anonymous donor paid for the recasting of two bells and the purchase of another, and they were rehung with three existing bells, so that a perfect peal resulted. The new rector also carried on his predecessor's enthusiasm, which had perhaps lagged as he got older, to renovate. In particular he supported Dr Rashleigh's campaign to have electric light brought to the village and to the church (which was lit by oil) especially. Miss Varwell was not a supporter of the introduction of electricity to the church, but she generously accepted that once it had arrived it actually improved the situation.

Father Drew also had the tithe barn painted and Trelawny Lowe generously allowed the church to continue using it for functions. As Hollow Park had been the personal property of Father Lowe, Father Drew clearly could not live there, and he reverted to using the New Rectory, which had been provided for his predecessor when Dr Rashleigh bought Parson Archer's house. His sister came to keep house for him and Emmie Varwell described her as 'the "compleat" hostess'.[19] She died in 1941 and that made Father Drew perhaps more lonely and isolated.

The church required little alteration after the work of Father Lowe, but Father Drew did in due course carry out one important change which his predecessor had not accomplished, which was to move the Easter Sepulchre

---

18 Varwell, *Throwleigh*, p. 123.
19 Varwell, *Throwleigh*, p. 35.

back to its original place on the north side of the church. Another scheme, which was carried out very early in Father Drew's incumbency, was to complete another project which his predecessor had left, which was the restoration of the lych gate. It was decided that this should be a memorial to Father Lowe, and Trelawny Lowe was instrumental in the instruction of the distinguished ecclesiastical architect Sir Charles Nicholson, although the gate was made and thatched locally. The only two thatchers left in the village carried out the work to its roof. It was dedicated on 3 October 1936 by Bishop W.F. Surtees of Crediton and a bronze plaque to Father Lowe placed on it.

There is no doubt that Father Drew appreciated the legacy which he had inherited. Miss Varwell became a devoted follower of him in his turn and she recorded him as saying: 'When I am going home from church in the morning, I often look across at the crucifix over Father Lowe's grave, and thank God for him and the lead he gave which has made it possible for me to carry on.'[20]

However, not only had Anglo-Catholicism acquired a harder cutting edge since Father Lowe's time, but Father Drew had none of his easy familiarity with people. He sought to transport that to which he had become accustomed in London to the rural fastness of Devon, and it proved difficult for the local parishioners to accept this. When the compilers of the Throwleigh Archive project interviewed those who had known Father Drew, they could find no one who was positive about him, although there clearly were some followers of his at the time, including particularly the Mesdemoiselles Varwell and a Miss Agnes Fox, who assisted Emmie Varwell with her book, was a keen photographer, and is remembered as having provided much finance for church activities: she lived at The Hey. However, it does appear that, even more than was the case in Father Lowe's time, the rector's supporters came from incomers rather than locals. The influx of elderly females to Shilstone Lane continued, and it became known as Petticoat Lane, or, behind the backs of the residents, as Old Maids' Alley.

20 Varwell, *Throwleigh*, p. 124.

Father Drew also ensured by this means a ready congregation. He was particularly keen on regular attendance and was wont to chide those who missed mass, or even worse, did not go at all. He still had control, direct or indirect, over property in the village and let some on what became known as 'daily mass tenancies'. These, which were unique in the experience of the writer, were arrangements whereby property was only let to those who were willing to come to mass daily and also to go to confession. An anonymous parishioner ('A') recalled a conversation with a lady in her 70s ('B') who had been ill. The exchange was as follows:

B: 'I'm having such a hard time.'
A: 'Really, what's the matter?'
B: 'Well, I'll have to leave. I've had a heart attack and I can't walk down to the church every day and back again.'
A: 'Why should you?'
B: 'I'm on one of the daily mass tenancies. I must let the House go to someone who can keep up the proper tenancy. Father Drew doesn't want me to stay.'[21]

Another lady, who lived in the Old Rectory, went so far as to ask for a certificate from the doctor to say she was unable to go to church, but this was refused.

Such tenancies continued for many years: in December 1961 for example an advertisement appeared in these terms: 'Daily mass tenant required to rent unfurnished bungalow in Devon village close to Anglo-Catholic Church', with an address given in Throwleigh.[22]

The villagers were particularly alarmed by the new rector's insistence on confession: Father Lowe had clearly heard confessions, and Faith records in her 1918 diary that she rode over to a nearby church to make hers, but Father Drew upset many of his parishioners by making direct requests of them. He also made it perfectly clear that he had no time for the Methodist Chapel or indeed for other Anglicans who were not of his outlook, telling one woman that she would go to Hell if she went to the Chapel, and another, who was an agnostic, that she would be sorry when she met her

---

21 Paget, *Throwleigh*, pp. 101–3.
22 In *Crux* for that month.

Maker. This intransigence led to arguments between the rector and some of his parishioners and as motor transport gradually became more readily available more people went to Gidleigh church, which was in any event nearer to parts of the parish than was St Mary, Throwleigh.

One of the problems was the contrast between the jocular Father Lowe and his generally rather dour successor, entirely convinced of the correctness of his own point of view, and without any instinct for the countryside. He appears always to have worn a cassock and cloak in the village, with biretta or curé hat as the case may be. One frequent visitor to the village recalled:

> Father Lowe was a hard act to follow. Father Drew's Service was like the Roman Catholic – Farm Street [the Jesuit church in London] nearer than Throwleigh. Everything that could go in, went in, in that tiny church – which I thought was quite extraordinary – all the ceremonial, everything you could possibly find. He used Latin for the consecration.[23]

In later years, Father Drew's successors were to be amazed by the number of candlesticks in the cupboards in the church, which no doubt had been used on Corpus Christi Day and the like.

Although comments such as that quoted were made, it is equally clear that Father Drew's support in bringing electricity to the village was much appreciated. It is also the case that the underlying tensions were not always understood by the outside world, and the attendance at mass was, for a tiny village the population of which had only risen to 350 in 1955, very impressive.

The Rural Dean of Okehampton, the Revd H. Beaumont F. Burnaby, was certainly impressed by what he saw. In the foreword to Miss Varwell's book he wrote: 'What a joy it must be to live in Throwleigh with its whole life radiating from the "Living Presence" within the sanctuary of the parish church.' In his inspection book for 1942 he wrote: 'Perhaps more than ever one felt the devotion of the churchpeople of Throwleigh to their sanctuary. Sometimes the Rural Dean finds visits to churches rather painful but visits to Throwleigh have (with one exception)[24] always been

---

23 See Paget, , *Throwleigh*, p. 103.
24 The exception is not recorded.

an inspiration and have had the effect of breeding encouragement and greater devotion to the causes of Christ.'

The following year Horace Keast's article on the village appeared in *Fiery Cross*, which was an insert for parish magazines produced monthly by the Church Union. At that time it was recorded that there was a daily mass attendance of 12, and there were 9000 attendances at church during the year, 5000 communions and 400 confessions. The village had a weekly holy hour (on Thursdays) and benediction (on Saturdays).[25] These are remarkable figures, although it does appear that many of the attendances were recorded by Father Drew's elderly female disciples from London and elsewhere.

It also appears to be the case that Father Drew had ill luck. In 1947 the roof of the church caught fire and was only put out by the efforts of the villagers, who brought water in buckets and jugs and removed valuables before the fire brigade could reach the scene. The sacristan, Miss Phyllis May, another of the rector's devotees, was actually in the church when the fire started above her head and was initially unaware of it: some of the village children raised the alarm when they saw smoke pouring from the roof.

On 17 September 1949 Princess Marie Louise opened the new hall which Father Drew had had built near the church. This was another example of his ability to get things done, but unfortunately the roof was insufficiently robust to withstand the heavy falls of snow which sometimes occurred in the area in the winter, and a few years later it collapsed. The Princess, who was one of the few members of the Royal Family with any close interest in Anglo-Catholicism, was frequently involved in such events and was entertained at Rashleighs.[26] Father Drew appears to have carried out little work to the parish church, having of course no private

---

25 Keast, 'Catholic Notebook – VII', in *Fiery Cross,* July 1943.

26 Princess Marie Louise (1872–1956), born Princess Francisca Josepha Louise Augusta Marie Hélène Christina of Schleswig-Holstein-Sonderburg-Augustenberg, who chose to use the names Marie Louise for private purposes in childhood, was the granddaughter of Queen Victoria: her mother was Princess Helena, daughter of the Queen. In 1891 Princess Marie Louise married H.H. Prince Aribert of Anhalt, but the marriage was annulled by a decree of her father-in-law in 1900, and she returned to England, where she had been born. In 1917 she relinquished her German titles and was thereafter known simply as Princess Marie Louise.

funds of his own, but a wooden statue of St George was installed after the Second World War.

The post-war years do not appear to have seen the conversion of the village to Catholicism as Father Drew must have hoped. The older generation of incomers was dying off and his own conception of the priestly role was increasingly seen as outdated even among Anglo-Catholics. He continued, however, in the same vein, and in 1961 contributed a series of articles to *Crux*, a magazine for Anglican Catholics, advocating the practice of communion in one kind and the use of the Missal.

In 1954 Ralph Sutton suffered a stroke and the use of the chapel at Murchington seems to have ceased about then. It later became dilapidated and in 1975 was sold for conversion to residential accommodation.

Father Drew did not retire until 1969, when he was some 84 years of age. He died three years later and was buried in Throwleigh churchyard near to the graves of his sister, of Miss Fox, and of other close followers: perhaps symbolically they are all in one corner. An obituary in the *Catholic Standard for Anglicans*, January 1973, by the Revd A.H. Simmons, Master of the Society of the Holy Cross (SSC), was fulsome in its praise. Father Simmons made reference to Father Drew's support for the Society for Retreat Conductors and to his own visits to Throwleigh after 1934, and wrote:

> Father Drew made his church a spiritual power house.
>
> He encouraged his people to the regular practice of prayer and meditation before the Blessed Sacrament, and the life of the church, in consequence, was second to none.
>
> His devotion to the missal was exceptional. He went around in his car with an extremely tattered, and much corrected, version of *The English Missal*, which was his constant study and his work on the Ordo, similarly painstakingly done, is well known by many of us.
>
> To some he seemed an alarming person, but underneath was an understanding heart: the heart of a good priest, a Catholic of unquestionable orthodoxy, one who loved the Lord Jesus Christ with a devotion others could not fail to acknowledge.

In the meantime, however, the storm which had been brewing under the surface for so long came to a head.[27] Upon Father Drew's retirement, it must have been clear to any objective observer that Throwleigh could not sustain a priest of its own. By this time the advowson had passed from the Sutton family to the Guild of All Souls, a venerable Anglo-Catholic institution which held the patronage of a number of livings. When Father Drew left, the Revd J.O. White, rector of Gidleigh, acted as priest-in-charge. He immediately changed the character of the liturgy to a more moderate form, abandoning incense but then recommencing its use for a time, after which some villagers complained and he ceased once more.

It seems likely that Father Drew had never had a Parochial Church Council: that would accord with the general view of Anglican Papalists, namely that the Church was a divine institution which could not be run by committees. However, one of the new priest-in-charge's first moves was to call a meeting and to establish a PCC. The churchwardens, Mr E. Ponting and Mr P. Baker, were unanimously elected and were representative of the Anglo-Catholic side.

Shortly after this, Mr White died suddenly, leaving the future unclear. The churchwardens wrote to Bishop W.A.E. Westall of Crediton, who was on the committee of the Guild of All Souls, asking that any new incumbent be appointed for Throwleigh only, which was a vain hope, and also that he continue to uphold the tradition of the church. About 40 other villagers were displeased at this and sent a petition to the Rural Dean calling for a return to Matins (which they seem to have thought was the general Church of England morning service). One of the anti-Catholic faction said that the villagers wanted 'an orthodox service, something they understood'. Another said that it was important that any new priest should have in effect a commitment to the Church of England, which it was felt Father Drew did not have.

The resolution of these serious problems was easier than at first appeared. The Revd Lewis Coulson was appointed vicar of Gidleigh and priest-in-charge of Throwleigh later in 1970 and then in 1972 he was made rector of Throwleigh and he and his wife moved into the New Rectory in Shilstone Lane. He is credited with having restored theological harmony

---

27 See Paget, *Throwleigh*, p. 104, quoting from the local paper of 28 January 1970.

to the village, through his pleasant personality and affability. The era of hard-line Anglo-Catholicism ended and a new, softer age of presentation took its place. He stayed until 1978, when he moved on to another living.

Subsequently the livings of Throwleigh and Gidleigh were initially held with that of the much larger village of Chagford, and in due course have been incorporated into a large circuit (the Whiddon parishes) with nine churches, so that the tradition built up has dissolved. Attendance is now not good, which is not surprising bearing in mind the size of the village.

Throwleigh had a much longer period of exposure to Anglo-Catholicism than many villages: there are many churches elsewhere which can still be seen in which empty votive candle stands are placed in front of dusty plaster statues of Our Lady, and an aumbry still has a lamp before it, but the doors are locked and parish communion is held once a month. In Throwleigh the residue of the long period from 1895 to 1969 still remains, although the memories are fading. The church is kept open, and the interior has been simplified, with the removal of the riddle curtains and reredos so as to allow for celebration facing the people, but the statues are still there, albeit being wooden they are less obvious than the gaudy painted plaster saints sometimes found, and there remains a notice by a pricket stand, written by Father Drew during the Second World War, asking for prayers for the reconversion of the Dowry of Mary. Unfortunately he did not achieve that result in this corner of the West Country.

2

St Bridget, Bridgerule, Devon, and the Kingdon Family

There have been a few incumbencies in the Church of England which have exceeded in length that of the Revd F.H. Kingdon in Bridgerule, Devon, but by any standards his devotion to one parish was exceptional. He was born in 1860, ordained deacon in 1885 and priest in 1886, appointed to the living of Bridgerule in 1888 and died in office at the age of 98 in 1958 after 70 years in the parish. He was also an uncompromising Anglo-Catholic from a family with a well-established High Church tradition which has produced many priests, including two of his brothers.

Bridgerule lies across the River Tamar which generally divides Cornwall from Devon. The church is out of the centre of the small village, on an incline on the eastern side of the river. Until 1844 the boundary between the counties coincided here with the Tamar, which meant that part of the settlement (West Bridgerule) was in Cornwall and the other (East Bridgerule, containing the church) was in Devon, but in that year a rectification in that and other areas took place and the whole village was united within Devon, so that after 1974, when the village of North Petherwin, somewhat south of Bridgerule, was transferred from Devon into Cornwall, thus ensuring that the river was the boundary in that area too, West Bridgerule was left as the only part of Devon on the Cornish side of the river.

The local influence of the Kingdon[1] family was very considerable: as

---

1 Spelled Kyngdon by some members of the family and Kingdom by others: the great railway engineer Isambard Kingdom Brunel received his second forename because that was his mother's surname, and she was a member of the family, although distant from the Holsworthy Kingdons.

well as Bridgerule, to which they held the patronage, they had acquired the right to the advowson of the neighbouring Cornish parish of St Anne, Whitstone. Until the closure of the Bude branch line, part of the Southern Railway's 'withered arm', in 1966, the two villages actually shared a railway station, Whitstone & Bridgerule, which was just in Devon.

Both villages are also near the remote coastal parish of Morwenstow, famous for its association with the eccentric poet-priest, the Revd Robert Stephen Hawker (1804–75). The question of whether Father Hawker had gone over to Rome on his deathbed, and if so whether he was in a mental state properly to make the decision, was one which exercised the Kingdons and others in the locality very much. To this day a picture of Hawker, taken a week before his death and portraying him in biretta, surplice and stole, is still displayed in Morwenstow Church with the subscription: 'Photograph taken a few days before his death – as a priest not a Roman Catholic layman'.

The Kingdon family was spread over Cornwall and Devon from at least the thirteenth century, although the church of St Hugh at Quethiock in East Cornwall was regarded as the family shrine. They were not noble but they were on the whole reasonably well off.[2]

The Bridgerule and Whitstone Kingdons were part of the Holsworthy branch of the family. This arm had been founded by Roger Kingdon who settled in the town in about 1730 and opened a store there.

Roger Kingdon's descendants were academically gifted: his son John was one of five generations to be Fellows of Exeter College, Oxford, the last of whom was the Revd Henry Paul Kingdon (1907–89), chaplain of the College and later a parish priest, and a man who left chaos in his wake wherever he went because of his disputatious nature.

John Kingdon, Roger's son, was vicar of Bridgerule from 1765 to 1808 and for the last 27 years of that incumbency he combined it with being rector of the adjoining Devonshire parish of Pyworthy.

---

2 See F.B. Kingdon, *The Kingdon Family* (Stanley Press, London, 1932), and A.S. Kingdon MBE, *The Kingdon Family – A Second Look* (published privately by the author, 1974). The latter in particular contains a great deal of information about the clerical Kingdons of the twentieth century.

John Kingdon's oldest son, another John (1768–1843) was rector of Whitstone from 1795 and was followed by his brother William, his father's third son, who married Jane Hawker, the sister of the vicar of Morwenstow. It was by this route that Frank Kingdon and indeed his father received his middle name: Frank was the great-nephew of the poet and also his godson.

The Revd William Kingdon was succeeded in Whitstone in 1864 by his son Robert, the father of Frank Hawker Kingdon.

The second member of the Kingdon family to be vicar of Bridgerule was Thomas Hockin Kingdon, the fifth son of John Kingdon and thus the brother of John junior and of William. He was a Fellow of Exeter College from 1794 to 1804. He was lord of the manor of Shebbear and was instituted to Bridgerule and Pyworthy in 1808. He remained as incumbent of Pyworthy until his death in 1853, but his oldest son Samuel Napier Kingdon took over as vicar of Bridgerule in 1844 and stayed until 1872. Samuel's son, the Revd Herbert Napier Kingdon, clearly did not want to take on the living and became the headmaster of Dorchester Grammar School: he had no desire to be a parish priest. It was he who appointed Frank Hawker Kingdon to Bridgerule in 1888.

The Revd Robert Hawker Kingdon (1832–1909), Frank's father, born in Whitstone and later vicar of the parish, married Mary Jane Chope in 1856: she was born in Bideford, Devon in 1835. By her he had five sons but no daughters. The sons were: Robert William Kingdon (born 1858), Claude Drewitt Kingdon (born 1859), Frank Hawker Kingdon (born 1860), Edward Owen Kingdon (born 1866) and Reginald Arthur Kingdon (born 1868). The older three were born during the time from 1856 onwards when their father was curate of Amersham, Buckinghamshire, and the younger two after he had returned to Cornwall in 1864 to become parish priest of Whitstone, where he was able to live in considerable style. The family had a number of resident servants, and in addition to his ecclesiastical duties the rector is recorded in 1871 as farming 40 acres.[3] The very large rectory in the village is now a school. A church hall in

---

3 For the non-agricultural, this is about 20 football pitches, or in other words a considerable area of land.

Whitstone was erected to his memory in 1910 and a crucifix marking his grave stands prominently above the churchyard.

The oldest son Robert died aged 13 in 1871. The penultimate son, Edward, became a doctor of medicine and practised in Holsworthy, the nearest town to Bridgerule. He married a Tasmanian lady and had three children, all of whom had Hawker as their last forename.

The other three boys were all ordained into the Church of England and all were staunch Anglo-Catholics. Also, they were all very long lived, with Frank the most so.

Claude and Reginald were both undergraduates at Keble College, Oxford, and neither married. Frank on the other hand did not immediately undergo further education, and he was married, to Jessie Freyberg (1854–1927), by whom he had two sons and three daughters.

Claude proceeded from Oxford to be curate of St Peter, Prickwillow, Cambridgeshire, from 1882 to 1887, and then had a short sojourn as curate of St Laurence, Northampton (1887–88) before returning to Prickwillow as vicar (1888–1917). While there he wrote a short pamphlet entitled *Prickwillow on the Fens* in 1892. Prickwillow lies just outside Ely: it is an archetypal nineteenth-century village of the type often found in that area, bisected by railway lines and with flat vistas in every direction except to the south west, where the Cathedral towers over the region. Claude described himself in the 1901 census as being an 'English Catholic priest': what the census enumerator made of that is not clear. The brick church, again a typical building for the area, was erected in 1868 and has lost the tradition it had during his incumbency. However, a new close recently constructed in the village perpetuates Father Claude's name: Kingdon Avenue is just off Ely Road.

After his long spell in the East of England, Claude returned to a very different area, Cornwall. He was curate in charge of St Teath, not far from Bridgerule, from 1917 to 1923, although that was a church with no strong Catholic tradition, but in that latter year he succeeded to the family living of Whitstone, so for a number of years thereafter he and his brother Frank were parish priests in adjoining villages, although of course in different dioceses. He became Rural Dean, retired about 1945, and died aged 90 in 1949. He was noted for his eccentric parish magazines, in which he bound

up ordinary parochial matters with cuttings and illustrations from elsewhere so that no two of the 60 odd copies were the same. He also rewrote
some of his sermons in verse form and so published them.

Whitstone church stands in a hollow in a rather isolated position well
away from the main road through the village. As well as Throwleigh,
Horace Keast visited Whitstone, and he wrote about it in the *Fiery Cross*
for July 1939. He was entranced by what he saw, from the holy well of St
Anne outside the church and her shrine in the vicarage garden, to the interior, of which he wrote: 'Everything in this ancient church shows the love
and care that true faith bestows.' A carved rood screen had been erected
and the Blessed Sacrament was reserved in the south transept chapel. The
interior remains today much as Keast saw it, but of course it is now part
of a much larger circuit. The surrounding churches such as Whitstone,
Week St Mary and Poundstock, all of which once had a flourishing Anglo-
Catholic tradition, now do not have services even every week and have
been levelled down to the churchmanship of those with whom they are
run. Reservation of the Blessed Sacrament has virtually ended in these
churches, although most are open for private prayer all day.

Reginald (usually known as 'Reggie') was the youngest and best known
of the Kingdon brothers. It was said that Frank was allocated a rural living
by the family on the grounds that he was less robust, whereas Reginald
was asked to work in the East End on the basis that he was in rude health.
Frank's longevity, however, belied that early assessment, although he
did complain when young of frequent bilious attacks which kept him
in bed for several days, but Reggie was throughout his life a man of re-
assuring bulk, generally with an endearing smile. After Keble he went to
Ely Theological College (which at that time was the leading such Anglo-
Catholic institution) and, for him, had the additional advantage of being
near to his brother Claude. He was ordained as a deacon in 1892 and as a
priest the following year.

Father Reginald Kingdon spent all his working life in two East End
parishes, apart from a short spell in 1914–15 when he was a temporary
chaplain to the forces. From 1892 until 1917 he was curate of St Augustine,
Settles Street, Stepney, which was later to be one of the churches which was
hit in the blitz and indeed it was never rebuilt. The parish, which at the

turn of the century had required a team of five priests to run it, was then united with that of St Philip, Stepney Way, which itself is now closed.

In 1917 Father Reginald Kingdon was appointed to his only living, St John, Isle of Dogs, where he stayed until his retirement back to Widemouth Bay in Cornwall in 1948. He died in 1955 aged 86.

The years when Father Kingdon was in the East End were marked by constant poverty and then by the horrors of the blitz in the Second World War, in which he bestrode the parish with a tin hat on his head instead of his customary biretta, but still with cassock, patrolling the air-raid shelters each night. The presbytery was destroyed by a direct hit from a bomb on 19 March 1941 and the church itself was battered but remained in use.

Between the wars Reginald Kingdon emerged as one of the leaders of the Anglo-Catholic 'slum priests' and he was perhaps an exemplar of that type: his parish was on the isolated island formed by a long loop in the Thames and was generally little known to the outside world. He was elected as a proctor in convocation from 1929 to 1935, and he was one of the Twenty One who defied Bishop Winnington-Ingram in 1929–30, along with the Revd A.F. Asher, then incumbent of St Augustine, Stepney, who had been a curate with Father Kingdon before succeeding to the living. In 1931 he was chosen as a foundation Guardian of the Shrine of Our Lady of Walsingham, and played a very substantial part in life there for many years before and after that date, leading many pilgrimages. When he retired from the Isle of Dogs, he became the first Guardian Emeritus. He also wrote a tract entitled 'How to conduct a children's mass',[4] intended, as he made clear, for 'those who use the Western rite in English'. He was well known for his loud voice and one parishioner recollected: 'the sermon was a real thumper'.[5]

Like his brother Claude, Father Reginald is commemorated, in his case by Kingdon House in Galbraith Street, on the island. Although some did not approve of the tone of his services, there was no one who did not respect his devotion to duty and to his parish.

---

4 Published by Faith Press, *c*1925.

5 See E. Hostettler, *The Anglican Church on the Isle of Dogs 1854–2004* (Island History Trust, 2004), p. 26.

Against this high public profile, Father Frank Kingdon was much less visible, but we know a great deal of his life because he and his wife left extensive (although not quite continuous) diaries for the years from 1883 to 1944: they are now in the Devon Record Office.[6] He was clearly a formidable figure and after his death one of his clerical contemporaries said he was: 'A gorgeous figure at such assemblies as Diocesan Conferences. In a very posh cassock and with a voice like a foghorn he would broadcast his views to the world outside.'[7] The loud voice was clearly a family characteristic and indeed was noted in his obituary as remaining strong to the very end: he conducted the Armistice Day services two weeks before he died.[8]

The census returns show that in 1881 Frank Kingdon was living in Kensington and working as what is described as a merchants' clerk. The diaries begin in 1883 and, prior to his marriage, it was Frank who kept them. The early years are an engaging mixture of piety and naivety, and reflect his doubts about the course his life should take. Initially he frequented St Matthias, Earls Court Road, but on 2 February 1883 he records attending the opening of St Cuthbert, Philbeach Gardens, which he termed 'such a jolly day'. Thereafter he seems to have divided his attendance between both those churches, but he also went on special occasions to festivals of the Confraternity of the Blessed Sacrament at various places, to St Barnabas, Pimlico (where he participated in an outdoor procession in February 1885) and to St Augustine, Queen's Gate. On some days he records his own failings in non-specific terms, and once he simply wrote 'peccavi' without telling the reader which sin he had committed.

The first mention of his future wife comes on 31 March 1883 (although he could of course have known her in previous years). On that day they and others walked together to Richmond. Jessie Freyberg was six years older than Frank Kingdon, a difference of which he makes no mention, although he does refer to her within the confines of the diary as 'dear old Jessie'. She was clearly involved in St Matthias and other similar churches in the area.

---

6 Reference D5179M-O/F/1–65.
7 See A.S. Kingdon, *Kingdon*, p. 73.
8 *The Times*, 3 December 1958.

Jessie Freyberg was the daughter of an auctioneer, James Freyberg, and had been brought up in the London area. In 1877 her mother Jane died and in 1880 her father remarried a lady called Julia Hamilton. Jessie and her brothers and sister then lived in Earls Court Road while their father and stepmother moved to Richmond and later to Hammersmith and began a large second family.[9] In 1891 her father and the second family emigrated to New Zealand.

Thereafter Frank saw Jessie frequently and on 24 June 1883 confided in her that he was determined to take orders. He was very close to his brother Claude, who was a deacon at that time and he visited him in Prickwillow and was then present at his ordination as priest in December 1883.

Frank had not of course gone to University at the conventional time, but in 1884 he started attending King's College, London in order to prepare for ordination, which required him to master Latin and Hebrew. Comments about that are interspersed with the continued friendship with Jessie: he records in April 1884 that he 'gave her such a pretty bunch of flowers' and in September of that year he walked with her to her mother's grave and they put on it flowers from a wedding they had attended the previous day. He was also assisting with missions and in November 1884 helped in that capacity at St Augustine, Haggerston.

By 1885 Frank was living at 31 Kempsford Gardens, Earls Court, very near Jessie, and continuing with his studies, his church work and what was becoming a serious romance. He was successful in his examinations, later living to be the oldest holder of an AKC, and proceeded to be ordained as deacon in the Diocese of Truro, on 30 June 1885. It is not clear why he served his title and first curacy at the church of St John, Penzance, as that was definitely not a church which was in the forefront of the Catholic revival. There were many others in Cornwall which were, notably St Mary, also in Penzance.

The diaries reveal, however, that the new curate had a heavy workload of daily visiting and engagements with parish societies and the like. He continued to be in close touch with Jessie and on 31 August 1885 he met

---

9 One of the children of this second family was Bernard Cyril Freyberg (1889–1963), later General Lord Freyberg VC, GCMG, KBE, DSO and three bars, KStJ, who was Governor-General of New Zealand for some years after his distinguished Army career.

her at Okehampton station and she stayed with him and his parents in Whitstone.

The parish in Penzance remained lively and in January 1886 a new mission room was opened. A cutting in the diaries displays a letter to the paper complaining that the Revd Frank Kingdon had allowed his Bible class to consume beer and to smoke, while earlier he had supported the Blue Ribbon Gospel Temperance Sunday. He has appended no comment to this criticism.

In early 1886 Father Kingdon was clearly making up his mind to marry Jessie, although the diary is less than explicit about when the engagement took place. In June 1886 he records that his ordination as priest was to be postponed until December, presumably because of the forthcoming wedding.

On 31 August 1886 Frank Kingdon went to sign the marriage settlement, an essential part of any Victorian middle-class nuptials, and the following day he and Jessie were married in Richmond, where her father was then living. Their honeymoon was spent touring, with the first two days visiting the cathedrals at Winchester and Salisbury: on both occasions he laconically notes 'bed at 10' without any further elaboration.

On 19 December 1886 Frank Kingdon was ordained priest. He continued to work hard in his parish, although there appears to have been no daily celebration there at that time. However, it seems apparent, although again the diary entries are somewhat elliptical, that there was a falling out between vicar and curate. He sought his brother Claude's advice but the situation could not be resolved: it may be that the younger man wanted to advance ritual developments at a pace unacceptable to the older. He retained a cutting from the local paper which set out the situation objectively in an edition of February 1887:

General surprise and regret was felt among the parishioners of St John's Church, Penzance some days ago when it became known that it was the intention of the Rev F. Hawker Kingdon to leave the neighbourhood in the spring. Among a section of the members of the church, sorrow is not altogether unmingled with indignation as it is understood that the causes which may have led to the approaching severance

of Mr Kingdon's connection with the parish are not of his own crea-
tion. Personally Mr Kingdon was popular in the parish, more especially
among the working classes.

In May 1887 he moved, but only so far as St Maddern, Madron, just
outside Penzance, at which church in a few years time George Gambier
Lowe was to marry. On 3 November of that year Father Kingdon records
attending the consecration of Truro Cathedral, and then on 5 December
1887 their first child, Mary Joyce Kingdon, was born.

It was early in the following year that a possible move to Bridgerule
began to be discussed. On 1 February 1888 he went to see the church and
the vicarage and recorded that they were both 'very nice'. This seems an
odd comment, as one would have expected that, having been brought up
in Whitstone, and with the Kingdon family connections in Bridgerule,
he would have been familiar with it in advance. Be that as it may, not
long after that he was formally offered and immediately accepted the living and he was pleased to note that at the same time Claude was offered
Prickwillow. After the long incumbency of the Revd Samuel Kingdon
in Bridgerule, there had been a succession of vicars who stayed only for
short periods.

On 5 April 1888 Father Hawker was instituted to Bridgerule by the
Bishop of Exeter. In fact he stopped off to see the Bishop on his way up
to London from Penzance. Thus began his very long association with the
parish.

At that time, when priests were often curates for many years, the
move to Bridgerule must have made others very envious. The amount of
pastoral work required was relatively light because of the small number of
people living in the parish, about 500 at the time. The vicarage was a very
substantial property indeed, which dated from the late eighteenth century
and is now a listed building in private occupation known as Glebe House.
It is set in extensive grounds and its size can perhaps also be grasped from
the fact that the stables and barns ancillary to it have now been converted
into seven self-contained holiday cottages. A room in those outbuildings
was even used as a meeting room for the parish during Father Kingdon's
incumbency, in lieu of a church hall. In order to run such a large estab-

lishment a priest clearly needed private means and the Kingdons were comfortably off. They were able to afford several living-in servants and, when appropriate, a nurse for the children as they arrived.

The family expanded rapidly after the move to Bridgerule. The second child was Robert Claude Hawker Kingdon, born 21 April 1890, and he was followed by Bridget Mary Kingdon, born on 23 December 1892, Jane Edith Mary Kingdon, born 27 May 1896, and finally by Frank Denys Kingdon, born 4 September 1898. By this time the diaries were largely being written by Jessie and it seems clear that the children had an idyllic lifestyle. Their parents were concerned and interested in what they were doing, the countryside was all around them, and their home circumstances were very pleasant. Jessie Kingdon was clearly a doting mother and, although her diary entries are largely factual, it is apparent that she was very distressed when in due course the boys went away to school, Robert to Charterhouse and Frank to Bradfield.

The area was still of course very remote and the North Cornwall Railway to Bude did not open until 1898: indeed Jessie records that Frank cycled over to witness the start of running on the line. The parents and in due course the children cycled all over the area, and there were many Kingdon relatives to visit, including Edward and his children, who were slightly younger than Frank's children. A horse and trap was the alternative means of travel: when Father Kingdon died, *The Times* said that he had not learned to drive a car until he was 80 and that when he was 96 the authorities suggested that he might relinquish his licence for everybody's safety. However, his daughter-in-law subsequently confirmed that in fact he had learned during the 1920s, although the second part of the story in the newspaper obituary was correct.

The church at Bridgerule stands above and slightly away from the village, in a substantial burial ground. It has a core from the twelfth and thirteenth centuries, but was substantially rebuilt in 1448 at which time it appears definitely to have been dedicated to St Michael, and is a fairly ordinary Gothic church of those periods, with a substantial tower in three stages topped by large crocheted pinnacles typical of the Dartmoor area and one aisle to the south added at the time of the rebuilding: the north has a transept only. Some features remain from before the rebuilding, including a lancet window and a font of great simplicity and antiquity which may be Saxon or Norman, or may even have been adapted from a pagan sacred stone. There had been various further rebuildings and renovations over the years, including the south-east wall in 1790 and early in the nineteenth century the provision of new pews, altar rails and pulpit. In 1878 there was a major restoration including the addition of an organ chamber at the east end of the aisle with a vestry behind it and the re-flooring of most of the church. A new pulpit was erected at that time in memory of the Revd T.H. Kingdon.

The new vicar was anxious to move the liturgical worship onwards and upwards, and to carry out further alterations to the fabric, but was equally sensible enough to take the changes gradually.

In 1913 Father Kingdon had published a record of his first 25 years as parish priest, with illustrations, including one of himself, and a poignant picture of his two sons as thurifer and boat boy. Neither was to follow the family tradition: both in due course went to Hertford College, Oxford, and Robert then joined the Malay Civil Service. The poignancy in the picture arises from the fact that, as with so many of his generation, he joined the Army and was killed at Vimy Ridge in April 1917 while serving with the Royal Field Artillery. His brother Frank also joined the RFA, but survived the war and indeed was awarded the Military Cross. He joined the Sudan Political Service and became Governor of the Upper Nile, before coming back to England in 1948 and then, in contrast, running the Eton College stores until his retirement in 1963.

It is clear from the diaries that from very early on in his incumbency Father Kingdon began daily celebrations of what he then called holy communion: the term 'mass' does not appear in his wife's diaries until about 1906 and later.

The rector recorded in his Silver Jubilee booklet that his first step was to raise £12 to pay off a debt on the windows. He next introduced six altar and standard lights for evening service, new superfrontals and a credence table. By September 1888, after he had been in office for about six months, a choir for men and boys was instituted and they were provided with cassocks and surplices. A surpliced choir was regarded with horror by the Protestant Leagues and was thought to be a clear mark of Ritualism: such a choir had been instituted by Father Kingdon's father at Whitstone some years before, and he noted after a visit there in 1886 that the choristers were coming in following a processional cross for the first time.

Bridgerule did not acquire its own processional cross until 1890: its arrival may have been delayed because of the need to raise more money following the tower being struck by lightening in late 1888, which required remedial works. The arrival of the crucifix caused two men to leave the church as a protest against its introduction.

Screens were regarded at this time as an essential, to separate the chancel from the nave and thus to emphasize the importance of the mysteries of the altar. Many churches in Cornwall and Devon had had such screens until the Reformation and some had already been restored. In 1890 a carved oak screen was inserted across the north transept and it was fitted up as a lady chapel for the early celebrations. A new organ was purchased and placed at the east end of the south aisle.

The year 1891 was of considerable significance in ritual advance. Then, for the first time, linen vestments were worn. It was also at that time that a carved oak rood screen was erected right across the church with a narrow loft and a large rood and six tall candlesticks surmounting it. The lower panels were fitted with paintings of the 12 apostles 'after those in Amiens Cathedral'. It would not be unfair to say that the workmanship was not of the highest quality and the figures in particular owe perhaps more to the vulgar East End Anglo-Catholicism of Father Reginald Kingdon than to the more refined style generally found in the country. There was nothing here of the exquisite and expensive mediaevalism of a Comper refurbishment. A parclose screen was also erected to form a chancel and carved oak choir seats were installed to replace the Victorian pitch pine.

The vicar was convinced that the proper dedication of the church was not to St Michael but to St Bridget of Kildare. He explained in his booklet that he had not fallen into the trap of considering that the name of the village was connected to that of the saint: the name clearly comes from the bridge over the river in the centre of the built-up area. However, he was adamant 'that the Saint under whose patronage the church was built and the first altar reared (sic) was S. Bridget also seems fairly well established'.

The reasoning may well have been faulty but he would not thereafter move from it. On 30 January 1891 Harry Hems carved a small statue of St Bridget, which was then erected in a niche in the porch: the cost was met by Mrs Dennis, the wife of the supportive local squire, Mr G.B. Dennis. It was shortly after that the Kingdons' third child was born and she was of course given the name of the supposed patron saint.

The next step in what was a very ambitious programme of refurbishment was the introduction of Stations of the Cross. Then in 1895 a baptistery was formed around the font by the erection of three carved oak screens with paintings, the latter being the gift of the Kingdons themselves to give thanks for their three children who had by then been baptized there. A cope was presented by a third party and used for the first time at the dedication of this work.

The next step was to enhance the chancel decoration, particularly of the roof, and a carved oak font cover was given and introduced. New stained-glass windows were installed both in 1896 and later in about 1908, but the work was again not of any high quality.

The first use of incense in the church was in 1899, for Mr Dennis' funeral and thereafter it was used liturgically on all festivals. This again shows how far ahead a remote country parish such as Bridgerule could be, as incense was still very rarely found in the Church of England at that time.

In 1900 carved oak angels were erected on the chancel roof and gates inserted in the screen. In 1902 a reredos, made in Antwerp at a cost of £200, was placed on the high altar: it depicted Jesus appearing to Mary Magdalene with angels looking on. The reredos incorporated a tabernacle with a door of beaten copper and brass: again, such a method of reserving the Sacrament was far ahead of most London churches at that time.

A reredos was also carved for the lady chapel and the altar there was also provided with six candlesticks. This reredos was, however, made locally, by the Mesdemoiselles Pinwell, the daughters of the vicar of Ermington in Devon, who carried out a great deal of work, some of very high quality, in the area, particularly at St Paul, Yelverton. Further enhancements to the roof and the introduction of yet more carved oak continued: some of the work to the gilding of the lady chapel roof was apparently carried out by the rector himself.

Bridgerule had come to the attention of those who were opposed to the Catholic Revival in the Church of England and there was a 'painful scene' between Father Kingdon and a woman who was attempting to garner evidence to put before the Royal Commission on Ecclesiastical Discipline. The Kensitites appeared at least once, but could not obtain entry to the church. There was also controversy in 1908, when a churchyard crucifix on the Bavarian model, raised on steps and beneath a wooden roof, was dedicated by the Bishop of Lebombo, in what is now Mozambique, in memory of Mr and Mrs Dennis. The Bishop was robed in mitre and cope, which was a considerable novelty at the time. Finally, shortly before the publication of the booklet Father Claude Kingdon presented an almost life-size statue of St Bridget, which was initially erected in a niche outside the lady chapel.

By the First World War the church had therefore been almost completely refurnished and little was done thereafter: indeed to this day it has remained in essentially the same state. The catalogue of changes has been set out in detail because it shows the revolution which the villagers saw in the way in which the liturgy was offered in their parish and there is rarely so much accurate information available as to how this was done.

Father Kingdon wrote: 'One thing seems incontestably proved: that ritual in general and incense in particular does not drive away people, as one so often hears, from their parish church.' He justified that statement by means of a helpful table in the booklet, and the value of that data has been increased since he subsequently added to it in manuscript throughout most of the rest of his long life, finishing only in 1952.

It would also appear that he was correct in indicating that he was successful in his ministry. It is frequently difficult to establish exactly how many were attending and whether there were any special features of the congregation, such as the incomers in Throwleigh. It does not appear that here there were any such particular circumstances. The number of Easter communicants was 18 in 1889 and did not rise above 40 until 1901. By the mid years of the first decade of the twentieth century it was around 70, and then went over 100 in 1911. Throughout the inter-war years it was almost always well over 100 and even after the Second World War it hovered around that figure. If one bears in mind that these were figures for communicants, so they excluded young children, and that the population of the village was only about 500, they are impressive evidence of the continuing impact of Father Kingdon. In the diaries various other figures are given from time to time, such as there being 20 at weekday evensong on occasion before the First World War.

Father Frank Kingdon's ministry bears some similarity to that of Father Lowe in Throwleigh. They almost certainly knew each other well. Both were affable, concerned men with a happy family life who each had considerable charisma. It appears though that Frank Kingdon was more successful at attracting the support of the villagers for his new style of services and the commitment that was required. He also had the advantage of living for so long that everyone in the neighbourhood respected and knew him. Shortly before his death he baptized a baby girl, as he had her mother, grandmother and great-grandmother.

After the First World War, while the refurbishment of the church was complete, there was a rather stronger line displayed by the vicar in support of Anglo-Catholicism. He does not appear to have had many contacts with London clergy apart from his brother Reggie, or to have participated in the Anglo-Catholic Congress Movement or in the devotion to Our Lady of Walsingham. He was, however, a member of some national bodies, such as the Federation of Catholic Priests, and, particularly, the Confraternity of the Blessed Sacrament. Under the memorial plaque to Father Kingdon, which is on the wall above the stall where he used to sit, hangs his CBS medal. There were meetings of the society both at Bridgerule and at other local churches, such as St Andrew, Stratton, near Bude, which has and had a strong tradition of Anglo-Catholicism. In June 1927 it is recorded that 60 attended vespers for the Confraternity at Bridgerule, which was followed by tea on the extensive rectory lawns. There was also always a procession and benediction on Corpus Christi Day to which others from outside were invited.

The Kingdons had suffered the tragic loss of their older son in the war, and the other children moved away. Mary married an army officer in 1918 and Bridget and Frank also married. The diaries begin to note illness on the part of Jessie which on occasion precluded her from playing the organ in the church, and then 1927 turned out to be a very doleful year for the family. Jessie's health declined and Frank took over the entries in the diary. By the autumn she was clearly very ill, and on 2 November she received holy unction. Two days later she died, and Frank recorded with his usual brevity: 'Dear Jess passed: 5.30 peace falls.'

As if that were not enough, within weeks Father Kingdon's youngest daughter Jane, who had not married, died in Hong Kong. Her father was then 67, and was left to soldier on in the parish for more than 30 years.

It appears that after the loss of his wife, Frank Kingdon drew closer again to his brothers. They were accustomed to go on holiday together every year to Widemouth Bay, south of Bude. At that time this was a very small development of bungalows: it has since expanded as a retirement and surfing centre. It fell within the parish of St Winwalloe, Poundstock, where a similar pattern of changes to the fabric and the services had occurred as at Bridgerule, but at that time there was no church at the new settlement.

The brothers used to talk about their various problems and plan their sermons for the year.[10] Frank kept commonplace books, one of which has survived, in which he stuck sheets from parish papers from other places to give him ideas for addresses: St John, Isle of Dogs and his brother's pithy prose features frequently, but he also used material from the well-known mission parish of St Michael, Polwatte, Colombo, Ceylon, and also from the Cathedral of St Peter, Charlottetown, on Prince Edward Island in Canada.

In 1929 two pious ladies, Miss Kirby and Miss Topham, had erected by a Mr Bright a small cruciform oratory of wood and asbestos in the garden of their bungalow at Madeira Drive, Widemouth Bay. It was dedicated to Our Lady and St Anne. During the holiday period the three clerical brothers were able to use it as a private chapel. In 1940 the same Mr Bright moved it to a plot on the edge of the development, in Leverlake Road, where it remains to this day, painted white with black facings, one of the

---

10 Revd J.G. Edwards, in *The Story of Poundstock Church and Parish* (published by the PCC 1979, 1988 and 2000) says that the three brothers preached identical sermons throughout the year, having planned them while at Widemouth, but that seems to be apocryphal judging by the evidence of the notebook which has survived.

most unusual buildings in use for Anglican worship, but because of its small size, well adapted to the congregation and cheap to run. The Blessed Sacrament is reserved on the altar, and there is a large statue of Our Lady and a small rood of figures from Oberammergau. The tradition of the little chapel was maintained by successive vicars of Poundstock, one of whom, the Revd Peter Richard Fallowfield Sanderson, who was there from 1956 to 1974, was for a time Director of the Apostleship of Prayer of the Catholic League, the most prominent Anglican Papalist organization, and was also a member of the priests' Sodality of the Precious Blood.

Following the humiliation suffered by the episcopate over the failure of the attempts to revise the Prayer Book in 1927 and again in 1928, new attempts were made in several parts of the country to introduce disciplinary measures against Anglo-Catholics: it was apparent to all that one of the features of the new Prayer Book, had it been authorized, would have been an insistence that no deviations were to be permitted from the authorized rites.

One of those campaigns was in the Diocese of Exeter and involved also, a few years later, the requirement which was made for a new parish priest at Throwleigh, namely not to reserve the Blessed Sacrament. Pressure was put on Father Kingdon, but he was a formidable opponent and countered by having printed and distributed a pamphlet written by him entitled 'The duty of the parish priest to reserve', in which he asserted not only that he should not be prevented from so doing, but that he had a positive duty so to act, particularly because of the needs of those who could not get to church. The pamphlet is not dated but internal reference means it must have been issued in about 1929.

He set out a classic Tractarian position very clearly: 'I did and I still do assent to the 39 articles but of course <u>not</u> as the man in the street misunderstands them . . .' He went on to set out that he was 'obediently reserving against my Bishop's will but (a) not against my oath (b) not against the Prayer Book (c) not against the law and canons of the Catholic Church in England'. He then referred to the Twenty One incumbents in London who had refused to comply with the directions of Bishop Winnington-Ingram to cease from services directly related to the Blessed Sacrament, one of which number of course was his brother Reggie, by declaring defiantly that there were Twenty One in London and he remained 'Number Twenty Two'.

As usually happened, the Bishop eventually backed off and Bridgerule was left to go its own way. One of the strongest cards that a priest such as Father Frank Kingdon had was that he was clearly well regarded locally and he had the backing of the parish.

It also appears that Father Kingdon was in touch with other priests in the provinces who were suffering similar pressure: in his papers is a copy of an open letter written in 1929 by the Revds Cyril Wilkins, Arthur E. Wykes and Russell D. Marshall to the Bishop of Liverpool.

Once that controversy disappeared, Father Kingdon simply continued in the way to which he had become accustomed. After the Second World War he became something of a curiosity because of his venerability, but it would be a mistake to consider that he was stuck in a Tractarian past: rather he had moved forward liturgically and theologically to the advanced position adopted by many Anglo-Catholics in the 1930s. The church interior remained something of a period piece, as he did not have the enthusiasm for Baroque fittings shown by many of his colleagues.

It would appear that his flock's regard for their priest did not diminish with the years and certainly his own figures for the period up to 1952 do not indicate a slackening in numerical support. After his death, a simple grave was set up in the churchyard and the plate mentioned above was erected over his stall.

The author has some residual memory of staying in the area in the 1960s, when the villagers remained very devoted to Father Kingdon's memory: the incumbents who immediately followed him were the Revds S.A. Piggott and P.L. Swaffield, the latter of whom is also buried in the churchyard. By the 1980s and another visit the living had been combined with Pyworthy as in years gone by: mass was still sung on Sundays with a thurifer in attendance. Today the church has to be kept locked, but inside it is much as it was in 1914. However, there is a sung Eucharist only on three Sundays out of four, and on the other matins is the only service, thus reverting once a month to the pre-1888 situation.

The impact of Anglo-Catholicism on Bridgerule appears to have been more long lasting and deeper than in many comparable places, but to have been much abetted by the personality of the priest concerned. The problem in rural areas in recent years has been that small parishes are served by a flying squad of priests who necessarily have to serve many churches and cannot devote the time and effort that Father Kingdon expended in promoting the Faith.

3

St Petroc Minor, Little Petherick, Cornwall, and Athelstan Riley

The era in which rich, independent, patrons took up the cause of Anglo-Catholicism and in particular altered the pattern of worship in churches with which they were connected and which they financed, has now long gone. Two of the more prominent of these patrons in the early twentieth century were Athelstan Riley, with whom this chapter is concerned, and Samuel Gurney, who is dealt with in the next section.

There were of course others, such as the seventh Duke of Newcastle, whose churchmanship influenced a whole swath of churches in Nottinghamshire, the tenth Duke of Argyll, who strongly promoted the cause of Anglo-Catholicism within the Episcopal Church of Scotland, including refurbishing the church of St Paul at Inverary, where his ancestral castle stands, and Sir Hubert Miller, squire of Froyle in Hampshire, who refurnished the village church with items he brought back from his continental tours and also had erected a new mission church in the parish.

John Athelstan Laurie Riley (1858–1945) never had to seek remunerative employment throughout his long and in many ways industrious life, during which even those who stood askance were impressed by his energy. There were some who made fun of him, for he could be described fairly as not being his own worst critic, and in particular he lacked a sense of humour so far as his own activities and personality were concerned. Short and slight, he was always correctly dressed, and never out of doors without a hat. In later years he often wore a fur-lined travelling cloak over his suit, which would itself be either dark, for town, or tweed, for the country.

Proper form in dress and address was of particular importance to him.

Athelstan[1] Riley, as he was always called, was the only child of a Halifax-born barrister, John Riley (1820–62), who had a successful practice in London, and his wife Mary Margaret Elizabeth, née Laurie (1833–1925). She was the eldest daughter of John Minet Laurie (1812–68), MP for the City of London, and they married in London on 23 July 1857. John Riley was the third child of another John Riley (1786–1856) who was born at Wadsworth, Hebden Bridge, married Elizabeth Hargreaves of Heptonstall, also near Halifax, and appears to have made the family money in land, banking, shipping, and through his directorship of the Lancashire & Yorkshire Railway. His substantial home was at Brearley House, Luddenden Foot, in the same area and he in turn was the second son of yet another John Riley, of Souter House, Wadsworth, Hebden Bridge.

Athelstan Riley did not in later years lay any great emphasis on his Yorkshire roots, preferring to stress other connections: his long friendship with Lord Halifax was of more interest to him than his own roots in that town.[2]

It was obviously from his mother's maiden name that Athelstan acquired his own third forename. Typically, he used that chance to adopt St Laurence as his patron: he decorated a number of buildings with which he was associated with the gridiron of the saint, and he named his oldest son after him.

Athelstan Riley was born in London on 10 August 1858, and was thus still a very young child when his father John died on 20 October 1862. He was the only child of the marriage. In 1867 his mother remarried Dr W.G. Hamilton Roe: later she was widowed for the second time, and married for the third.

Athelstan Riley lived as a small child in Hastings, and went to prep school in Hampstead and then on to Eton. From there he went up to Pembroke College, Oxford, in 1878, taking his BA in 1881 and his MA

1 It is not clear why he was given this unusual name, but it was perhaps a sign of the revival at that time of Historicism: Athelstan was a Saxon King.

2 The reference in his obituary in *The Times*, 19 November 1945, to the effect that he 'never forgot' that he came from West Riding stock appears to be belied by the other evidence of his life.

two years later. It appears to have been at Oxford that he was first touched by Anglo-Catholicism, which never thereafter released its firm hold upon him. He claimed later not to have covered himself in academic glory while at university, and he did not take an honours degree: he did not follow his father, who had been at Cambridge.

There is no doubt that Athelstan Riley was rich, albeit he was also, like many who are well off, thrifty in small matters. However, although wealthy and undoubtedly enjoying the privileges which came from that status, he was serious minded and anxious to inform himself on ecclesiastical matters. His support for a very English, but at the same time mediaeval and antiquarian, liturgy in the Church of England was unswerving and he was a founder member of the Alcuin Club in 1897, which reflected those views of his as well as those of many others within the Anglo-Catholic Movement at that time: Riley was even nicknamed 'Sarum' after the ancient rite of Salisbury.

It is not surprising that in due course Riley became a patron of Ninian Comper, whose designs in the pre-First World War period embodied precisely Riley's own thinking. It is said that the two were introduced by the Revd (after 1905 the Revd Dr) Salisbury James Murray Price (1858–1926), a wealthy priest with strong mediaevalist leanings, who had been born in Scotland but was brought up by his widowed mother in England. Price had also graduated from Pembroke College, Oxford, although he did not go up until 1881, the year that Riley took his degree, and they may not have met there. However, Price's initial curacy was at Holy Trinity, Ely (1884–87), where he later employed Comper in his first substantial furnishing, at the small church of St Peter in that city, and he was then chaplain in Beirut (1887–88), which post was no doubt obtained through Riley's contacts. He was next curate of Coveney, near Ely, from 1888 to 1890: Riley had acquired the right of patronage to that church in 1883. In 1893 Price went to be rector of Kingston, Cambridgeshire, and then in the following year to his most substantial post, vicar of All Saints, the parish church of the small town of St Ives, then in Huntingdonshire, where he stayed only until 1899. In both churches he again employed Comper.

In 1883–84 Athelstan Riley had built for himself a substantial property known as 2 Kensington Court, which was constructed on part of the site of the former Kensington House. It was designed for him by T.G. Jackson, whose only London house this was. The cost was £7800 odd, a very large sum for the time: Riley was of course still unmarried at that period. The editors of the *Survey of London* remark that the property was 'among the first in Kensington to manifest the enthusiasm of artistic architects in the 1880s for Flemish buildings of the fifteenth and sixteenth centuries'. However, Riley ensured that it had a number of personal touches: all around the exterior run ornamental stringcourses bearing his initials, made by Doultons. It was that ostentatious streak which made some distrust him.

At this time, Riley was very involved with the Near East and with relations with the Orthodox and other Eastern Churches. He made his first visit to Russia in 1881 and then in 1883 he went to Greece. His travels in that region led him to eat yogurt far before it was fashionable and to smoke cigarettes from Cyprus. In 1883 he had commissioned from Gregory, a monk on Mount Athos whom he had met when visiting the monasteries there, a specially inlaid wooden door, which was hung in Kensington Court between the dining room and, a characteristic Riley touch, a private chapel, which was provided in due course with cedar panelling designed by C.E. Kempe and with a sixteenth-century Flemish sculpted reredos of alabaster, which was framed by Comper and is now in the church of St Mary in Cavendish, Suffolk.[3] The oratory is no longer in existence.

The remainder of the accommodation (which was extended later) was suitably lavish and included a small drawing room with a plaster ceiling incorporating both Riley's initials and the gridiron of his patron saint. A statue of St Laurence was added to the exterior in about 1890 when a small gable was erected at the rear following additions. The furniture was equally exquisite: much of it had been accumulated by Riley on his foreign tours, but it included a grand piano which was also designed by Jackson and was inlaid with satinwood, ebony, tortoiseshell and mother of pearl. In later years the property was converted to a hotel and much altered.

---

3 The connection with Cavendish arose because Athelstan Riley's daughter, Morwenna Brocklebank, lived in that village for many years both before and after the death of her husband in 1944. The reredos is said to have been badly over-painted at some point.

In 1884 Athelstan Riley presented himself to the Archbishop of Canterbury and offered to go at his own expense to visit the Assyrian Christians of the Middle East: he soon thereafter left for Syria and the Caucasus and on his return later that year published his report under the title *Narrative of Visit to the Assyrian Christians in Kurdistan*. He was then closely involved with the affairs of the Mission to the Assyrians until its demise in 1915.[4] In 1887 he published his first substantial book, *Athos, or the Mountain of the Monks,* which has been described as somewhat pedestrian, but was groundbreaking in its choice of subject so far as the English-speaking world was concerned and reflected the increased interest in the Eastern Church being shown in the Church of England as a result of the efforts of travellers such as Riley and another wealthy enthusiast, W.J. Birkbeck (1859–1916), later squire of Stratton Strawless, Norfolk, whom Riley had met at Eton. The book is still cited and was recently re-printed. In 1917, after Birkbeck's death, Riley was to edit and publish a book of essays and articles by his friend, under the title *Birkbeck and the Russian Church*.[5] In the period between 1890 and the First World War Birkbeck was the leading contact between the Church of England in general and the English Church Union in particular and the Russian Church, and Riley occupied a similar position in relation to the non-Orthodox Eastern churches, especially the Assyrians. Both were trusted friends of Lord Halifax, the President of the ECU. Salisbury Price also introduced Birkbeck to Comper and the result was that Comper carried out work to the church of St Margaret at Stratton Strawless: after leaving St Ives, Price only had one beneficed employment, which was as curate in this Norfolk parish from 1902 to 1903.

On 30 April 1887, in the same year as the publication of his book on Mount Athos, Riley married. His bride was the comprehensively named Andalusia Louisa Georgina Charlotte Molesworth, whom he called 'Anda'.

---

4 For a comprehensive and detailed account of this curious episode in missionary activity, see J.F. Coakley, *The Church of the East and the Church of England: A History of the Archbishop of Canterbury's Assyrian Mission* (Clarendon Press, 1992).

5 See also R. Birkbeck, *The Life and Letters of W.J. Birkbeck* (Longmans Green, 1922), and J. Bibbee, *Anglo-Catholicism and the Orthodox East: William Birkbeck and the Quest for Unity 1888–1916* (Anglo-Catholic History Society, 2007).

She was not rich, but she was the daughter of a nobleman and a priest, which was no doubt a matter of some importance to Riley. Her father was the Revd Samuel Molesworth, eighth Viscount Molesworth of Swords, County Dublin, and Baron Philipstown, in the Irish peerage (1829–1906): he had inherited the title from his uncle, who in turn had inherited from his second cousin. From 1876, Viscount Molesworth was the incumbent of St Petroc, Little Petherick in North Cornwall and it was this connection which led to Riley's involvement with Cornwall in general and that village in particular. Little Petherick lies on an arm of the River Camel, between Padstow and St Issey, and had then and for the next century a population of something under 200. The village lies in a dip in the land, through which the sinuous main road runs.

The wedding of Athelstan and Andalusia Riley took place at St Barnabas, Pimlico: the bridegroom gave what was almost certainly an address of convenience at 221 Ebury Street, Victoria, so as to establish residence in the parish, as he was in fact living at Kensington Court at the time. No fewer than six witnesses signed the marriage certificate, including Sir Hubert Miller of Froyle and sundry relations. The officiant was the Revd H.M. Myddleton Evans, then a curate at St Agnes, Kennington, who later went over to Rome while parish priest of St Michael, Shoreditch.

Andalusia's parents were married at the British Embassy in Paris in 1862, and she was born in that city on 6 February 1863. Although her father had taken his degree in 1853, he was not ordained priest until 1866, which was not a common pattern at that time. Andalusia was named primarily after Andalusia Grant Carstairs (1809–88), a former singer also known as 'Anda', who in 1844 married Sir William Molesworth, Bart. (1810–55), a radical MP who sat for East Cornwall and then other constituencies, was for a short time before his death a Government minister, and was the head of another, and at that time more prosperous, branch of the family. He was a well-known figure for his time, perhaps because his Radicalism was unusual in one of his background.[6]

6 It was somewhat strange that the name was so perpetuated, as Andalusia née Carstairs was very unpopular with most of the Molesworth relations because of her alleged lowly origins, her professional singing career and her earlier marriage to a man three times her age. Her forename was taken from that of her own mother, but how that lady was given it remains unclear. See A. Adburgham, *A Radical Aristocrat: The Rt.*

Louisa was the name of Andalusia's paternal grandmother. The names Georgina and Charlotte came from her mother, Georgina Charlotte Cecil Gosset (1839–79) who was born in Dublin but was the daughter of George Bagot Gosset (1810–40), an army officer with land holdings in Jersey: it was from this family connection that Riley's close involvement with that Channel Island began.

Andalusia's maternal grandmother was born Charlotte St Clair Douglas in Belfast in about 1808 and after the early death of George Gosset she remarried the Marchese de Vinchiaturo, a Calabrian, who then left her widowed for the second time. It was no doubt a source of some admiration from Riley that his wife had a grandmother with such an exotic title: Andalusia was living in London with the Marchesa in 1881, and the old lady died in Chelsea in 1888, the year after the wedding: she left some of her French antique furniture to her granddaughter, who placed it in her sitting room at Kensington Court. The Revd Viscount Molesworth had remarried one Agnes Dove in 1883.

The Molesworth family had had a connection with the Little Petherick church, which was properly called, with a mediaevalism which would have appealed to Athelstan Riley, St Petroc Minor of Nansfounteyn, for many years. There were two branches of the family, of which Samuel represented the senior, but by the late nineteenth century more impoverished, branch. From 1848 to 1862 the living was held by the Revd Hugh Henry Molesworth, of the junior branch, who was the cousin of Sir William and succeeded to the baronetcy on the latter's death in 1855.

The Revd Hugh Molesworth had been influenced by the then relatively new Oxford Movement. He had the church rebuilt entirely.[7] It had been erected originally in the fourteenth century, but by the mid-eighteenth century had fallen into disrepair and had been partly rebuilt, with a new

---

Hon. Sir William Molesworth of Pencarrow and his Wife Andalusia (Tabb House, Padstow, 1990).

7 One of his predecessors was the Revd Richard Lyne (rector 1812–34), who was an ancestor of Father Ignatius Lyne, the unconventional Benedictine revivalist. However, Richard Lyne, unlike Father Ignatius, was strongly anti-Roman, as was conventional for his era. Interestingly, however, another of the many Molesworths who were in Anglican orders, the Revd Paul William Molesworth, who held the living of Tetcott, the family seat in Devon, went over to Rome in 1854.

stone tower erected in 1750. However, the work cannot have been carried out with any great competence, as by 1858 the enthusiastic priest-baronet had the entire church pulled down and then reconstructed by the architect William White, who built a number of other churches at that period. It thus represented a realization of the ideal of a mediaeval church, but constructed to what were then modern standards. The rector is commemorated by a small stained-glass window in the church, erected many years later, and anachronistically showing him in eucharistic vestments, which he never in fact wore. He also added to and altered the rectory, which had originally been a small thatched house.

Sir Hugh Molesworth was succeeded by the Revd G.W. Manning (parish priest, 1862–76), who stencilled all the internal walls of the church with texts in black, green and red. He in turn was succeeded by Andalusia's father, who carried out only minor changes to the fabric of the church such as the insertion of two new windows and the construction of a vestry. He also built a new wing on to the rectory. The Viscount's churchmanship has not been recorded but it would not appear that it necessarily followed that of his relative Sir Hugh: the very comprehensive *Church Traveller's Guide* of 1897 does not contain an entry for the church.

In 1898 Viscount Molesworth resigned the living: he died at Bath in 1906. The advowson was alienated from the Manor of Porton, to which it had been attached since about 1264, and was acquired by Athelstan Riley, who was always anxious to acquire such rights in order that he could thereby influence the tone of the liturgy. He was to effect over the succeeding years a very considerable change in the furnishings and churchmanship of Little Petherick, as he did in other places, particularly Coveney, near Ely in Cambridgeshire, of which he acquired the advowson in 1883, very soon after coming down from Oxford, when the Rokeby Estates were broken up. He presented Father Myddleton Evans, who had officiated at his wedding, to Coveney, although the latter stayed in the Fens for only a short time (1884–89): Father Salisbury Price overlapped with his time during his curacy, although it is difficult to see why a tiny parish such as that required two priests. It is surprising that Comper was not engaged to work there, although extensive renovations were carried out. Riley also held a number of other rights of patronage, including Cranham in

Gloucestershire, Helpringham in Lincolnshire, Littleham (near Exmouth) in Devon, and the important London church of St Augustine, Kilburn.

Riley also increased his influence over patronage later when he and his good friend Lord Halifax became trustees of the Society for the Maintenance of the Faith, which held a number of advowsons across the country.

In the meantime, Athelstan and the Hon. Andalusia Riley were proving that, although they spent relatively little time together because of the many internal and external journeys made by him, they were together often enough to create a large family. Their first child, Laurence Athelstan Molesworth Riley, was born on 9 January 1888 in Kensington. He became a noted plant collector, fathered a son, Laurence Eyre Riley (1919–97, born in Guernsey), and died young, in 1928. However, because the child was born outside matrimony, as a result of an association with one Charlotte Eyre Thompson, Athelstan Riley cut his son off completely from the family and treated him as if he no longer existed. Even his obituary, in 1945, claimed that he had had four sons and a daughter, expunging Laurence from memory.

After a stillborn daughter in 1891, Athelstan and Andalusia's second child, and the only girl who lived, was Morwenna Mary Andalusia Riley (known always as 'Fluffy'),[8] born on 12 May 1892 in Cornwall. She married Harold Brocklebank in 1920: he died in 1944, she in 1970 and the marriage was childless.

Morwenna was followed by Christopher John Molesworth Riley, born in Kensington on 20 February 1894: he became an army officer, married twice, and had two children of his first marriage. He died in 1958. In October of 1895 Andalusia gave birth to another boy, who lived only a day and was never named, and then she had Hubert Cecil Charles Riley, who was born in Kent on 19 September 1896. He never married and ran his own school in Westgate-on-Sea, Kent: he died in 1970. There was scarcely time to draw breath before the fifth child, John Harold Douglas Riley, was born on 30 August 1897: he married but had no children and died in 1968. Finally, and perhaps as something of an afterthought, there

---

8 The name Andalusia has been perpetuated in various descendants since.

arrived the splendidly named Quintin Theodore Petroc Molesworth Riley on 27 October 1905. He became a naval officer and noted polar explorer,[9] married late and had a daughter and a son, but the latter lived only a few days. He died in 1980 of injuries received in a motor accident.

In addition to the six children who lived and two who did not, Andalusia also had six miscarriages. There were in fact remarkably few grandchildren from so many children.

Throughout this early period of marriage Athelstan Riley continued to travel and also to concern himself with many church-based committees and campaigns. Andalusia only accompanied him occasionally, but recorded her thoughts in ill-punctuated and often trenchant diaries which she sent home. She did not take Athelstan as seriously as he did himself, and is reported to have said that whenever he could not think of a rhyme for one of his hymns he ended the line with an Alleluia: she certainly recorded in her holiday diary that what he insisted was an eastern church looked to her more like a mosque. She also used what is now a dated and rather evocative expression of her husband (whom she always referred to as 'Athelstan' without abbreviation) saying that one morning he felt somewhat 'seedy', and stayed behind, which perhaps indicated a break for her from the incessant church crawling.

In the autumn of 1888, only months after the birth of his first child, Riley was off to Kurdistan to report again for Archbishop Benson, a trip he had already undertaken in 1884 and again in 1886: on his return on this occasion he persuaded the Sisters of Bethany to send a few of their nuns to the region, but their stay was relatively short and unsuccessful.

Riley was prominent in the English Church Union, the Anglican and Eastern Churches Association (founded in 1906 as the Anglican and Eastern Orthodox Churches Union)[10] in which the Papalist Revd H.J. Fynes-Clinton was also a leading light, and many other such bodies, including

---

9 See Jonathon Riley, *From Pole to Pole: The Life of Quintin Riley* (Antony Rowe Ltd., Chippenham, 1998), which has much interesting information on the family as well as on Q.T.P.M. Riley's career.

10 The Association was the product of the union of the Anglican and Eastern Churches Union and the Eastern Church Association, the latter of which had been founded in 1864 by John Mason Neale. Riley was largely responsible for engineering the merger.

the pioneer Association for the Promotion of the Unity of Christendom, which had been founded as long ago as 1857 but had lost most of its influence when Roman Catholics were forbidden to participate in it. In 1898 Riley published another book, entitled *A Synopsis of Oriental Christianity*, which was reprinted in 1902, and in 1901 and 1908 he wrote successive volumes entitled *Pontifical Services*, the first of which was illustrated by miniatures of the fifteenth and sixteenth centuries and had an introduction by Father W.H. Frere CR (later to be Bishop of Truro), and the second of which was accompanied by pictures of sixteenth-century woodcuts.

At this period he also wrote a book, which went into several editions over many years, entitled *A Guide to High Mass Abroad: Being a Manual for the Use of English Churchmen Attending the Celebration of the Eucharist in Catholic Countries*. This had the text of the mass in parallel columns in English and Latin with learned digressions such as 'Notes on the Asperges'. Later, in 1922, he published a similar book relating to the Orthodox, entitled *A Guide to the Divine Liturgy in the East, being a Manual for the use of English Churchmen*. He also contributed to all manner of publications, such as, for example, the foreword to a book by the Revd G.A. Cobbold, of St Bartholomew, Ipswich, entitled *Why I am an Anglo-Catholic*.

Although Riley was primarily interested in narrowly ecclesiastical matters, he also was very much involved in the divisive education debates of the 1890s. The Education Act of 1870 had brought about the provision of many Board Schools: it was specifically provided that 'no religious catechism or religious formulary of any particular denomination shall be taught in [any such] school'. This was coupled with difficulties in relation to the so-called Voluntary Schools, that is those which had been set up before 1870 by the churches themselves, which found themselves financially disadvantaged vis-à-vis the new Board Schools.

Riley was elected to the London School Board for the Chelsea Division, and strongly advocated definite Anglican teaching being given in state schools. He came much to public attention as a result of this and so the 1894 election, in which he stood again, attracted a great deal of controversy. To the surprise of many of his neighbours he decorated the façade of his elegant house in Kensington with numerous bills supporting his candidature. He succeeded in being re-elected and Lord Halifax was so delighted he presented him with a small silver cup with Riley's arms engraved upon it. The Boards were abolished under the Education Act of 1902, but further fierce controversy surrounded the Bill of 1906, brought in by the new Liberal Government under pressure from Nonconformist interests. Riley remained interested in the subject and in 1911 he co-edited a book on the subject, entitled *The Religious Question in Public Education.*

In 1897 it was also proposed that he be elected a Proctor by his old Oxford College, but that proposal in the end fell through. This episode showed the regard in which he was held, as he had never taken an honours degree nor been a Fellow of the college.

As can be seen from the places of birth of his children, the Rileys split their time principally between London and Cornwall, with interspersed travelling. He began to participate more fully in Cornish church affairs, but his involvement with the Duchy became far more pronounced once his father-in-law had left Little Petherick and he had taken control of the right to appoint his successor.

Riley's first appointment as rector of the village was the Revd Hildebrand Samuel Barker, who was the first priest at Little Petherick to wear eucharistic vestments, which at that date were still very rarely found in the country. He is described as a man of considerable zeal and talent, but he died suddenly in 1901. He was still a young man: he came to Cornwall from two curacies in Devon, at Bideford and St John, Torquay, respectively. He was commemorated by a brass in the pavement of the lady chapel showing a priest in appropriate vesture.

Father Barker was succeeded by the Revd William Margetson, who stayed until 1909. He had undertaken training at St Stephen's House, Oxford, then beginning to establish itself as a centre for the Anglo-Catholic Movement, and then had two other curacies, one at St John, Clevedon, Somerset, being immediately before his move to Little Petherick. After leaving Cornwall he had a number of other posts, which culminated in his appointment in 1925 as Provost of St Mary's Episcopal Cathedral, Edinburgh. For a short time during 1903–04 he even had a curate, the Revd E.G. Winstanley, which would appear to have been an extravagant appointment bearing in mind the tiny population of the village.

During these two incumbencies, Athelstan Riley began a further restoration of the church, only 50 years or so since it had been completely rebuilt. The stencilling on the walls was removed and under Comper's direction, as an old guidebook puts it, 'the church [was] restored as far as possible to its original condition before the troubles of the sixteenth century despoiled it'. That comment was aspirational rather than rooted in solid fact, as of course it had been almost entirely rebuilt in 1858.

The work was very extensive. A new altar was placed in the lady chapel and the wooden altar which dated from the time of the Revd Sir Hugh Molesworth was enclosed within it. A carved and gilded reredos was erected over the altar, containing figures of Our Lady, St John the Divine, St Petroc, St Francis and St Anthony of Padua, which was the gift of Father Barker's family: he died during the restoration. An organ gallery was erected at the west end of the church and a new organ supplied for it. The entire church save for the chancel was reroofed internally in the old Cornish style, using plaster panels. A new vestry was built over the small one provided by Andalusia's father. In the chancel a complete remodelling took place with a new high altar, and the stalls erected by Sir Hugh Molesworth were moved into the lady chapel and many new oak benches provided for the body of the church.

The most significant alteration to the church, and that which perhaps informs the observer most about the thinking of the patron and his architect, was the erection of a most elaborate wooden screen and rood loft right across the church, painted and gilded on the west side. It is an important example of Comper's work at this time, and it displays many motifs which he used elsewhere: the rood images are flanked by the fiery six-winged seraphims, and over the lady chapel entrance is the image of the thrones, a wheel in a wheel, full of eyes round about. The screen also incorporated the arms of the diocese, the county and of Riley himself, whose initials, joined by rope, are also found. The carving was largely carried out locally and the work was complete by 1908.

Thus the interior of the church was very significantly altered and has remained so since although the artistic and theological insights upon which it was based have long since disappeared. Comper's vision of beauty and mediaevalism, shared by his wealthy patron, is now anathema to those who build or refurbish churches.

Over the same period in which the restoration took place, Riley acquired for Little Petherick a fabulous collection of vestments and ornaments, mostly but not entirely of continental origin and dating from the sixteenth century. They included a modern silver hanging pyx, an unusual method for reserving the Blessed Sacrament as aumbries were more common and tabernacles were coming into use, but one characteristic of the thought of Riley and of Comper and justified by them on historical grounds. The pyx was designed by the Revd Walter Wyon, then at St Issey, Cornwall, and later rector of Ufford, Suffolk. The little church thus possessed a collection of ecclesiastical finery almost unparalleled in this country, and certainly not equalled in a similar parish. In 1899 Riley had written and published a hymn to St Petroc, a Cornish saint who had died at Bodmin: his feast day, 4 June, was marked thereafter in the parish church.

Riley's development of the parish was not confined merely to the church itself. The rectory at the time he became patron had 40 acres of glebe and was itself a substantial property, which is now a hotel and is known as Molesworth House.

Riley rented this from the rector from 1898 to 1909 and during that period extended and altered it quite considerably: he then acquired property in Jersey and treated that thereafter as his main country residence, but when in Cornwall he stayed at St Mary's, one of two small houses (the other being Bridge Cottage) which he had had built in 1904/05 on the glebe land. They were designed by the Plymouth architect T. Rogers Kitsell, who also carried out work in that area for some of the Anglo-Catholic churches. Plymouth was known during this period for advanced Anglo-Catholicism, particularly during the incumbency of the Revd Charles Rose Chase at All Saints (1878–98) and later when the Revd Maurice Child and others were at St James the Less. The rectory was let after the Rileys vacated to a Mr G.T. Skilbeck, who became a benefactor to the church on his own account.

It appears that the two cottages were intended for retired clergy but in fact were never used in that way. Further construction took place to produce cottages for the coachman and gardener (now called Glebe Cottages), which he ensured had a feel of the Holy Land about them, to remind him of his travels in that region. As if that building was not enough, Riley himself in 1907 designed and had constructed a village hall for the parish, which has proved to be a successful and long-lasting facility.

On 28 September 1908 Fidelity Trust Ltd. was incorporated under the Companies Acts and on 26 March 1909 Riley conveyed property to it, which appears to have included Tregonna House, which was near the rectory at Little Petherick. Thereafter he sat on the board of the Trust and it appears to have been used as a vehicle to assist ecclesiastical purposes, and in particular to hold the property of monastic communities who were forbidden to own their own land: others also gave money. The definition of the Church of England provided in the articles is indicative of the donor's thinking: it was referred to as that part of the Catholic Church in communion with Canterbury, and in the event of a split the gifts were to be used for that part which upheld the doctrines which were promulgated prior to the Great Schism of 1054. Unfortunately no full list of Athelstan Riley's many donations to churches and institutions appears to have survived.

Apart from his other concerns, Riley was also a member of the committee which was responsible for the acclaimed and, for its time, revolutionary *English Hymnal,* the first edition of which was published in 1906: the moving spirit behind the enterprise was the Revd Percy Dearmer, then at St Mary, Primrose Hill, who was a leading exponent of the English Use. Birkbeck was also co-opted on to the committee which produced the book, most of the meetings for which were at Kensington Court. It is perhaps surprising that Riley and Dearmer, neither of whom held a modest view of their own abilities, did not fall out, but they appear to have got on well and later, when Dearmer owned a Riley car, he nicknamed it Athelstan.

Although, somewhat surprisingly, his grandson recalled him as not being particularly musical,[11] Riley contributed seven translations from the Latin and one from the Greek: these included 'Hail O Star that Pointest', which was thought by some to be dangerously mariolatrous. In addition three of his original hymns were included, namely 'Come, let us join the Church above', 'Saints of God! Lo, Jesus' people' and, by far the

---

11 See J.R.C. Riley in J. Park, *Athelstan Riley: Patron of St Petroc Minor, Little Petherick* (published by the author, 1982), pp. 58–9. This book again assists with family matters, especially in its extracts from diaries.

best-known, 'Ye watchers and ye holy ones', which is still frequently sung today. In 1915 Riley published a book entitled *Concerning Hymn Tunes and Sequences,* which had an introduction by the distinguished organist and composer H. Walford Davies.

Although Riley was generally on the English Use side of the fault line in Anglo-Catholicism which divided those who looked back to the Middle Ages from the Western Use side who looked much more to the post-Counter Reformation Church of Rome, he was, like many at the time, entranced by the vision of revived Benedictinism being propagated by Abbot Aelred Carlyle on Caldey Island. There is no doubt in fact that Carlyle was an illusionist and a dreamer, with irresponsible and dark streaks, but he was remarkably persuasive and there were many otherwise level-headed enthusiasts for Anglo-Catholicism who were entranced by what they saw of the Community. Riley and others of his associates were highly regarded by Carlyle as supporters because of their ability to back with finance the schemes he devised, which became increasingly grandiose. After a visit to the island in 1907, Riley gave to the Community a silver hanging pyx beneath a canopy of three crowns, also designed by Ninian Comper.[12] He then famously wrote in the Caldey magazine, *Pax,* that 'Caldey is to me the greatest phenomenon in the Anglican Communion at the present day'.[13] He then, rather more prosaically, offered to lend the Abbot a machine for making concrete blocks, which he had been using at Little Petherick, in order to assist with the construction of cottages on the island. It is also said that this machine was used in the making of the ugly, and therefore controversial, concrete shell which was made to safeguard the oratory of St Piran at Perranporth in North West Cornwall.

Riley was not the only leading Anglo-Catholic to fail to see the lack of sound foundations for the enterprise, veiled as they were by the omnipresent mediaevalism and thick clouds of incense. Samuel Gurney donated the bells for the tower, and Lord Halifax, after being present at exposition of the Blessed Sacrament and compline in the chapel, wrote to his daugh-

---

12 This is now in St Mary, Penzance, after a number of moves.

13 Quoted in P.F.Anson, *Abbot Extraordinary* (Faith Press, 1958), p. 120. The article was in *Pax,* June 1910.

ter, 'It really was the chief dream of my life realized.'[14] In 1908 Halifax, Riley, Birkbeck and Samuel Hoare, later a leading Member of Parliament, were all on the island together. Halifax reported to his daughter that Riley had tried to get in to the mass at the other end of the bench so as not to disturb him, but had succeeded in falling over the Abbess of Malling, who was 'enclosed' in a curtained box 'for all the world like an old hen in a coop'.[15]

Following the defection of Abbot Aelred and most of his community to Rome in March 1913, difficult problems arose in relation to the owner-ship of the property on the island, most of which had been built with the aid of subscriptions from Anglo-Catholics. A committee of arbitration was set up with Halifax and Riley to represent Anglicans and the Duke of Norfolk and the Bishop of Menevia to represent the Roman Catholics. Riley was notably more conciliatory than Halifax: eventually agreement was reached, which included the retention of property at Pershore, to which the remnant from Caldey who had not gone over moved. The sums of money paid to the Anglican side were vested in the Fidelity Trust and the interest was paid to the community which was re-established at Pershore.[16]

One of Riley's more attractive characteristics was a determination not to give up, whatever the difficulties. Even after the debacle of Caldey, he strongly supported the efforts of the small remnant to continue, and he and his colleagues on the Pershore Helpers Committee (established 1916) were instrumental in persuading the Revd Denys Prideaux to take his vows and to accept the abbacy, which was a vital step in the future development of the community. Riley himself donated the furnishings of the altar at Pershore in 1914, in a rather more English idiom than was to be the case with later additions, particularly after the move to Nashdom in 1926.

It is clear that Lord Halifax, the acknowledged lay leader of the Anglo-Catholic Movement, continued to repose great confidence in Athelstan Riley and confided in him over both ecclesiastical and personal matters.

---

14 Letter of about 1908, quoted in J.G. Lockhart, *Charles Lindley Viscount Halifax, Part Two* (Geoffrey Bles, the Centenary Press, 1936), p. 208.

15 Lockhart, *Charles*, p. 207.

16 See *Jubilee Book of the Benedictines of Nashdom* (Faith Press, 1964), p. 13. The Trust also held money for other communities.

By 1909, following the completion of the restoration of the church, Athelstan Riley was looking for wider fields of influence than Little Petherick. In that year the Revd Ernest George Winstanley, who had already acted as curate in 1903–04, was appointed as rector, and he remained in post until his death in early 1944; the duties were not onerous and he was regarded as a good and faithful parish priest. As with his predecessor, he came from a curacy at St John, Clevedon.[17]

In August 1911 Lord Halifax called a conference at his Yorkshire home, Hickleton, which was ostensibly to deal with Prayer Book Revision, which was thought to be a pressing issue at that time, following the Royal Commission on Ecclesiastical Discipline (to which Riley had himself given evidence). In fact the need for expedition proved to be illusory and completed proposals did not appear until the 1920s. However, much of the conference was in fact taken up with the affairs of the Caldey Benedictines: Abbot Aelred attended and a great deal of effort was devoted to prevent him and the other members of the community from defecting to Rome. Temporary success in that respect was achieved, but in addition a manifesto was prepared which was published by the Alcuin Club and edited by Riley. It was entitled *Prayer Book Revision: The irreducible minimum of the Hickleton Conference showing the proposed rearrangement of the order of Holy Communion together with further suggestions.*[18]

As the book showed, those present at the Hickleton Conference pledged themselves to resist, and to refuse to employ, any revised form of the Book of Common Prayer which relaxed the existing directions of the Ornaments Rubric, altered the substance or use of the Athanasian Creed, sanctioned the giving of communion to those not confirmed, failed to restore a 'better and more primitive' order for the administration of communion, including (a) the linking together of the preface and sanctus, the existing prayer of consecration and prayer of oblation and the Lord's Prayer and (b) the placing of the exhortation, confession, absolution and comfortable words 'in their proper place' after the communion of the priest, sanctioned the

17 The fact that Father Winstanley was married would appear to give the lie to one of the Revd Colin Stephenson's good stories, at p. 78 of *Merrily on High* (Darton, Longman and Todd, 1972, reissued by Canterbury Press, 2008), which relied on the assertion that Riley had a 'mania about [clerical] celibacy'.
18 This too has been recently republished.

postponement of baptism beyond the time appointed in the existing Book, failed to provide for unction of the sick, interfered with or failed to recognize continuous reservation or failed to direct prayers for the dead. This shows clearly the line being taken at that time by 'advanced' but still mainstream Anglo-Catholics.

By this time, Riley's domestic life was moving away from Cornwall, although he retained the use of the cottage, St Mary's, thereafter. In the early years of the century he had become enthused about the Channel Islands, to which he was introduced through his wife's connections, and thought very seriously about purchasing the island of Sark, with its peculiarly mediaeval system of government. To him, a feudal title was a *sine qua non* of any purchase and he also looked seriously at Cyprus as a place to live.

However, these ideas did not proceed, and in 1909 he purchased the manor of Trinity in the north east of Jersey. He immediately had very extensive work to the house carried out by the architect Sir Reginald Blomfield, and thereafter used it as his principal country home. The house was of a variety of periods, and Blomfield's first proposal was quite conservative, but then Riley had him substantially remodel it with high roofs, such as were found on the nearby Cotentin peninsula in France and in particular overlooking the harbour at St Malo. The roofs were of grey Delabole slate from Cornwall which contrasted with the pink Jersey granite. He also incorporated in it materials purchased from a fifteenth- or sixteenth-century house on the island called L'Ancienneté. The Greek-made door, the Jackson piano and many bookcases were taken to the Manor from Kensington.[19]

More importantly, so far as Riley was concerned, the acquisition gave him the right to call himself 'Seigneur de la Trinité', which he proceeded to annex to his name thereafter on all possible occasions. His insistence upon the title, which in many ways was of little more than symbolic importance, was the subject of a considerable amount of ribaldry on the part of those who knew him and led to many jokes using play on the expression Holy Trinity. It also gave him an entrée to *Burke's Landed Gentry*,

---

19 See an interesting article on the house by Marcus Binney in *Country Life*, 7 August 1986.

which was a matter of importance to one of his cast of mind. He was worried during the negotiations for the purchase that the vendor (Captain Graves Chapman Swan) had not had the approval of the Crown when he had himself bought some years before, and so he successfully petitioned the Privy Council to ensure that he could be admitted to the twice-annual Assize d'Heritage in Jersey and could use the title.

Riley had his bookplate altered: initially it showed the house as he bought it, but then it had on it the house as altered, but both had a knight in armour in the foreground.

The manor carried with it the obligation, as a service of grand serjeanty, to present the Sovereign with two mallards when he visited Jersey. On 21 July 1921 Athelstan Riley was able to perform this service for the first time: it was just the sort of gesture in which he rejoiced. He was also appointed at various times to be a Commander of the Order of King George I of Greece and of the Serbian Order of St Sava.

On 29 February 1912 Andalusia died in Kensington of pulmonary tuberculosis: she was still only in her late 40s and it was only just over six years since her last child had been born, but she had been in poor health for some time, accentuated by the strain from her continual pregnancies.[20] It is said that straw was laid on the street outside to deaden the noise of horses passing while she was so ill. It is a reflection on her husband's self-importance that even on the death certificate he insisted on describing himself with the addition of his Jersey title.

One feature of the rectory in Little Petherick, after it was altered by Riley, was a revolving summer house on a flat roof, which was itself provided with a lawn: the invalid was carried to it by a wooden footbridge over the public highway, the main road between Padstow and Wadebridge.

The funeral was in Jersey and Andalusia was buried there, but later commemorated at Little Petherick in spectacular fashion. Athelstan Riley never remarried and the burden of bringing up the younger children fell on domestic staff and schools. He was domestically wholly incompetent and was Victorian in his approach to children: there was one occasion when, most unusually, he took the very young Laurence for a walk, but

---

20 The death certificate does not bear out Jonathon Riley's assertion in his life of Quintin Riley that she died of rheumatism, if indeed one can so die.

he then returned several hours later without the child, whose presence he had completely forgotten. The boy was later retrieved from a police station. His grandson recalled him as interested, but 'never generous with his gifts [to the family] or lavish with his affections'.[21]

Laurence had followed his father to Eton, but perhaps because of the lack of appropriate piety there, the other boys were all sent to Lancing.

From Andalusia's death until the end of the First World War, Riley busied himself with writing, committees and the like: he became involved in a particular row with his previous collaborator Percy Dearmer when the latter favoured allowing women, particularly the charismatic Maude Royden, to speak in churches as part of the National Mission of Repentance and Hope in 1915. Riley was predictably opposed to this development and said that if this were allowed 'disaster must inevitably follow'.[22] He continued to be on good terms with Salisbury Price and visited him at Tintinhull, Somerset, in which he lived after about 1903. Comper was employed there also, to design a churchyard war memorial cross in about 1920, although Price held no official position in the parish. After his death in 1926 a memorial to him was erected in Littleham, another Riley parish, and was appropriately enough designed by Comper.

Riley was not of course immune from the effects of the hostilities, and his son Christopher (Kit) was injured in action. The war also impacted on remote Little Petherick in an unexpected way: a Belgian refugee (reminiscent perhaps of Agatha Christie's Poirot), named Wilhelm, carved a statue of St Petroc which was placed next to the high altar.

Although Riley was in many ways of a conservative way of thinking, he was not immune to some new ideas, particularly if he was thereby enabled to advance the causes in which he believed. He was particularly concerned that in the long term it was not sustainable for a village as small as Little Petherick to have its own priest. In 1918 he corresponded with the Bishop of Truro in an attempt to allow Father Winstanley to hold the adjoining (and generally rather Low Church) parish of St Issey in plurality, but this did not occur then and indeed did not happen until 1967. He also put

---

21 See Park, *Athelstan*, p. 58.

22 See D. Gray, *Percy Dearmer: A Parson's Pilgrimage* (Canterbury Press, 2000), p. 150.

forward a more ingenious suggestion, which was that the Oratory of the Good Shepherd, an association of celibate priests whose members were bound by a rule of life but were not in community, should be invited to take over four Cornish parishes, including it would appear Little Petherick, and run them together: however, this too failed to proceed further.[23]

Riley's politics were idiosyncratic: in 1884 he had written from Pembroke College to a correspondent: 'I am an anti-Liberal ('Conservative' or 'Tory' do not express what I mean, being mere party names) simply because I am a Christian man; and I have never yet known a man with really Liberal principles who was *thoroughly* sound on matters of faith.'

Over the years, however, he had from time to time been asked to stand for parliament in the Conservative interest but to this point had never put himself forward. He was, perhaps surprisingly, a supporter of women's suffrage, but only for the educated. The end of the First World War saw the franchise greatly extended, with all men and all women of 30 and over being given the right to vote, in contrast to the limited and somewhat arbitrary but certainly all-male electorate which had existed before the hostilities.

At that time, and indeed until after the Second World War, the Universities of Oxford and Cambridge had their own representation, with the right to vote being exercisable only by senior members. In 1919 a by-election was called at Oxford after one of the two sitting members was elevated to the peerage. Riley was prevailed upon to stand as an Independent, although making it clear that his sympathies were entirely to the right politically. He issued a manifesto address which began, with the candidate's usual self-importance, by saying 'My name is at least familiar to nearly every voter, whether it raises sentiments of hostility or of friendship'. He went on to excoriate both Conservatives and Liberals and to denounce Socialism. His basic point was that authority was needed in 'a country which has become dangerously unstable' and that 'in the shifting of political power to the uneducated masses lies our great peril'.

This appeal was unsuccessful. Riley came third out of three, with 1032 votes. The election was won by the distinguished historian Professor

---

23 See G. Tibbatts, *The Oratory of the Good Shepherd* (OGS, 1988), p. 25.

(later Sir) Charles W.C. Oman (1860–1946), who polled 2613 standing as the Official Conservative candidate, and thus triumphed by a large majority over the Labour representative, the equally distinguished classicist Professor G. Gilbert Aimé Murray (1866–1957), who received 1330 votes. This short and slightly embarrassing essay was the end of Athelstan Riley's direct political involvement.

At about this time, Riley compiled his own curriculum vitae for the Archbishop of Trebizond, with whom he was corresponding in French. It is worth quoting almost completely, as it shows the breadth of his interests and achievements, but also why some thought him pompous and self-satisfied:

> Athelstan Riley, Seigneur de la Trinité (an ancient feudal property in the Island of Jersey); Commander of the Order of King George of Greece; Order of St Sava of Serbia; Member of the House of Laity in the National Association of the Church of England; Vice-President of the English Church Union; Fellow of several Learned Societies including the Society of Antiquarians (sic); Chairman of the Anglican and Eastern Churches Association; Chairman of the Alcuin Club, a society for publishing liturgical documents. He was educated at Eton, the chief public school to which the sons of the nobility and gentry of England are sent, and subsequently graduated at the University of Oxford. Has travelled all over Europe and in Turkey and Russia; visited the Holy Mountain of Athos as a young man in 1883 and wrote an account of the monasteries; in 1884 was sent out to Kurdistan by Archbishop Benson to visit the Archbishop's Mission to the Assyrian (Nestorian) Christians. Was Chairman of the Committee which was occupied with the education of Serbian theological students during the Great War. Has recently made himself responsible for the religious necessities of the Russian refugees and arranged with the Anglican ecclesiastical authorities to place a large Anglican Church in London at their disposal for Orthodox Worship.[24] Was at one time connected with the State

---

24 This was a reference to St Philip, Buckingham Palace Road, which was later demolished in order to make way for an extension of Victoria Coach Station. It is shown just before complete demolition in the history of that Station, R. Paramor, *Hello ... Coastal* (Venture Publications, 2007), p. 88.

Primary Education and is a strong supporter of Religious Education in the State Schools. He is best known to the Orthodox Prelates visiting England as the Archbishop of Canterbury's lay representative and is a member of various conferences between Orthodox and Anglican theologians. [After listing publications, it continues:] Mr Athelstan Riley married a daughter of the Viscount Molesworth, by whom he has several children. His son and heir [i.e. Christopher, as Laurence was regarded by then as *persona non grata*] is a Captain in the Royal Guard. He lives partly on his property in Jersey.

In 1919 the elderly Lord Halifax decided to resign as President of the English Church Union, which under his leadership, ably assisted by the efficient Secretary, H.W. Hill, had enjoyed a golden period. Riley was an obvious candidate to succeed him, although there were some who thought a younger man was required. He, however, refused to stand and eventually Lord Phillimore, a compromise candidate, agreed to accept the position for one year only. The following year, the problem reoccurred and Riley again refused to stand, but was then persuaded to do so only on the self-imposed condition that he set out his manifesto first: he, however, came to that position without knowing that Halifax had agreed to support Sir Robert Newman. Riley's sponsors then, in his absence abroad, nominated him without disclosing his letter of policy and he had to withdraw his candidature by writing publicly to the *Church Times*.[25]

In 1921 Riley was a founding delegate to the Central Council for the Care of Churches, and proposed its first President, Bishop H.E. Ryle. He served on that body for ten years. His antiquarian cast of mind was very similar to that of Dr F.C. Eeles, the long-serving Secretary, although the latter had a long-standing feud with Comper, which would not have accorded with Riley's views.

Although by the post-war period Riley was spending less time in Little Petherick, it was still a place where he felt at home and where he and Andalusia had spent much of their married life. He decided that although she was buried on Jersey, he would commemorate her in Cornwall in some style. He thus instructed Comper to build out a small chantry chapel to

---

25 See Lockhart, *Charles*, pp. 263–4.

the south of the high altar, in which was provided an altar with Italian reredos and a sarcophagus with a bronze figure of his late wife. This was an extremely rare addition to a church by this date: he also provided a fund for the saying of mass annually for her soul and (prospectively) for his own and this was held by the Fidelity Trust.

Halifax, still involved in church matters, retained his regard for Riley and when he thought that he would be unable to continue with the Malines Conversations in 1925, he pressed for Riley's inclusion in his place.[26]

The next years were, however, dominated, so far as Athelstan Riley was concerned, by the slow moves to provide for a Revised Prayer Book, culminating in the parliamentary defeats of 1927 and 1928 and the consequent humiliation of the episcopate.

Riley, with Lord Halifax, would have been perfectly content had the bishops authorized the use of the Prayer Book of 1549 as an alternative to that of 1662, but by the end of the 1920s he and his party were being out-flanked by more militant Anglican Papalists, who made it clear that they would not be bound by any state-imposed liturgy and in any event were unwilling to obey direct instructions from the episcopate to cease from Roman-inspired devotions. His own rather moderate and English Use outlook was becoming dated and the English Church Union was losing influence to the more militant Anglo-Catholic Congress, which attracted more young blood and was brilliantly orchestrated by the Revd Maurice Child: in addition Hill had retired as secretary of the ECU when Halifax resigned in 1919 and his successor, the Revd Arnold Biddulph Pinchard, was less effective. Riley was very much taking a back seat.

By 1932 there was strong pressure for the two bodies to amalgamate: Halifax by then had returned to the Presidency although his great age made him unable to control matters as closely as before. On 30 December of that year the now nonagenarian Halifax wrote to Riley: 'I really cannot tell you how, in all these difficulties in relation to the Union, I miss you.'[27]

Halifax's last service to the cause of Anglo-Catholicism was to bring about, from 1 January 1934, the joinder of the two organizations: he died on the 19th of that month. He had altered his perspective as the

---

26 See Lockhart, *Charles*, p. 311.
27 See Lockhart, *Charles*, p. 366.

years went by rather more readily than had the younger Riley. The latter was being passed by and left behind as times changed: unlike Halifax for example, he, an inveterate writer of epistles to the newspapers, had not signed a letter of support for the Twenty One priests who had defied Bishop Winnington-Ingram of London in 1929.

The Association for the Promotion of the Unity of Christendom was another organization which was being left behind as new groups came into existence which were more definitely focussed on union with Rome. At a meeting of the Union at the turn of the century, the Revd Spencer Jones had delivered a sermon which sparked into existence the Anglican Papalist movement, with which Riley had little sympathy.

On 27 January 1921 Riley wound up the APUC at a meeting, purportedly on the grounds of the absence of any Roman involvement, but that had been the case for many years. He does not appear to have consulted the wider membership (such as it was by then) before taking this drastic step.[28] Its work was taken over by the Church Unity Octave Committee, which was a definitely Papalist grouping.

The Oxford Movement Centenary in 1933 was marked with the publication of a rash of books, one of the better of which was *After the Tractarians* by the Revd Marcus Donovan, which is described as being 'from the recollections of Athelstan Riley' and contained a lengthy preface by him condemning Liberalism in the Church.

As well as Little Petherick (or as he almost invariably referred to it ' St Petroc'), Riley was also involved with the nearby parish of St Endellion, where the church is now best known for its references in the poetry of Sir John Betjeman and to its music festivals. The magnificent building, built to cover the shrine of St Endelienta, had from at least the thirteenth century a college of priests known as prebendaries.

For some reason which is not clear, but probably was as a result of its remoteness, the college was not suppressed at the Reformation and was not affected by the Dean and Chapter Act of 1840, which dispensed with many surviving non-residential prebendaries. The survival of this

---

28 M.D. Chapman, *The Fantasy of Reunion: The Rise and Fall of the Association for the Promotion of the Unity of Christendom* (Anglo-Catholic History Society, 2003).

mediaeval establishment made it a predictable attraction to Athelstan Riley and he acquired the patronage to two of the three non-residential prebendaries, those of Bodmin or Kings and of Trehaverock: Lord Clifden held that of Marnays. The fourth prebendary was the rector.

Riley's enthusiasm for St Endellion increased after the appointment as rector in 1917 of the exotically named Revd Fortunato Pietro Luigi Josa: he was born in Rome in 1851 and ordained in what is now called Guyana in 1874. He then became Archdeacon of Demarara before retiring to England. His wife wrote a guide book to the church, indicating that her husband had begun its move towards Anglo-Catholicism. Father Josa, however, died in 1922.

Athelstan Riley visited the church and its festivals frequently when in the West Country and was an enthusiastic supporter of the plan, put into effect by Bishop Frere in 1929, to give new life to the College. Riley served at the altar as the rehabilitative statutes were brought into effect with a Eucharist on 2 May 1929, and was named in the document setting out the constitution. The revised statutes required the prebendaries to visit the church once a year, to assist the rector and to celebrate the Holy Communion with special intention for the College at least annually.[29] The prebendaries also had restored the right, unique in the Church of England, to wear a fur cape called an almuce, which had otherwise been made obsolete in 1571.

The tone of the church moved further in the direction which Riley supported when the Revd A.W.G. Murphy became rector in 1932. He substantially reorganized the interior in accordance with contemporary moderate Anglo-Catholic thought.

Although Riley went to Cornwall less often, and spent correspondingly more time in Jersey, he was still there for a considerable part of 1935 and again in 1937, and his son John continued the family traditions by using the house there named St Mary's. Athelstan Riley continued to travel frequently, usually by liner, although later he took the aeroplane

---

29 See E. Stark, *Saint Endellion* (Dyllansow Truran, 1983), and *The Patrons of the Prebends of the Collegiate Church of St Endellion* (Dyllansow Truran, 1990). Father Edwin Stark was himself a Prebendary of St Endellion and for a time was parish priest of Blisland, on the edge of Bodmin Moor.

on occasion to Jersey. In 1934 he was made an Honorary Fellow of his old college, Pembroke, and donated to it a number of Syriac manuscripts he had acquired on his journeyings. He still lived in style, often staying in London at his club, the United University, and playing at the feudal lord in the Channel Islands. He was also a member of the Athenaeum. He attended meetings of the Société Jersiaise, the local learned antiquarian group and even had an honorary chaplain to the manor of Trinity, the Revd Francis Moat (who was also a Prebendary of St Endellion, on the nomination of Riley), and who died in 1936. The house had its own chapel which had a carved altarpiece of German origin and was consecrated by the Bishop of Winchester on 4 May 1914.

Another revival instituted by Frere when he was Bishop of Truro was that of a diocesan pilgrimage, to a different church every year. In 1938 the place chosen was Little Petherick, and Riley was obviously there.

By this time, Athelstan Riley was an old man and increasingly deaf. In December 1938 he flew to Jersey and remained there until the following June, when he returned to London for the Church Assembly. In July 1939 he returned to Little Petherick for what transpired to be the last time, and on 14 August flew back to Jersey from Exeter. There he was overtaken by events outside his control, for in June 1940 the Germans occupied the island and he was of course thereafter unable to escape. It is not clear why he did not leave before then, when the danger was clear: he may have been unwell.

The last years of Athelstan Riley's life were clearly unhappy. He was a frail old man, unable to communicate much with the outside world, and deprived of many of the luxuries to which he had always been accustomed. German officers were billeted on the manor house, and in 1942 he moved to one of the lodges, with his butler. In 1944 he had to go into a nursing home. He was fortunate that he had some protection from his daughter-in-law, Yvonne, née Lemprière, the Dame of Rozel, who was Christopher's second wife. She spoke very good German and was able to try and mitigate on his behalf some of the problems which inevitably arose.

By 1944 the right to present to the living of Little Petherick had been transferred by Riley to himself and his daughter (and oldest surviving child) Morwenna Brocklebank. He was obviously unable because of his exile actually to exercise the right when in 1944 Father Winstanley died. He had been parish priest for 35 years and was much respected. In later years he and his wife had lived in a small cottage near the church. His widow presented the church with a reredos for the high altar, also designed by Comper although by then in a more mature style, depicting the Risen Christ with Saints Alban, Petroc, John, Peter and Katharine and Our Lady, and the parishioners subscribed for a new bell for the tower, the others (one of which had been given by Riley) being rehung at the same time.

Father Winstanley's successor was the Revd R.E.S. Houlston, who became the first incumbent in the twentieth century to live in the splendid rectory. He had been priested in 1915 and spent much of his ministry thereafter in and around Birmingham: he may have wanted a country living because he suffered badly from asthma. By that time it was something of an anachronism that a village as small as Little Petherick should have its own priest and as early as 1934 the civil parish had been amalgamated with that of neighbouring St Issey.

Athelstan Riley died in Jersey on 17 November 1945. His son Quintin and his grandson John were both able to visit him very shortly after the island was liberated in early 1945 but by then he was scarcely aware of his surroundings. He was buried in Jersey, but his heart was taken to Little Petherick and placed in the chantry chapel near to Andalusia's sarcophagus, with a commemorative plaque. He left to the benefice the two cottages which he had built in the village, the last of his generous gifts to the parish. He was also commemorated by a window depicting St Laurence and others, in the church of St Andrew, Helpringham. Quintin's son, born at this time, was named Peter Athelstan, but sadly died after only a few days of life. He also had a daughter, who was named Noel Andalusia.

Quintin, although quite unlike his father in that his life was spent in the military and in exploration, had become closer to him as he got older and had inherited his own peculiar brand of anti-Roman but still ritualist Anglo-Catholicism: in later years he was a member of the General Synod and fulminated in particular about the prospect of women priests.

Athelstan Riley's son Christopher, who had served in both wars, succeeded to the title of Seigneur and he and after him his son Major John R.C. Riley continued to live in Jersey.[30]

Fidelity Trust Ltd. is still in existence, although it was reconstituted under a Private Act of Parliament in 1977. This was necessary because decisions in other similarly constituted trusts had indicated that the way in which it had been arranged contravened the rule against perpetuities, a notoriously difficult legal principle which has over the years provided a trap for many.

Little Petherick has no war memorial: it was one of the very few so-called 'Thankful Villages' which lost no men in either World War. In 1948 the advowson passed to John H.D. Riley, who had the closest local con-nections, but in 1949 he passed it on to Keble College, Oxford, which already held a large number of such rights.

Father Houlston continued in the parish until 1955, when he was suc-ceeded by Canon Edmund Alban Clarabut. He had been a curate at the well-known Anglo-Catholic Church of the Annunciation, Brighton, from 1913 to 1922 and had then held other positions, including the incumbency of the nearby church of SS. Protus and Hyacinth at Blisland, Cornwall, from 1935 to 1939, before going to East Africa: he was Archdeacon of Zanzibar from 1942 to 1954, after which he came back to England and took on Little Petherick.[31] He was a member of the Sodality of the Precious Blood from 1936 onwards, which fact reflects his views. It was only on his retirement, in 1967, that the logical step was finally taken of the vicar of St Issey holding the two livings in plurality.

It was a further consequence of Canon Clarabut's retirement that the rectory was put up for sale in 1969 as it was no longer required. The foot-bridge over which the Hon. Andalusia Riley had been carried to the roof garden was dismantled and two teak candlesticks were fashioned from it for the church; the pillars which supported the bridge remain in situ. The

---

30 J.R.C. Riley became Chairman of Channel Television and a Senator and leading figure in Jersey: he died in 1998.

31 His father was the Revd Ernest Blaxland Clarabut, who was a well-known Anglo-Catholic priest who had been vicar of Walthamstow and was later himself at Blisland. It is notable that as late as 1940, after Father E.A. Clarabut left Blisland, the Bishop of Truro was attempting to ensure that any new incumbent there did not reserve the Sacrament.

church was also given altar rails which were fashioned by local designer Herbert Read, who had also assisted with the furnishings at Throwleigh.

The church is now part of the United Benefice of St Merryn with St Issey and St Petroc Minor. The interior is well kept and remains an astounding memorial to the patron. The fact that both the clergy who now serve the church are women would not, however, have pleased him.

Athelstan Riley was a man of his time, but as he grew older he became something of an anachronism. By the outbreak of the Second World War, the age when gentlemen could devote themselves to good works and scholarship was fast disappearing. His view of the Church of England as a non-Roman but Catholic body with its own liturgical standards based on mediaeval precedents was also becoming much less widespread than had been the case before the First World War. However, the effect which he and others like him were able to produce by expenditure and influence was very considerable, particularly in a small parish like Little Petherick, where he clearly did not ignore the secular needs of the inhabitants either. The long-term effect, however, was not the universal acceptance of the Catholic Faith within the Church of England which he foresaw.

4

St Swithun, Compton Beauchamp, Oxfordshire, and Samuel Gurney

Samuel Gurney (1885–1968) is perhaps little remembered today, save by some for the mention of him in Sir John Betjeman's poem *Anglo-Catholic Congresses*:

> We recall the triumph, that Sunday after Ascension,
> When our Protestant suffragan suffered himself to be coped –
> The SYA[1] and the Scheme for Church Extension –
> The new diocesan's not as 'sound' as we'd hoped,
> And Kensit threatens, and has Sam Gurney poped?

Samuel Gurney was in many ways a similar figure to Athelstan Riley. Both were wealthy, although Gurney less conspicuously so than Riley, and thus were untrammelled by the need to earn a living, and both were convinced Anglo-Catholics and willing to further the cause of that interest within the Church of England. However while Riley had an influence on many churches in England and elsewhere, Gurney's direct impact was restricted to the small village of St Swithun at Compton Beauchamp in Oxfordshire (formerly, and in his time, in Berkshire).

Samuel Gurney's family background was, however, quite different to that of Riley and much more similar to that of Riley's friend William John Birkbeck. Both Gurney and Birkbeck came from that entwined Norfolk

---

1 Seven Years Association: it was set up by the Church Union after the 1933 Anglo-Catholic Congress to prepare for the projected 1940 Congress, which never of course took place, but had been planned for 7–15 July of that year.

company of Quakers and former Quakers who were principally involved in banking, and from whom in due course Barclay's Bank was to emerge. Birkbeck married a relative of Samuel, Rose Katherine Gurney, and lived eventually at Stratton Strawless, near Norwich.

Samuel Gurney was the eighth and last child of John Gurney (1845–87) and his wife Isabel Charlotte, née Blake Humfrey (1851–1932), whose biographer in due course he became.

John Gurney was a banker in Norwich: the bank with which he was concerned had been founded in 1775 as a purely family business but in 1866 was reconstituted as a new partnership thereafter known as Gurneys, Birkbecks, Barclay and Buxton, thus uniting all the principal families of the group. In 1868 he left the family home, Earlham Hall, and bought for his own occupation Sprowston Hall, on the other side of Norwich. In 1871 he married Isabel, a noted local beauty, whose father, who had been born Robert Blake, had lost a leg in the Peninsular War and retired back to Norfolk. He had adopted the additional name of Humfrey in 1847 when he inherited the estate of a wealthy parson of that name who lived at Wroxham on the Broads.

The Gurneys, as was the custom at the time, almost immediately began a family. The first, Sybil, was born in 1873 and married the Hon H.D. Napier. The second child and oldest son, John Nigel, known as Nigel, was born in 1874 and became a banker but died young, in 1902. The second daughter Laura, born in 1875, married Edward Gurney Buxton, another of the local bankers.

The next son was Eustace, later Sir Eustace, Gurney (1876–1927), who married Agatha Lee Warner, of a family who were squires of Walsingham. In due course he and she moved to Walsingham Abbey and he was soon a vocal and unrelenting critic of the innovations brought about by the Revd Alfred Hope Patten after he became parish priest of Great and Little Walsingham with Houghton St Giles in 1921.[2]

Eustace was followed by Hugh, later Sir Hugh (born 1878), who became a distinguished diplomat, Robert (born 1879), who became a scientist, Julien (sic), who lived and died in one day in 1881, and finally, after

---

2 See Michael Yelton, *Alfred Hope Patten and the Shrine of Our Lady of Walsingham* (Canterbury Press, 2006).

a gap of four years, Samuel, born on 30 June 1885 at Sprowston, who was named after his paternal grandfather.

It appears that the Gurney family life prior to the premature death of John in 1887 was happy and varied, although the evidence for that statement comes mainly from the saccharine portrait painted by Samuel in his only substantial published work, the 1935 biography of his mother, which was rather pretentiously entitled *Isabel Mrs. Gurney, afterwards The Lady Talbot de Malahide.*[3]

John Gurney was certainly a benefactor to the City of Norwich: a particular scheme of his was the conversion of the former Norman castle, which had been used as the prison, into a museum, a use which it retains to this day. Another, which was effected while he was Mayor of the City in 1885–86, was the building of a new highway, named Gurney Road in his honour, across Mousehold Heath, giving views of the cathedral. In July of 1886 he entertained the Prince and Princess of Wales when they visited Norfolk for the Royal Agricultural Show: Samuel Gurney, who was then of course only a baby, records that the Prince took Isabel Gurney on his arm and accompanied her to the show but makes no comment which indicates that that well-known royal roué showed his appreciation of the local belle.

Although obviously a man of enterprise and energy, John Gurney suffered throughout his life from poor health, which was accentuated by a fall from his horse in 1881. Soon thereafter this led to blindness. He taught himself Braille and his public and private duties continued unabated thereafter as did his family life. It appears that Samuel was conceived while his parents were in Cannes for the winter of 1884–85, where they had also spent the preceding year.

It was perhaps inevitable given the fact that Samuel was the youngest child and that his father died when he was less than two years old, that he was thereafter devoted to his mother and his filial piety is very well demonstrated in his book of her life: she was, it is only fair to say, a woman of courage and some distinction in a number of ways. One aspect of life in which she did not influence him was religion: she remained of a

---

3 S. Gurney, *Isabel Mrs. Gurney, afterwards The Lady Talbot de Malahide* (Jarrold & Sons Ltd., and Simpkin Marshall Ltd., 1935).

central Church of England outlook, tending towards the Evangelical, and was somewhat apprehensive of the ritual which she encountered through him in later life. The only Anglo-Catholic in the Norfolk family appears to have been the Revd Joseph John Gurney, Samuel's uncle, who was said to have been a great friend of Father Stanton of St Alban, Holborn. He was parish priest of St John de Sepulchre (now closed) in central Norwich.

For the ten years or so after John Gurney's death, Isabel continued to live at Sprowston, to bring up her children and to engage in works of charity among the local population. In due course the boys, including Samuel, went away to Eton: there appears to have been no shortage of money even after the demise of the head of the family. She was also an accomplished artist.

By the end of the century Isabel Gurney began taking a house in London every year for the 'season'. Samuel, as by far the youngest, continued to receive special treatment, in 1897 being taken to the South of France and to Italy after being ill. By 1898 his mother had decided that Sprowston Hall should be handed over to Nigel, who was by then in the bank. She therefore took a house at 28 Grosvenor Place, near Buckingham Palace, and Samuel began his involvement in London life, in the vacations from Eton.

In 1901 Isabel remarried. Her new husband was Richard Wogan, 5th Baron Talbot de Malahide (1846–1921). As with the Molesworth family, his title was from the Irish peerage: Malahide Castle is in County Dublin, very near to Swords, from which the Molesworths took their own title. Lord Talbot was a widower with a son and in addition to his peerage he was hereditary Lord High Admiral of Malahide and the Seas Adjacent, just the sort of meaningless but picturesque detail which fascinated Samuel Gurney (and would have impressed Athelstan Riley even more). Gurney himself says, revealingly, that his mother 'was delighted with the beautiful name that was to be hers'.[4] What he meant of course was that she was pleased to be the wife of a peer.

In consequence of the marriage Isabel moved to live most of the year at Malahide Castle. Lord Talbot was a diehard Unionist and the next

---

4 Gurney, *Isabel*, p. 83.

years were to be exceptionally difficult for him and for all those of his cast of mind. However, he was also very fond of travelling and over the period between then and the First World War he and his wife, sometimes accompanied by Samuel, frequently went abroad. Samuel had gone on from Eton to Trinity College, Oxford, and in 1905 accompanied his mother and stepfather to Egypt during his Christmas vacation. Later, in 1911, he was to go with them on a round-the-world tour, visiting China, Japan, Hawaii and then the United States.

On graduation, Samuel appears to have had no particular plans. He certainly showed no interest in or inclination for the family banking business, nor did he appear to want to settle in Norfolk, as did his brother Eustace and his sister Laura. Eustace in fact was to follow his father as Mayor of Norwich in 1910, and was knighted the next year.

Eustace was also, however, instrumental in the foundation in 1908 of the Medici Society, with his wife's cousin Philip Lee Warner, who was already in business as a publisher. The purpose behind the new organization was to bring artists' work to the appreciation of a wider public, and to sell the work for 'the lowest price commercially possible'. The business was originally set up as a society properly so called: in other words, by paying a subscription, members were entitled to prints as they were published. However, this was soon altered and a limited company was formed in 1911, which sold reproduction paintings and the like and then in the 1930s diversified into greetings cards. Samuel Gurney became a director of the company, introduced no doubt through his brother's interest, and was able thereafter to use that connection to benefit the Anglo-Catholic Movement in a number of respects. Philip Lee Warner continued to publish books on his own account and on behalf of the Society, some of which, such as lists of Old Rugbeians and Old Etonians (representing his school and that of the Gurney boys) had little to do with the central purpose of the Medici Society.

It is clear that by the time he came down from Oxford Samuel Gurney was thoroughly infused with Anglo-Catholicism. It is not clear whether he first encountered this phenomenon in Norwich, where there were a number of churches which had taken up its ideals, or whether this occurred at Oxford.

While at Eton and again while he was at Oxford, he had known slightly Ronald Arbuthnott Knox, one of the sons of the strongly Evangelical Bishop of Manchester, E.A. Knox. Ronald Knox was born in 1888, so was a few years younger than Gurney. It is apparent, however, that they became friendlier after Gurney had gone down and was living mainly in fashionable Albemarle Street, off Piccadilly in the Mayfair area, an address he retained throughout his life, but while Knox was still up at Oxford. In November 1908 they went together to hear the Abbot of Caldey preaching at All Saints, Margaret Street, and the following summer they actually went to the island, where they were entranced by what they saw. Knox went again, at least once with Vernon Johnson, who later became Father Vernon SDC[5] and still later a notable convert to Rome.[6] Samuel Gurney presented the monks with the bells for the abbey. Knox graduated in 1910: he had been up at Balliol.

What is apparent is that the course of Gurney's life altered radically in that year, 1910. His mother was not attuned to his interest in the Catholic faith, but he refers in his biography of her,[7] rather coyly, to a letter she wrote to him on 15 October 1910 in these terms: 'I think much of you and your theological difficulties, and I feel that the true Quaker and Huguenot spirit is with you . . . still . . .'[8] This may well indicate that he had thought at that time of going over to Rome ('poping' in Betjeman's terms) but if that were so nothing came of it and as the years went by he became more embedded in the Church of England.

That letter by his mother was written after a momentous holiday in June 1910. Gurney had invited Knox to accompany him to Oberammergau for the Passion Play, with which they were both very impressed: Knox insisted on attending an Anglican service, whereas Gurney went to a Roman Catholic mass, no doubt using Athelstan Riley's guide to assist him. They went on to Belgium, where in Bruges they met another party led by the Revd Maurice Child, whom Knox at least had already met in Plymouth

---

5 The Society of the Divine Compassion, now defunct, was an Anglican brotherhood of Franciscan inspiration and Socialist leaning. Father Vernon was a very popular preacher of the time, but was led to Rome by the example of St Thérèse of Lisieux.

6 See Chapter 10.

7 Gurney, *Isabel*, p. 121.

8 The family had Huguenot as well as Quaker ancestry.

when Child preached there: there is more detail on Father Child in the next chapter. All three of them were impressed by the piety which they saw in Bruges: Belgium was seen as very attractive by many Anglicans of that time because of the devotion of the population and the lack of political pressure which had badly affected the Roman Church in France. Alfred Hope Patten, then still a layman, was another who was impressed by what he saw in Bruges at around this time and remained devoted to the town throughout his life.

The meeting between the three men was the catalyst for the foundation of the Society of St Peter and St Paul, usually referred to as SSPP, which was an important factor behind the move of the main part of Anglo-Catholic opinion towards a Western as opposed to English Use. That generalization conceals as much as it shows: there were many who regarded SSPP propaganda as being overtly pro-Roman, whereas in fact, although the overlay of liturgy and furnishing was entirely continental, the underlying tone was of loyalty to the Cranmer liturgy, and later some of the more ultramontane Anglicans denounced its followers for that reason. Certainly, after the possible wobble in 1910, Gurney never showed any signs of following the example of Knox, who was to go over to Rome in 1917. The reference in the Betjeman poem was perhaps more a joke at his expense than any reference to real doubts which Gurney had during the period of the Congresses.

Knox and Child got on particularly well, because each had a ready turn with words which could be both amusing and sarcastic. Child is said to have been instrumental in persuading Knox to accept the position of Chaplain and Fellow of Gurney's old college, Trinity, which he accepted by letter from Namur.[9] In 1912 Child and his friend the Revd Vincent Baker moved to Devon to be curates at St James the Less, Plymouth, and Gurney went down to stay in the summers before the First World War in a sumptuous car, a Talbot (appropriately), known as 'the Light Ford', which allowed him to take his friends around the area.

Thereafter Gurney was able to use the Medici Society to give indirect support to the SSPP, which although founded shortly after the Belgian

9 See E. Waugh, *The Life of Ronald Knox* (Chapman & Hall, 1959), pp. 103–4. Samuel Gurney is acknowledged as a source in the Preface.

meeting, did not manifest itself to the world until 24 February 1911, when the *Church Times* contained an advertisement for altar and servers' cards. Indeed the connection with the Medici Society was initially very strong: the first address for the SSPP was 7 Bruton Mews, Bond Street, which was in fact nothing other than the back entrance of the Society's own premises: it was not possible for purchasers to move internally from one vendor's counter to the other and they had to go out, round the corner and then in to the other door. This arrangement was, however, only temporary, because in late 1911 the Society moved to 32 George Street, Hanover Square, which then later became their offices, and a shop was opened at 302 Regent Street, near to All Saints, Margaret Street. Gurney became honorary secretary of the Society and was able, because of his financial independence, to devote a great deal of time to it. While Knox provided much of the early writing together with the Revd N.P. Williams, Chaplain of Exeter College, Oxford (known as 'Nip'), and with Child, who also used his brilliant gift for propaganda, Gurney carried out a great deal of the design work, which meant that everything produced by the Society was to the very highest standards, even though produced on a strict budget.

Norman Powell Williams was undoubtedly a significant intellectual presence for the SSPP to have supporting them: in 1927 he was to be appointed Lady Margaret Professor of Divinity at Oxford, and he appears to have collaborated well with the others, coping with Child's barbed comments although he was notoriously thin-skinned. Williams' biographer said of him, with masterly understatement, that 'None of those who knew him well would deny that he was a difficult person',[10] and even his widow in her personal memoir of him said: 'I am not going to pretend that he was an easy person with whom to live. [His illnesses] combined with the effects of an unhappy childhood,[11] together with his amazing intellect and memory, were all factors which made him temperamental, extremely sensitive, and easily hurt, and, therefore, very quick to take

---

10 See E.W. Kemp, *N.P. Williams* (SPCK, 1954), p. v.

11 His parents were first cousins who were on difficult terms. His father, the Revd Thomas Powell Williams, was at one time parish priest of the well-known Anglo-Catholic church of St Mary, Tyne Dock, South Shields.

offence.'[12] Williams also had continual financial problems, as he was very extravagant in his personal expenditure.

Ironically, the first commission executed by the SSPP was for a copy of the Prayer Book of 1549 for Lord Halifax, who liked Maurice Child whereas others stood back. Thereafter a torrent of publications followed, many of which were cleverly edited by Gurney. Ronald Knox had been ordained as deacon in 1911 and adopted an additional forename, in accordance with the prevailing fashion among his contemporaries, in his case that of Hilary, and was ordained priest the following year. He produced a number of lampoons, including *Absolute and Abitofhell*, which was reprinted by the SSPP in 1912, and *Reunion all Round*, published in 1914, made by Gurney with infinite care and skill to resemble a seventeenth-century pamphlet. He used for these purposes an elderly retired engraver named W.M.R. Quick.

Although the SSPP was primarily a publisher, it also held an annual high mass, usually at the now closed church of St Thomas, Regent Street. The liturgy used was that of the Book of Common Prayer, suitably disguised by Roman rubrics, Latin vestments and passages said *sub silentio*. Sir Hubert Miller of Froyle sang the Ten Commandments from the west gallery and Samuel Gurney fasted from the night before until the late morning, so as to be the sole lay communicant required by the 1662 Book, a typical SSPP legalism. Frederic Hood, later Principal of Pusey House but then still a layman, was a server at some of these events.

The SSPP were also much assisted by the input of the ecclesiastical furnisher and stained-glass designer Martin Travers (1886–1948).[13] It is possible that Gurney had met Travers, who was his near contemporary, in Norwich, a city to which the latter had moved in about 1897, but certainly they knew each other by 1911, when Travers designed a first mass card for the SSPP for the Revd Humphrey Whitby, then a curate at St Columba, Kingsland Road, Haggerston: he was later to be vicar of St Mary, Bourne Street, Pimlico, where he perfected the SSPP method of saying mass using

---

12 See M. Williams in Kemp, *Williams*, p. 69.
13 See R. Warrener and M. Yelton, *Martin Travers (1886–1948): An Appreciation* (Unicorn Press, 2003).

the words of the Anglican Prayer Book but in such a way that an observer would think that he was at a Roman service.

Gurney and Travers became friends and in 1912 the latter invited the former to a tea party to celebrate the completion of a commission of an exquisite window for a small church in Chesterblade, Somerset.

The publications of the SSPP covered a wide variety of subjects, mainly of course liturgical or devotional but also encompassing a number of cleverly illustrated stories. However, there were two pamphlets which were definitely out on a limb so far as the bulk of the production was concerned: these were *Foundations of National Glory* (1915) and *Golden Opportunities* (1916), both of which were collections of addresses made by Samuel Gurney's mother and obviously printed only because of that family tie.

After Lady Talbot moved to live principally in Ireland, in 1901, she became very involved in charity work. She had already, in 1891, been appointed as a Lady of Grace of the Order of St John of Jerusalem for earlier good work, but once established in Malahide Castle, she became, in 1908, President of the Mothers' Union for the United Dioceses of Dublin, Glendalough and Kildare. The pamphlets were the product of her main-stream Anglicanism as put before the fiercely Protestant Church of Ireland ladies, who would have been astonished had they seen the rest of the SSPP output. Lady Talbot moved on, in the difficult situation in which those of her and her husband's political situation found themselves in Ireland at that time, to become very involved with the Red Cross, as local President, and hosted large fetes at the castle. It was for this very significant and energetic series of charitable initiatives that in 1920 she was appointed a Dame of the British Empire in her own right.

In the meantime, neither the outbreak of the First World War nor the troubles in Ireland had of course passed Samuel Gurney by. The SSPP con-tinued production unabated, but gradually some of their associates joined up and of course there were casualties in time. One particular friend of both Gurney and Knox was the Hon. Edward ('Ted') Kay-Shuttleworth, born in 1890, who died in action in 1917 and plays a part later in this chapter. Child served for a time with the Forces in France.

In 1916 Gurney was in Ireland and joined the Officers' Training Corps at Trinity College, Dublin, while living most of the time at Malahide.

Initially he was rejected for military service as unfit, and was then trapped in the College by the Easter Rebellion, which he appears to have regarded with distaste equal to that shown by his stepfather and mother. He then re-applied to the military and was assigned to a training unit at the Curragh.[14] His mother then pulled strings via Lord Leicester, whom she knew, to ensure that the commission he was entitled to as a result of his training was with the 2nd/6th (Cyclists') Battalion of the Norfolk Regiment, and he joined them in late 1916. He was temporarily promoted to Captain but discharged as Second Lieutenant in early 1919. The regimental records make it clear that that battalion remained in England throughout the remainder of the hostilities and Gurney did not therefore have to suffer the horrors of the Western Front. He was photographed in his uniform in a photograph in his book, accompanying his mother to a charity event.

After the war, Gurney returned to the Medici Society and to the SSPP. The mood in the Anglo-Catholic Movement was confident, particularly after the first Congress, in 1920, proved such a success. In 1919 a private limited company, the Society of SS. Peter & Paul Ltd., was incorporated with Gurney as the majority shareholder, but the Society continued in existence to disseminate literature. The limited company dealt with all trading and publishing, and it may be that the new structure was an attempt to protect the members of the Society from any personal liability in the event of defaults in payment. The finances were always very shaky, because the number of titles was very large and thus the stock had to be immense. As time went on, the SSPP was largely absorbed by the new Anglo-Catholic Congress, of which Gurney sat on the committee, and in 1924 the limited company was reconstructed with the writer Kenneth Ingram as managing director: this coincided with Gurney moving out of London to live principally in the country. The Society itself lost its independent existence at that time and the company was wound up in 1929, although the name was revived in 1940 for a charitable trust set up by Father Humphrey Whitby.

---

14 The statement in his army records to the effect that he had taken an active part in putting down the Sinn Fein Rebellion was, on Gurney's own account, a grossly exaggerated version of what actually occurred.

In 1921 Lord Talbot died and Isabel decided to leave Ireland: her step-son took over the castle and shortly thereafter married. Isabel decided to return to London and took a lease of 38 Buckingham Palace Mansions.

It was at this time that Samuel Gurney bought a property at Compton Beauchamp and began a transformation of the village church. Compton, rather like Little Petherick, had a population of fewer than 200, many of whom lived not in the village proper but in the adjoining hamlet of Knighton. It lies in the Berkshire (now Oxfordshire) downlands, eight miles from Wantage, with its Tractarian tradition and its convent, and with ready access to the then Great Western Railway main line. It had a moated manor house in which an earlier Dowager Duchess of Craven had previously lived, and a substantial Victorian rectory with a garden. Gurney had been taken one day by friends to see the manor house, which they were considering buying and indeed subsequently did. He looked over the hedge and saw the rectory, which immediately appealed to him as a prospective residence for himself, but it was then occupied by the Revd Charles Pepys and not for sale.

Pepys was rector of the parish only from 1919 to 1922 and then moved on to Aylesbury. The Revd Alan John Fosbrooke Hobbes, the vicar of adjoining Ashbury, took on Compton as well at that time. The rectory, which Gurney wanted but had thought he would never be able to buy, was therefore put on the market by the Church Commissioners, in an early example of the rationalization which has taken place in many other villages since. Gurney was able in 1925, following complicated negotiations with both the Commissioners and with the Craven Estate, which owned part of the land around, to buy the house and garden and an additional area of about 20 acres which had been glebe land. The Craven Estate was by far the largest landowner in Berkshire at that time. This property became and remained Gurney's home, although he retained his flat in Mayfair and from it he was able to set himself up as the de facto squire of the village.

It is a measure perhaps of the snobbish element in Gurney that he never referred to the village by the name which everyone else used. He preferred to refer to it as Compton Regis, a name which had fallen into desuetude well before the twentieth century, and he noted also that it had been known as Compton-juxta-Album-Equum, for it lies very near to the Vale of the White Horse: it had in fact had other names as well over the centuries.

The house he purchased was built of chalk stone in Tudor Revival style in 1849. Although Gurney himself said that it was 'on a very small scale',[15] in fact it was a substantial property for a bachelor, albeit one who frequently entertained his by now ageing mother. He had it completely renovated and redecorated, filled it with antique furniture, and built new thatched cottages for the gardener and for the chauffeur: his way of life remained comfortable. In post-war years Bishop Eric Kemp took his wife and young children to tea with Gurney, and the children were fascinated by the fact that their host had a dumb waiter in the middle of the tea table. He enjoyed good food, although he himself was a vegetarian.

In July 1936 Gurney acquired the rood figures from the war memorial at All Saints, Clevedon, designed by Comper, as the parish were replacing them with larger figures, and erected them in his garden.[16]

It was clear that Gurney from the very start of his life in Compton Beauchamp decided to refurnish the church. It is equally clear that he must have been abetted in this by Father Hobbes, who remained priest of the two parishes until 1934, when he moved to All Souls, South Ascot, and was replaced by the Revd E.G. Mortimer, who remained until 1959 and is commemorated by a tablet in Ashbury Church.

By this time too the style of the Anglo-Catholic Movement, and the SSPP in particular, was a pastiche Baroque, designed to bring about the illusion that the Reformation had not happened and that the Church of England had developed in the same way liturgically as the Roman Catholic Church on the continent of Europe. Interestingly, and perhaps because of the difficulties brought about by the family connections, Gurney had relatively little directly to do with Walsingham, where Father Hope Patten's establishment of the Shrine of Our Lady exemplified this tendency.

---

15 Gurney, *Isabel*, p. 164.

16 This comes from the inscription on a photograph by Samuel Gurney's nephew David Gurney, taken in 1942 and now in the National Monuments Register. It does not really fit with the statements in the generally excellent gazetteer in A. Symondson and S. Bucknall, *Sir Ninian Comper* (Spire Books, 2006).

Samuel Gurney was also lucky in that he knew Martin Travers well enough to give him essentially a free hand in the refurbishment of the church: further, there was no substantial congregation to object and certainly no one who would stand in the way of a man with Gurney's connections and obvious wealth.

The little church at Compton before Gurney's additions was very clearly described in the *Victoria County History of Berkshire, Volume IV,* which by coincidence was published in 1924, shortly before the re-furbishment began. It is evident that at that time there was no history of advanced Anglo-Catholic worship in the church, although the 1897 *Church Travellers' Guide* does indicate there was a celebration of the Eucharist each Sunday: at that time the rector was the Revd John Edgell (1887–1906), who had followed the very long incumbency of the Revd G. Carter (1850–87). It appears to have been a typical country parish, the advowson to which had been held by the Craven family since 1846. The only indication that the Oxford Movement had had any effect on the building is that the VCH refers to the existence of a modern painted rood on the wall above the chancel, with the Commandments, Lord's Prayer and Creed on either side. There were also Victorian altar rails and a pulpit. The most striking recent addition to the church at the time when Gurney moved there, however, was vine leaf decoration on the walls of the chancel, which was carried out in about 1900 by Lydia Lawrence, who was the niece of Judge Bacon, a County Court Judge who was then the tenant of Compton House and had succeeded there his father, Sir James Bacon, the last Victorian Vice-Chancellor of the High Court. Lydia Lawrence was a member of the Kyrle Society, founded 1877, which was an organization devoted to 'brightening the lives of the people' by decorating buildings and planting flowers.[17]

The church is of cruciform plan with a low tower, and is hidden from view by the manor house: the construction material is large blocks of local clunch, and the roof is of stone slates, giving a pleasant vernacular appearance. The walls are plastered within, which allowed scope for the

---

17 Simon Jenkins, *England's Thousand Best Churches* (Penguin Books, 1999), is laud-atory about Travers' work for Gurney but wrongly attributes the Lawrence work to the same patronage.

new furnishings to be displayed and there were a number of significant monuments. The nave is only 37 feet by 15 feet, the chancel 26 feet by 13 feet and the two transepts about 12 feet square. Parts of the fabric date back to the thirteenth century but rebuilding had taken place at various times, including the reconstruction of the south transept as recently as 1911, which was a memorial to Judge Bacon. There had been an earlier, Norman, building on the same site.

The exact sequence of events in the comprehensive refurbishment carried out after Gurney's arrival in the village is not clear, because a number of Travers' drawings are not dated. It is apparent that what Gurney sought to create was an Anglo-Catholic ideal in a sort of bubble insulated from the rest of the Church of England and, in his mind, forming an example to it.

It may well be in fact that prior to carrying out any work at Compton, Travers refurnished the north chapel at the nearby church of St Mary, Ashbury, where Father Hobbes was also parish priest This was carried out in 1927 and was a memorial to Evelyn, Countess of Craven (1849–1926), who had lived for many years at Ashdown House in the village. She had been widowed as long ago as 1883, but had retained a full household: it appears that she was a pious woman, as in the 1901 census she had a resident private chaplain, the Revd Cuthbert Trower.

The Ashbury work complements that at Compton Beauchamp. The chapel was separated from the nave by a turned wooden screen with a gate in it and a new rectangular reredos was made with a rood on it, against a dark red background, edged in gilt and black. The chapel was dedicated to St Hubert, the patron saint of hunters, as the Countess had been a famous devotee of field sports and was a Master of Foxhounds even at an advanced age. A relief of St Hubert was added over the altar and he was depicted in the window of the chapel. The use of such a patron carried with it a whimsical touch which was characteristic of Travers' inventive mind.

However, although there can be little doubt that Travers received this commission because of his previous work for the SSPP, the designer was not able to take forward other designs which he produced for a charming high altar and also a war memorial chapel for the south transept of the church perhaps because Gurney was not willing to pay for work at Ashbury when he had such extensive plans for Compton Beauchamp. If all the work had been carried out, it would have transformed the interior.

It is clear that by the time Samuel Gurney's mother died in early 1932, extensive work had already been carried out to the interior of the church at Compton: he specifically says in his book that 'it was during Isabel's residence that Mr Martin Travers was employed to carry out his striking scheme for the high altar and rood figures, as well as the Lady Chapel at the west end under the tower'.[18]

It seems likely that the first phase of the renovation was the replacement of the painted rood, which was on the wall above the entrance to the chancel, and of the various inscriptions around it, and the erection of a typical Travers style rood in its place, which looks particularly striking against the white wall of the tympanum. That was carried out in 1927, and was followed by the new high altar and reredos, for which the design as carried out was dated that year.

The altar was enclosed within plain riddels in the English style which on the face of it is at odds with the Baroque feel, but in fact looks quite fitting. The reredos is of gold with a sunburst motif in the centre, in front of which was a large domed tabernacle. There were two, rather than six, Baroque-style candlesticks.

The reredos, and indeed the golden frontal which matched it, looked rather more opulent than in fact they were. Travers was a master of using cheap materials to give the impression of something more authentic, and here his chosen material was embossed Sanderson wallpaper painted gold and varnished. A notice on the sanctuary wall still informs the passer-by that the altar contains relics of SS. Vital and Victorinus of Assisi, authenticated by Bishop M.S. O'Rorke, Hope Patten's great supporter: the items were formerly in Walsingham and are an exception to Gurney's general lack of involvement with the shrine there. Peter Anson famously portrayed this altar in his seminal chapter *Back to Baroque* in his groundbreaking work *Fashions in Church Furnishings*.[19] He even supplied a visitor and a

18 S. Gurney, *Isabel*, p. 162.

19 Second Edition published by Studio Vista, 1965, Chapter XXX. The picture is on p. 324.

server in period costume, but unfortunately he added a tester above the altar which was on one of the designs, but was never constructed.

The next addition was the lady chapel. It would appear that this was done in or before 1931, rather than in 1934 as is usually cited. The church was too small for a conventional lady chapel unless the transepts were used for that purpose, but Travers solved the problem by designing a tiny altar under the tower in an old porch, at the west end. Above it was installed a shallow relief of Our Lady with the Infant Jesus and he used an altar stone which may have dated back to the Norman building and which had been discovered during the 1911 work to the south transept. Under the altar was placed a feretory chest with a relic of St Placidus, a sixth-century martyr.

At some time, and it is not clear exactly when, a tablet in memory of Ted Shuttleworth, designed by Travers, was hung in Compton Beauchamp. He had originally designed such a tablet for St Mary, Bourne Street, in 1918 and it is not clear why it was not used there or how it came to be in Berkshire: Kay-Shuttleworth seems to have had no connection with the parish.

Lady Talbot de Malahide died on 22 February 1932. She had been ailing for some years but had been well enough to start a branch of that quintessence of Anglicanism, the Mothers' Union, in the village. Her ever dutiful son had requiems said for her at Earlham, Norwich, where she was buried, at St Peter, Eaton Square, at Little Walsingham and at Compton itself. He also decided to commemorate her in St Swithun by the placing in the church in 1934 of a font cover in a free interpretation of those mediaeval originals found at Great and Little Walsingham, and Travers was called back to do that: it carries an inscription asking the reader to pray for her soul, although it seems doubtful that her own interpretation of the Faith would countenance such a course.

There was some existing mediaeval glass in the east window, and Travers retained that but replaced most of the window with a new design which was intended to complement the high altar. It shows Mary with the baby surrounded by sundry cherubs and the like.

The window was installed in 1937, and in the same year a relief of St Swithun, former Bishop of Winchester (died 862), was erected to the south of the chancel arch. St Swithun is depicted wearing a cope, which is divided to represent sun and rain, and the morse shows the sun itself. The saint carries a model of the church. The weather references reflect the legend that it rained for 40 days continuously when it was sought to move St Swithun's body from the Cathedral graveyard to the interior, against the wishes of the deceased. It was thought thereafter that if it rained on St Swithun's Day (15 July) it would rain for 40 more days immediately thereafter. Although this plaque is cleverly thought out and beautifully executed, it is perhaps too sentimental for modern taste, or even for the date when it was erected.

The Second World War did not cause the renovations to cease, although understandably there was a pause and for some of the war years Gurney stayed at Pusey House in Oxford. In 1947 Travers designed wooden screens to both transepts. In the south transept, which had originally been the chapel of St Edward the Confessor and is now the vestry, he also had fabricated a wrought-iron grill in front of a blocked-in window, which was worked with the monograms ER and RC and had attached to it a beaten copper figure of St Edward holding his ring, which he is said to have given to a beggar.

The north transept was dedicated to the Good Shepherd and has a small altar with wrought-iron candlesticks, and six matching hearse or lych lights used for funerals. A small Christus Rex figure was placed on the wall.

Travers died suddenly in 1948, and left a number of unexecuted projects which his assistants carried forward to completion using his plans. These included further work at Compton Beauchamp. In about 1950 the south transept was provided with oak vestment cupboards and a vestment press: they would have been more often found in a much larger church. The Victorian pulpit and communion rails were taken out, probably before the war, and the final element of the comprehensive refurbishment were new altar rails, installed in 1951 but again designed by Travers, although not as set out in his 1927 design for the high altar. The executed work has elaborately decorated filled rails rather than the simple oak design originally proposed.

In addition to the other work, Gurney and Travers saw to some minor matters. A missal desk in Baroque style was installed, which was specially designed to hold a leather-bound copy of the Anglican Missal, which had of course been produced by the SSPP during Gurney's involvement with that organization. The hymn books both at Compton and at Ashbury bound together the English Hymnal and its 'party' supplement, the English Catholic Hymn Book, and were decorated with gold leaf embossed representations of the respective patron saints, although, true to form, the splendid representation of St Swithun with sun and rain was encircled by a reference to Compton Regis.

Although 1951 marked the end of Martin Travers' involvement with the church, which the artist himself regarded as second only to his transformation of Cranford for Maurice Child, dealt with in the next chapter, it was by no means the terminal of the beautification and Gurney remained the power behind the scenes. In 1952 a local sculptor, Ulrica Lloyd, made and coloured a shield over the porch showing the arms of the Province of Canterbury and another over the north transept window depicting the arms of the Diocese of Oxford. She also made an external statue of Our Lady for Ashbury. In the same year a large painting of the Good Shepherd by Sir Noel Paton (1821–1901) was hung in the north transept chapel, and Ulrica Lloyd carved a relief of the Holy Trinity on a Sumerian stone excavated in Iraq to be placed above the altar there. At about the same time the lettering on the graves in the churchyard were repainted in black and red.

Finally, as late as 1967 birds, an owl, a bat and some insects were added to the vine mural by Anthony Baynes and T.L.B. Hutchinson.

There is no doubt that the interior of the transformed church is stunning. However, further thought is then perhaps required. Gurney was attempting to turn the church into something it never was, and that he managed satisfactorily. However, by the early 1950s, when the work was completed, the Liturgical Movement was just beginning to make its presence felt. Compton Beauchamp was redesigned for a Church in which the Parish Communion Movement, still less Vatican II, were distant and unwanted developments.

However much the work is admired and respected, there is bound to be an element of selfishness, or perhaps more exactly self-indulgence, about what occurred here. Samuel Gurney treated the church as his own private chapel, and the villagers were therefore given no option but to accept the way in which the Faith was then presented to them. The harshness of that expression of opinion is perhaps mitigated by the fact that he was obviously a generous and kind-hearted man who was benevolent towards those living around. He invited the villagers to garden parties on the weekend nearest to the feast day of St Swithun, when there was a procession followed by a short outdoor service, which is said to have required the villagers to carry a life-size statue of St Swithun, which normally stood in Gurney's bedroom, down the stairs and over to the village green. It was playing at being the Anglo-Catholic squire, but well intentioned. As with Athelstan Riley, it is easy to see the comic side to the way in which he behaved.

Gurney became more centrally involved in the Church of England as the years went by. He was a member of both the Athenaeum (as was Athelstan Riley) and the National Liberal Club (which Riley certainly was not) and when in London was accustomed to stay at one and eat at the other if not at his flat. He remained devoted to the cause of reunion, although not from a narrowly partisan perspective, and he was a prominent member of the Archbishops' Council on Foreign Relations and a founder of the Nikaean Club, which existed to afford hospitality to ecclesiastical visitors from abroad.

Gurney was Chairman of the Incorporated Church Building Society for some time and wrote a commendatory preface to their 1947 book entitled *Fifty Modern Churches,* depicting buildings very different from those in which he himself was accustomed to worship, or even thought others should. One of his successors in that post was his brother, Sir Hugh Gurney. In 1957 Samuel, perhaps more appropriately, was one of the founding members of the Friends of Friendless Churches, the moving spirit behind which was Ivor Bulmer-Thomas. He was a member of the London Diocesan Advisory Committee for the Care of Churches. He was also involved with the Metropolitan Drinking Fountain and Cattle Trough Association, which had been founded in 1859 by his namesake and grandfather, and many other bodies. Regrettably all his voluminous papers, which passed to his nephew Oliver, do not seem to have survived the latter's death.

Samuel Gurney was also directly involved over the years with a number of parochial missions and the like. In 1930, for example, he was the chairman of the 'Congress of Youth', which was designed to interest young people in Anglo-Catholicism and was run in the parish of St Mark, Swindon, not very far from Compton Beauchamp, under the aegis of the Revd A.G.G. Ross, who had been vicar of the parish since 1903 and prior to that had been curate from 1892 to the Revd the Hon. J.M.G. Ponsonby (later Lord de Mauley), who had established the tradition of worship. The area was at the time of the Congress almost entirely populated by employees of the Great Western Railway and their families and it appears that Gurney was able to adjust his normal style to the challenge posed by an almost entirely working-class area. Most of the meetings were in fact in the church hall of the daughter church of St Luke.

An unusual aspect of Gurney was that he was heavily influenced for many years, beginning even before the publication of his book in 1935, by the American Protestant evangelist Dr Frank Buchman (1878–1961) and his Oxford Groups, later known as Moral Rearmament or MRA. MRA was not a new sect but appealed to all established Christians: however, Gurney's enthusiasm was not shared by most Anglo-Catholics because of its emphasis on individual conversion, and this was, for an utterly conventional man, singularly out of pattern with the rest of his life.

Samuel Gurney died on 6 July 1968 aged 83. He lived at Compton Beauchamp to the end and, fittingly, is buried in the churchyard there. He never married: there is no double meaning implied by that statement. The interior of the church is his memorial, but as ever there is another aspect to it. The refurnishings are beginning now to show their age rather badly and damp has affected some parts of the building. They now look like a period piece rather than an aid to modern worship.

Both Compton Beauchamp and Ashbury are now within a team ministry based in the nearby town of Shrivenham. The electoral roll of Compton now contains fewer than ten names and there are not even weekly services at the church. Thus the individual tradition of a church, built up over many years, is inevitably diluted by the lack of commitment shown to it by a priest who has to adapt to the services expected by other churches which have nurtured different patterns of worship.

The tabernacle at Compton Beauchamp is empty although it is now back on the high altar after some years when it was on a shelf in a transept.

It is difficult to resist the conclusion that Gurney treated the little church as his personal plaything, but it is still worth appreciating.

5

St Dunstan, Cranford, Middlesex, and Father Maurice Child

The Revd Maurice Child (1884–1950) was, in his time, one of the best known of Anglo-Catholic priests. He was also as criticized by some as much as he was admired by others, which makes any balanced appraisal of his life very difficult. He was an omnipresent negotiator and spokesman on behalf of the Catholic Movement in the Church of England between the Wars, often described as its *eminence grise*, or more frequently as its *enfant terrible*. Nowadays he is known only by the cognoscenti, and also perhaps by those who saw his portrait in oils, which was hung in the former Maurice Child Hall, which is geographically in Hayes, Middlesex, although within his former parish of Cranford.

The only church of which Maurice Child ever held the living was that of St Dunstan, Cranford, which is now near the sprawl of Heathrow Airport but in 1935, when he moved there, was still in what was then the deepest rural Home Counties, and seemed very far away from London.

One of Maurice Child's characteristics was to spread around himself and his doings an air of mystery and intrigue, when the facts underlying were often straightforward and not at all complicated.

Even his background appeared to be a subject of some speculation among those who knew him, but in fact it was one of straightforward, middle-of-the-road, educated, Anglicanism. He was born in Old Alresford, Hampshire, on 17 August 1884, and all his immediate family also came from that county. He had two older siblings: Edward Courtney Child, born 1882 in Upper Clatford, and Gladys Mary Child, born in 1883, also in Old Alresford. Edward became an officer in the Royal Navy, and in 1915 married Winifred Robinson. Gladys married Sidney A.G. Hill, also a naval officer, in 1912: that family later adopted the surname Geary-Hill.

Maurice Child was the third generation (at least) of Anglican clergy. His father was the Revd Edward Child (1846–86) who died at the age of only 40 when his children were very small. Edward Child was born in Appleshaw, near Andover, and was the son of the Revd Thomas Child (1808–81). Edward Child went to Christ's College, Cambridge (BA 1869, MA 1871) and was curate of Amesbury in Wiltshire from 1870 to 1873, being ordained priest in 1871. He then moved to be his father's curate at Upper Clatford, Hampshire, from 1873 to 1882, when he moved to his final position as curate of New Alresford. He died, however, in Thanet, where he may have gone for health reasons.

Thomas Child, who was born at Hurstbourne Tarrant, also in Hampshire, was a graduate of Queen's College, Oxford (BA 1828, MA 1835). He was ordained as deacon in 1831 and as priest the following year and was then curate of Appleshaw until 1863, when he finally obtained his own living as rector of Upper Clatford. His wife Mary, née Fielder (1808–50), had died when his children were still young but he was assisted domestically in later years by her unmarried sister, Elizabeth. Another son, Alfred, who was older than Edward, was also ordained and was eventually rector of Rotherfield in Kent.

Maurice Child's mother was Minna Mary Pain (born 1857 in Westover, Wherwell, also near Andover). She married his father in 1881, so the marriage was a very short one, and she was then widowed for many years. Minna Child was the daughter of Charles Pain (1821–1902) and Mary Ann Pain, née Lywood (1831–1911), who had married in 1852. Charles Pain was born in Broughton and his wife in Barton Stacey, both nearby. He had farmed in Wherwell in quite a substantial way: at the time of the 1881 census it was recorded that he employed 27 men and 8 boys. They were prosperous enough also for Minna to be sent away to school near Salisbury, which was unusual for a girl at that time. The Lywood family were also substantial farmers and certainly at one stage Mary Ann's father had employed 40 men.

Following the death of her husband, Minna Child moved with her young children to Lower or Goodworth Clatford, which is very near Upper Clatford where her father-in-law had been rector. In 1891 she was living there with her two younger children and with a school governess as a boarder, but she is described as living on her own means, and was able to afford two servants. Edward was then boarding at a preparatory school in Southampton. At some point Minna moved to Winchester for a time: the young Maurice went to Kingsgate House, a school which was often used as a feeder for Winchester College. He was there for three years as a day boy and then for five as a boarder. One of his contemporaries recalled him as rather a whimsical child, who believed that the baying of a dog indicated death because he could recall a dog yowling as his father died. He was also somewhat delicate at that stage, although also mischievous and sometimes in trouble from the teaching staff, not least because of his inquisitive nature, which remained with him all his life.[1]

In about 1893 Minna moved to live back with her parents in Stockbridge, Hampshire, to which they had retired. This was a place where Maurice spent much of his spare time, and he absorbed the local atmosphere. The village had 13 public houses for a population of 800, and it was also patronized by River Test fishermen, and, most particularly, by the horse racing fraternity. There were a number of stables in and around. The young Maurice demonstrated at that early stage in his life another characteristic which remained with him, namely the ability to relate to all sorts of men and women, particularly men with a somewhat raffish nature. He also became very involved in local amateur dramatics.

Maurice Child moved on from Kingsgate House on a scholarship not to Winchester but to Sherborne, where his life seems to have been rather uneventful, although culminating in his appointment as House Captain, save that he was fed Protestant tracts which aroused in him a reaction in opposition: he became there an Anglo-Catholic and had a particularly Anglican devotion to King Charles the Martyr, which would have been looked down upon by those who were more Roman in their spirituality. He made the acquaintance of the Revd Charles Latimer Marson (1859–

---

1 See the obituary in Canon A.F. Hood, *St Mary's Bourne Street Quarterly*, Spring 1950, pp. 18–28 for this and many other reminiscences which have been used in this chapter.

1914), an Anglo-Catholic Socialist and pioneer collector of folk songs, who was then parish priest of Hambridge, near Langport in Somerset, and frequently stayed with him there.

From Sherborne, Maurice Child went on to St John's College, Oxford. He had already imbued the ethos of Anglo-Catholicism before he went up and by the time he came down, he was thoroughly immersed in its ways. He took only a pass degree, eschewing honours in order to spend a great deal of time racing, hunting, driving a four-in-hand, and in archery. He was also an official of the Oxford University Motor Club; cars were then very new and regarded with distaste by many of his contemporaries. He founded a new society called the Whip Club, which met in St Giles after mass on Sunday. His combination of piety and field sports was an unusual one, as appeared then to his contemporaries and to us today.

Among Maurice Child's contemporaries at St John's was Magnus Laing, who was himself later ordained and was successively a curate at St Saviour, Hoxton (1909–20), in the Bahamas, and then at St Mary, Bourne Street (1921–25), where he met up again with Child.

Child took his BA in 1908 and his MA two years later, and proceeded for training at Cuddeston: interestingly he did not go either to Ely or to St Stephen's House, Oxford, both of which were then the best-known Anglo-Catholic strongholds. At Cuddesdon he met many of the future leaders of the Church of England, including N.P. Williams: he remained very devoted to the College although he provoked fun at the earnestness and 'clerical voices' of some of the students there. This remained a constant theme: he disliked pomposity very much.

On one occasion, at a gathering, a parson who did not know him came up and said, 'I wonder if you can tell me which is Maurice Child?' Child drew himself up to his full but diminutive height and replied: 'I can't see him anywhere.' His questioner then asked, 'Tell me, what is the truth about that man?' only to receive the answer: 'The trouble really is, he is not *spiritual*.' He clearly had a sense of humour which extended to himself, unlike some others already discussed.

Another who was at Cuddesdon with Child was William George Vincent Corbet Baker, who had been at Trinity College, Oxford and became a great friend.

107

Child was ordained deacon in 1909 and priest in 1910 to serve in the Diocese of London, by Bishop A.F. Winnington-Ingram. There were some problems, because Child announced publicly prior to his ordination that he proposed to teach and to practise the invocation of the saints, but even more consternation was caused when he sent Cardinal Bourne £1 towards the fund for completion of Westminster Cathedral. Bishop Winnington-Ingram was, however, far more accommodating to his maverick ordinand than would have been many of his peers.

It was of course in the summer of 1910 that Child met Ronald Knox and Samuel Gurney in Bruges and thereafter became involved in the SSPP.

Maurice Child served his title and his first curacy (1909–12) in London. Technically he was at St Andrew, Haverstock Hill, Hampstead, but in fact he spent his time at the far more liturgically forward daughter church of St Silas, Kentish Town. The building in use at that time was a simple mission church dating from 1884 rather than the soaring church by E.C. Shearman, which was in fact constructed in 1911–12 during Father Child's curacy: the mission church then became, and remains, the church hall. The foundation stone was laid on 16 December 1911 by the ubiquitous Princess Marie Louise, and she in fact returned the following year for the consecration, by which time Maurice Child had left.

The priest in charge of St Silas (later from 1912 the first vicar) was the Revd G. Napier Whittingham, an uncompromising Anglo-Catholic who was anxious to move the church forward into the ranks of what were then termed 'advanced' churches. He was also a Socialist, which was unusual among the clergy at that date. He was assisted in his aims by his allocated curates, who were Father Child and Father Vincent Baker, who was of a similar cast of mind and with whom Maurice Child shared accommodation at 47 Queens Crescent, Kentish Town, and thereafter in various places for about nine years thereafter.

During this period Maurice Child lived principally in what was then an almost entirely working-class area of London, albeit his own home was in a much more salubrious street, and he also seems to have retained a more fashionable address as well. It was while he was at Kentish Town that he showed a typically extroverted aspect of himself, causing *Crockford* to enter him in the 1910 edition with the forenames Maurice Charles

Francis Hugh Dominic, although he had been given only one Christian name at baptism. It was characteristic of him that whereas others, even Ronald Knox, took one additional name on ordination, he took four.[2] The additional names were not continued in later copies.

Father Napier Whittingham was married. Child was a strong advocate of celibacy for the clergy, and would never attend, still less conduct, the marriage of a priest, but unlike some of his frame of mind he was unfailingly courteous to clergy wives and made very good friends of many of them.

In 1911–12 Child was off wandering, with Vincent Baker. He had always been fascinated by travel and when still at school he asked Thomas Cook if they could arrange for him to visit Kerguelen Island, which was the most remote place he could find in his atlas.

The two priests travelled right round the world, and on the voyage between Cape Town and Hobart in Tasmania he was able to see Kerguelen, if not to land there. Later they crossed the Andes on mules and it is said that Child played some part in the expedition of 1912 to Peru organized by Yale University and the National Geographic Magazine, under the leadership of the American explorer Hiram Bingham, who the previous year had discovered the lost Inca city of Machu Picchu. The exact part played by Child in this is not clear, and he is not mentioned either in Bingham's own book on his expeditions or in his biography.[3] Child himself subsequently wrote that he had arrived in the city of Cuzco by mule at a time when it was swarming with American explorers, but did not elaborate further. As a result of this expedition he was elected in 1915 as a Fellow of the Royal Geographical Society, an unusual distinction for a priest

In 1912 Child moved out of London. He became a curate at St James the Less, Citadel Road, Plymouth, which was then a leading Anglo-Catholic centre in a city which was in the forefront of the Movement, but was destroyed in the bombing of the Second World War. The parish priest of what was then a thriving church was the Revd Reginald (known

2 He did not, however, follow the example of one priest whose name Canon Hood does not reveal, who took the names Marie Immaculée.

3 See H. Bingham, *Inca Land: Explorations in the Highlands of Peru* (Constable & Co., 1922), and A.M. Bingham, *Portrait of an Explorer: Hiram Bingham, Discoverer of Machu Picchu* (Iowa State University Press, 1989).

as Rex) Miers, but in fact Child and Baker, who also moved down to the West Country at the same time, were put in charge of the small mission church of St Michael, Central Road, West Hoe. It was here that Child started to put into effect the ideas which he was beginning to have expressed through the SSPP. It is thought that the first pastiche Baroque altar in the Church of England was introduced by the Revd W.J. Scott in St Saviour, Sunbury, about ten years prior to this.[4] However, at Plymouth Father Child introduced two such altars which had resonances of South America about them, perhaps as a result of his Peruvian trip.

They were the forerunners of many others elsewhere in the country as the Back to Baroque style gained acceptance. The architect of this work is not known, but it may have been T. Rogers Kitsell, who built the cottages at Little Petherick for Athelstan Riley and who was at about this time working in the mother church of St James. Unfortunately, although the building on West Hoe still exists and is now in use as an Orthodox church, it has had periods of disuse including a time as a factory, and the altars have long since been destroyed.

Although Child appears to have enjoyed his time in Devon, he was essentially metropolitan. Further, he was becoming increasingly involved with the SSPP, which was to enjoy a period of creative flowering over the next few years and, although several of the early volumes were printed in Plymouth under his direction, it was much easier for all concerned if he were in London most of the time.

In 1914, therefore, Child moved back from Plymouth to become curate of Holy Trinity, Sloane Street, which was not particularly known as an Anglo-Catholic centre, but was in an area of London he liked. It has even been suggested that he moved there as a form of cover to enable him to continue his activities with the SSPP. The probability is that it was a convenient opportunity to move back to London as he got on well with the rector, the Revd Dr H.R. Gamble, although Child thought some of the customs rather fussy and 'High Church' in the derogatory sense. Baker took up a position in 1915 as curate of St Thomas, Regent Street, where the SSPP masses were generally held.

---

4 This church was later replaced and the furnishings disappeared.

It was during the three years or so that Maurice Child was at Holy Trinity that much of the best work produced by the Society of St Peter and St Paul emerged. He himself wrote a great deal, as did N.P. Williams, but much of what came out was anonymous and it is not now possible to be dogmatic about authorship.

What is clear is that, when in 1916 the benefice of Holy Trinity became vacant on Gamble's departure to be Dean of Exeter, Child attempted, with his usual liking for behind the scenes manoeuvring, to ensure that Williams was appointed, but this scheme proved unsuccessful and its most notable consequence in the long term was that Child introduced Williams to Miss Muriel Cazenove, the daughter of one of the churchwardens: she later worked in a secretarial capacity for the Catholic Literature Association of the Church Union.[5] Williams was then an advocate of clerical celibacy, which he had advocated in print, but after consulting far and wide he resolved to abandon this principle and eventually, in 1926, married Miss Cazenove.

One tract which was produced of which the authorship appears clear is *Decently and in Order: Suggestions for a Method of Saying Low Mass* by 'Didasculus', which was one of Williams' pseudonyms. He laid out there a series of principles with which Child and others agreed and which formed the basis of the SSPP case. They were as follows: (1) 'The ceremonial to be followed ought to be that known as "modern Roman" . . . Not so much because it is "Roman" as because it is the simplest, most convenient, most easily studied and (to modern minds) most intelligible method of rendering Divine Service.' He went on that it was necessary to consider 'how best we can adapt the directions for the Roman Mass to the Communion Service of the English Church'; (2) 'In accordance with the principle, recognized by English law, that a man is to be considered innocent until he is proved guilty, we shall assume that the Prayer Book is Catholic unless and until it is proved to be Protestant'; (3) having concluded that a vernacular mass was there to stay, 'the goal which we shall set before ourselves will be, not a return to the Roman Mass in Latin, but the restoration of that magnificent version of the Roman Mass which is contained in [the Book

---

5 See E.W. Kemp, *N.P. Williams* (SPCK, 1954), p. 28.

of 1549]'; (4) 'We shall endeavour to depart as little as possible from the way of doing things which actually is observed in the vast majority of "Catholic" Churches of our rite . . .'; (5) 'A bi-lingual rite is a liturgical and literary monstrosity.'

This manifesto shows very clearly that the SSPP was far more moderate than alleged by its detractors and has perhaps been asserted since. It may be that many have been misled by Peter Anson's comments in *Bishops at Large* referring to 'lawless Papalist clergymen associated with the [SSPP]'.[6] That allegation has also been made by Bishop Eric Kemp in his entertaining and illuminating recollections *Shy but not Retiring*, where he wrongly calls those who followed the SSPP, 'Romanizers who basically used the Roman missal either in translation or in the original Latin'.[7]

In fact the SSPP was promoting the use of the Anglican Prayer Book with Roman ceremonial overlaid, so that the observer thought he was seeing a Roman Catholic service but in fact was listening (to the extent that the service was audible) to Cranmer. This was far removed from the position of many Anglican Papalists, who believed that the only way to effect visible unity with Rome was to start by effecting invisible unity, in other words by adopting wholesale Roman standards of liturgy and discipline. That was the line to be taken later by Father Drew at Throwleigh, Father Beresford at Newborough and by many others. Child and his group were on the other hand strongly opposed to the interpolation of parts of the Roman canon into Anglican services.

In 1916 the SSPP released the first of two volumes entitled *Pictures of the English Liturgy*, both brilliantly illustrated by Martin Travers and both now rare and collectable: the second followed in 1922. There were a number of different versions, but in essence volume 2, which came out first (a typical Child piece of legerdemain), described low mass and volume 1 high mass. The first was a counterblast to a volume sponsored by the proponents of the English Use, called *Illustrations of the Liturgy* by C.O. Skilbeck and with an introduction termed 'The Present Opportunity' by Dr Dearmer, a man, like Athelstan Riley, with little sense of humour, especially at his own expense. Child's riposte was entitled *The Lost Opportunity* and was

---

6 P.F. Anson, *Bishops at Large* (Faber & Faber, 1964), p. 89.
7 E.W. Kemp, *Shy but not Retiring* (Continuum, 2007), p. 38.

suitably derogatory about what he and his friends called 'British Museum Religion'. In volume 1, some years later, the introduction used almost exactly the same words as had Didasculus in 1916, but it seems unlikely that Williams wrote this as by then he had drifted away from the position he had occupied with the SSPP and as the years went on he became more central and liberal in his thought.

It was the slightly sarcastic tone of much of the SSPP literature which attracted the most attention. This was undoubtedly the product of Child's slightly reckless sense of humour and although it made a number of people laugh, it also alienated others who thought that such things were not the subject of jokes. It is well known that advertisements were placed for Ridley and Latimer votive candle stands and Lambeth incense. Bishops who interfered and the more minor dignitaries of the Church of England who fussed then became targets: Child's response was an advertisement in the *Church Times* for 3 September 1915 which included tracts such as *Mary in the 39 Articles* and *Between Two Extremes* by 'Tractarian', all described as 'half price to Bishops and Rural Deans'.

One of the master strokes pulled by Child was that on its tracts the SSPP described itself as 'Publishers to the Church of England'. This at the same time appeared to the unwary to give it some quasi-official status but also played on the more familiar description of 'Publishers to the Holy See'.

There was considerable discrimination in the Army against those of an Anglo-Catholic inclination who sought to become chaplains. This, however, gradually relaxed as the war went on and there were shortages in that as in other spheres. Many of the stories told about Child are apocryphal, and this almost certainly includes the account[8] that when he was interviewed by the Chaplain-General and asked what he would do for a dying man, he replied: 'Hear his confession and give him absolution.' He attributed his rejection to the fact that the correct answer was: 'Give him a cigarette and take any last message he may have for his family.' However, he did subsequently spend a short period on secondment in France, working in a canteen for the YMCA.

---

8 E. Waugh, *The Life of Ronald Knox* (Chapman & Hall, 1959), p. 135.

In 1917 Child moved from what had never been more than a tempo-rary resting place at Holy Trinity to a much more congenial parish the other side of Sloane Square. He became one of the curates at St Mary, Bourne Street (then Graham Street), under the then newly appointed vicar, Father Humphrey Whitby. Whitby was wealthy, austere, and also the greatest exponent of the SSPP method of saying mass. He was a consider-able student of Cranmer, and spent much of his life writing a book on the 1662 rite which was never in the end published, but at the same time the services were overlain with elaborate ceremonial derived from modern Roman precedents. Whitby was not a man who had many friends, but Maurice Child became his closest: despite this they never used Christian names when addressing or referring to the other and indeed called each other 'Mister' rather than the more modern 'Father'.

The close association between Child and Baker came to an end: Child, like Whitby, was never tempted by Rome, but of course Knox had gone over in 1917 and Baker also converted a year or two later, becoming a priest of the Oratory. Ronald Knox is supposed to have said that there were only two possible religions, that of the Holy Father and that of the unholy Child. Ronald Knox had lived with Child and Baker for much of early 1917, at 209 Ebury Street, Pimlico.

Maurice Child was at St Mary during exciting times when it became the SSPP model church, following refurbishment and adaptation of the high altar by Martin Travers in 1919 and the years following, and the installa-tion of a number of shrines. In due course the church was extended by H.R. Goodhart-Rendel, at which time, shortly before Child left, Father Whitby bought 30 Westbourne Street, then the Pineapple public house, and had it converted into clergy accommodation. Child lived there for a short time: the life at Bourne Street suited him as he was in central London and thus able to mix in a variety of spheres, which he enjoyed, he was able to continue with his work for the SSPP and the church, its ethos and its staff were agreeable to him.

When Child arrived in 1917 the Revd John Francis Bloxam had already been a curate in the parish for ten years and he was to remain there until the year when Child himself moved on, 1922, when he was appointed parish priest of the then notorious slum church of St Saviour, Hoxton.

Bloxam was, however, away for part of the earlier time that Child was there, serving as a Chaplain in the Army, for which he was awarded the MC with Bar. This valour was a contrast to his earlier life: he had been part of a covertly homosexual set at Oxford and had written an unpleasant and decadent piece entitled *The Priest and the Acolyte,* which was published anonymously in the only edition of a magazine entitled *Chameleon,* and told the story of a priest who became infatuated with a young server and then, following discovery of the passion, poisoned them both with an adulterated chalice. Authorship of the article was then attributed to Oscar Wilde, who knew Bloxam, but it has made of the real author something of a cult figure among those who sympathize with the spirit behind the article. It is not clear whether Child knew anything of his colleague's past: today he is remembered by a statue of St Joseph in St Mary, Bourne Street.

In 1919–20 Child went off on his second world tour, this time accompanied by Archibald Frederic Hood, who had been ordained in 1918 and was later to move to Pusey House, where he spent many years as priest librarian (1922–34) and then Principal (1934–51). Hood was also well off and was a congenial companion. They had an adventurous time with expeditions on many South Sea islands to areas not usually visited by Europeans. It is clear that Maurice Child had funds available to him beyond any stipend he received: that again was a source of mystery to his contemporaries, but it probably amounted to little more than some family money from the Child side. He was certainly an eventual beneficiary under the will of his Pain grandfather, but that inheritance would not have fallen in at this time as it was subject to the rights of others. He himself, when interviewed later, said that all the money he had he had made himself, and certainly he bought and sold property quite frequently.

It was while Child was at Bourne Street that the first Anglo-Catholic Congress was held, in 1920. The secretary of that event was the Revd H.A. Wilson, then a curate at the nearby church of St Matthew, Westminster.[9] Father Wilson also organized the 1923 Congress: both were enormously successful and the consequence was that a new permanent organization

---

9 See T. Jones, *Father Wilson of Haggerston: A Life Simply Offered* (Anglo-Catholic History Society, 2008), and H.A. Wilson, *Received with Thanks* (Mowbray, 1940).

came into being, entitled not surprisingly the Anglo-Catholic Congress, which was to arrange subsequent national meetings and also the many local events which were springing up.

In 1921 the Revd Magnus Laing, the contemporary of Child's at Oxford, moved to Bourne Street. Bruno Scott James, a former Nashdom monk who later went over to Rome and became the first priest of the Roman Catholic parish church in Walsingham, knew them both. Although a snob and somewhat bitter about his Anglican past, Scott James was quite complimentary about Father Laing, saying: 'He belonged to the extreme right wing of the Church of England, and there was no doctrine of the Catholic Church, and no extra-liturgical devotion of strongly continental, if not Mediterranean, flavour that he was not prepared to champion and adjust to the teaching of the Church of England.'[10] Despite his early prominence in Anglo-Catholic circles, however, Laing left Bourne Street after a few years, married, took a country living, and died young. It may well be that his then ultramontanism jarred rather with the inherent Anglicanism of Father Whitby.

In 1922 Child left Bourne Street for Pusey House, Oxford, then under the principalship of the distinguished patristic scholar Dr Darwell Stone: Hood moved there in the same year. There could hardly have been another figure who shared Child's ecclesiastical outlook who was less like him than the grave, unworldly and taciturn Stone. The constitution of Pusey House provided that priests went for an initial year as Probationary Librarians. Child arrived in October 1922 and almost immediately was the subject of a complaining letter from Lord Phillimore, the now elderly former President of the English Church Union. He said that he had heard that Child said mass in the 'Graham Street style', that is partly silently, and that he deplored that fashion (as did Lord Halifax, a churchwarden at St Mary, although his increasing deafness made it difficult for him to distinguish whether or not the words were spoken out loud). Stone defended Child.[11]

Child served a very short time at Pusey House, the rather stiflingly intellectual tone of which would almost certainly have bored him in the

---

10 B. Scott James, *Asking for Trouble* (Darton Longman, and Todd, 1962), p. 32.

11 See B.A. Orford and W. Davage, *Piety and Learning* (Pusey House, 2002), pp. 54–5.

long term, as before his year on probation was spent he was offered, and accepted, what was now to be a full-time paid position as Secretary of the Anglo-Catholic Congress. The exact sequence of events at this time is not clear, as it appears that Father Child again went off travelling: he is said to have visited India and Burma during this period, staying in state in Bombay with the Governor, Lord Lloyd, who was one of his many friends. Certainly in 1924 he was the secretary of the first Anglo-Catholic pilgrimage to the Holy Land, which was what nowadays would be called a spin-off from the 1923 Congress. It was led by Bishop Roscoe Shedden of Nassau, later vicar of Wantage, and was remarkably successful: in consequence of it, Child was made a Knight Commander of the Order of the Holy Sepulchre by the Orthodox Patriarch of Jerusalem.

Over the next years, Maurice Child's formidable powers of organization and advertisement were strained but never found wanting. He arranged the 1927, 1930 and 1933 Congresses, the last of which was the largest and most lavish, in a way which was not only efficient but was effectively publicized and has been well documented. He continued as Secretary of the Church Union after the merger, with effect from 1 January 1934, of the Anglo-Catholic Congress and the English Church Union: this joining together, which now looks like an inevitable development, was delayed until that time because of the distaste among many of the more moderate rank and file in the ECU for the more advanced stance taken by the ACC, and by a certain lack of trust in the tactics and personality of Maurice Child himself. However, his fingers remained in many pies, and he knew a very large number of those who mattered in and out of church circles. One of the consequences of his extraordinarily busy life during this period was that he wrote little save for those publications issued by the SSPP, many of which were anonymous: his best known was a defence of the neutrality of the Vatican, issued during the First World War. He also penned over the years a large number of pieces for newspapers: he had an acute journalist's eye for absorbing and relaying information about foreign countries in particular, after his many trips abroad.

In addition to the Congress, Child was also one of the main opponents put up by the Anglo-Catholic party to resist the Revised Prayer Books of 1927 and 1928, making his points clearly and effectively and was a proctor in the Canterbury Convocation: he was the first unbeneficed priest to be so elected.

If that were not enough, Child's then London living accommodation, Eaton Place Cottage,[12] in a mews behind Eaton Square, was a centre of entertainment for those from a wide variety of backgrounds, many of whom were not ecclesiastical. One of the many good stories about Child was that a guest at one of his parties was surprised to see there the Lady Margaret Professor of Divinity at Oxford (that is the shy and aloof Williams) in deep conversation with the film star Tallulah Bankhead, over a cocktail. The décor in his London property was very modernistic for the time, with garish colouring on the walls, and this again deterred some. He shared the accommodation there with a lawyer named Eric Walter Dean (1906–93).

Child had got to know the Dean family when he was at St Mary, Bourne Street, which they attended. Despite living in a generally affluent area, the family was working class and not at all well off, and when Child was asked by Sir Charles Hyde, a philanthropist and proprietor of the *Birmingham Post* and one of his many friends, to nominate two boys who could be financially assisted through school and university, he chose Eric Dean and his brother Francis John Michael Dean, known always as Michael (1915–2003). Eric was later called to the Bar and certainly for a time was employed by the Board of Trade. In 1935 Michael Dean was able to go up to University College, Oxford, and after attending Pusey House and there coming under the influence of Canon Hood, he decided to proceed to ordination. Child's confidence in the intellectual promise of his protégés was therefore perfectly justified.

In addition to his hospitality in the West End, Maurice Child was a member of the Bath Club and of the Athenaeum, and was always seen at the Derby. He continued his foreign travel and became particularly fond of Spain, adding bull-fighting to circuses as an area of expertise.

There are certain features of Maurice Child's personality and attributes which are mentioned by almost everyone who published recollections of

---

12 It appears that Father Child moved there in about 1925–26: earlier editions of the London telephone directory give his address as in Westbourne Street, near St Mary, Pimlico. He had earlier had a flat in Sloane Street and for a time lived in a bijou house at 209 Ebury Street, also in Pimlico. His mother had moved from Hampshire and lived for many years in Eltham in South East London: she died in 1938 aged 81.

him. It is always said (and the many surviving photographs bear this out) that he was short and slightly overweight. He never wore a clerical collar even with a cassock and wore his cassock as little as possible: when out he would answer questions as to what he did by pretending to be a bookie or a loss adjuster. He was never conventional in the sense of accepting the then very rigid class distinctions and the etiquette which depended upon them.

One person who did know Child was Bruno Scott James, who said of him: 'He was a fine preacher with a very attractive voice, and he had great charm of manner, but he sometimes liked to affect a rather bizarre and not very clerical dress that did not appear to further his apostolate. Nevertheless, he did good work among delinquent young men, over whom he was said to exercise a somewhat salutary influence.'[13]

Another who knew him, and indeed was a participant in the 1924 pilgrimage to Palestine, was the writer and later editor of the *Church Times,* Sydney Dark. In his own autobiography, written in 1941 when Child was still alive, he says of him: '[He is] a tubby humorous little priest, whose life has been influenced, to his considerable cost, by Mgr Ronald Knox, who was an Oxford friend of his.[14] Mgr Knox contrived to combine piety with flippancy and finally went to Rome to escape himself. Maurice Child has retained his flippancy in the Church of England. He is an able man, a charming host, a delightful companion. But flippancy has made his life a failure . . . I always feel about Maurice that at heart he is very sad and is always trying to laugh it off.'[15]

Those were hard words to write about a man who was still very well known in ecclesiastical circles and indeed at that time had just resigned as Secretary to the Church Union.

The opposite point of view was put by another well-known priest and writer, the Revd Desmond Morse-Boycott, who produced a very large number of books with common themes and much purple prose, but

---

13 Scott James, *Trouble*, p. 34. It seems, however, that in fact Child's solution to the problems of delinquent young men was often nothing more sophisticated than urging them to join the armed services.

14 This does not appear to be strictly accurate. Knox and Child knew each other well after Oxford: Child had come down before Knox went up.

15 S. Dark *Not Such a Bad Life* (Eyre & Spottiswoode, 1941), pp. 205–6.

who knew Child well. In *They Shine Like Stars,* published in 1947, Child was almost the only living Anglo-Catholic whom he discussed in his discursive history of the Oxford Movement and its successors. He wrote of him: 'I feel that he has, in his own way, made more Anglo-Catholic history than, perhaps, anyone else and also because he was, whilst doing so, the very perfect opposite of the grave old Tractarian ... He was rebuked as pleasure-loving, as overgiven to hospitality, as an adventurer in the realms of ecclesiastical politics ... Where did he stand ... this priest whose sermons sparked like November crackers; whom opponents feared and friends worshipped; who subscribed to every good cause in cash and comment, kind or caustic; who never slept, apparently, and yet, after a strenuous evening entertaining the bright and the nit-wits of Church-minded London, could be found on his knees at dawn?' Morse-Boycott continued that of the two schools of thought about Child, he fell into the camp which regarded him as touched by sanctity, a conclusion to which he had come through knowing him very well.

He concluded that: 'Behind the "eye-wash" of the jazzy home; the bountiful wine-bin; the luxuriance of a setting in which a Leading Lady, a Bright Young Novelist, or a Film Star would be at home, gleaned the gold of Christian living and renunciation, even as behind the whitewash on the walls of St Sophia gleam the mosaics of the days of Faith.'[16]

It may well be that one of the factors which influenced the strong feelings that many clearly had about Child was the unspoken suspicion that he was a homosexual. He was certainly very flamboyant (a word often used at that time as a code for gay) in his personal dress, but that of course means nothing. In his seminal article *Un-English and Unmanly: Anglo-Catholicism and Homosexuality,*[17] David Hilliard specifically discusses Child, and synthesizes the opposing views of him very fully thus: 'Maurice Child [was] the "mystery man" of the Anglo-Catholic Movement [and] was regarded by critics as a flippant and pleasure-loving "sybarite" and by admirers as a dedicated priest of remarkable ability. Child was of a type

---

16 This part of the description was recycled (as was much of Morse-Boycott's writing) from a newspaper article he had written anonymously about Child.

17 In *Victorian Studies,* Winter 1982, pp. 181–210.

that popped up regularly in Anglo-Catholic circles between the wars. A strong believer in clerical celibacy, he was also rich, witty, versatile, a *bon viveur* – nicknamed "the Playboy of the Western Church". In London he lived with a male companion at a series of fashionable addresses,[18] where he entertained friends from many walks of life. His glittering parties bore little resemblance to the usual clerical social gatherings.'

It is clear that Hilliard, without actually saying so directly, was implying very strongly that Child was indeed homosexual. However, there appears to have been no scandal or other untoward behaviour and the fact that he was generally thought to be at his best pastorally with young men is no proper evidence of any misconduct, especially since he ministered to many women as well. Child was punctilious about many matters, especially money, and well aware of problems which arose in the lives of some of his acquaintances. It would appear that whatever his orientation, any allegation of impropriety is unfounded or at the highest unproven.

It was against this background that, in 1935, Child accepted the living of St Dunstan, Cranford, the patronage to which was held by Lord Berkeley. It would seem that he did so with a view to his eventual retirement as Secretary of the Church Union, although he did not in fact resign from that post until 1940 and thus combined the two positions for about five years. It was the only church of which he was ever parish priest and his incumbency was to be cut short by his untimely death in 1950.

It is now almost impossible to visualize what Cranford was like when Child moved there in May 1935. Of all the locales in England, it has changed perhaps the most.

Prior to the First World War, there were large areas of Middlesex which were still very rural, and the small villages had rustic churches which were often hidden from view. As the tide of suburbia engulfed them, different solutions were adopted to meet the challenge.[19] At Greenford, which became the most populous parish in the Diocese of London, a substantial

---

18 That does not appear strictly correct. He certainly shared the accommodation in Eaton Place Cottage with Eric Dean, but it does not appear that they lived under the same roof elsewhere.

19 See R. Walford and J. Morris, *The Growth of New London in Suburban Middlesex and the Response of the Church of England* (Edwin Mellen Press, 2007).

new building was erected next to the tiny ancient parish church, which was then used for early services only. At Perivale, the old church was made redundant and a new church built nearby. At Northolt the old church was renovated and refurbished but new churches later sprang up around.

When Child went to Cranford, the spread of new building was still some distance from the small village, which then had a population of little more than 750, but was approaching rapidly. Close by was the hamlet of Heath Row, which has now disappeared under the tarmac of the airport runways. The M4 now bisects the parish and the building of approach roads to it has distorted the original road pattern very extensively. The rural nature of the setting of the church in 1935 was compounded by the fact that St Dunstan was adjacent to Cranford Park with its great house, owned by the Berkeley family since 1618, and some distance from the small village. In fact, in the past the church had been seen more as a private chapel for the house and the rector as the Berkeleys' private chaplain: as late as 1876 no one was allowed into the park to visit the church save by permission or to attend services and the key was kept at Cranford House.

As Maurice Child arrived, this quasi-feudal arrangement had already disappeared. The Berkeleys vacated the property at about the time of the First World War and then in 1932 sold the house and its park to Hayes and Harlington UDC, who in 1935 sold it to Middlesex County Council, but took a lease back and administered it jointly with Heston and Isleworth Borough Council, to which part of Cranford had been transferred in the meanwhile. In 1945 the house, save for the stable block which remains and is extremely close to the church, was demolished, to Child's chagrin and over his protests. The park, however, remains open to the public and has not been built over, although it is now hemmed in by motorway and airport.

The new rector was also somewhat unlucky so far as his accommodation was concerned. The Old Rectory lay about 440 yards east of the church and had been improved and extended over the years: part of it was timber framed but had been faced with brick in about 1774. There was also a glebe of some 14 acres and the grounds were extensive enough for parish functions to be held and the scouts to camp there.

In 1939 the Air Ministry compulsorily purchased both the rectory and 11 acres of the glebe under an Act of Parliament with a view to extending Heston Airport: this never in fact took place. Father Child protested about this and ensured that it was provided in the legislation that three acres were in return to be given as a site for a new rectory. That did not happen and a question was asked in the House of Commons on the subject. The local authority was also difficult, as was the Inland Revenue, and in due course Father Child succeeded before the King's Bench Divisional Court in his contention that the costs of opposing the legislation were a deductible expense against his income. At a lunch on 21 May 1939 to mark the 951st anniversary of St Dunstan, the guest speaker was the former Lord Chancellor, Lord Sankey, who expressed his sympathy for the parish in the loss of the rectory.

Later, litigation ensued, as a result of which in 1958 a three-acre plot was eventually provided as a site for a new house, but that was then itself subject to compulsory purchase to be used for the M4 motorway.

The short-term solution was that Father Child himself acquired two semi-detached suburban houses, 131/3 Roseville Road, on the so-called Arsenal Estate, near the church but today separated from it by the M4, and it was in those unglamorous surroundings that Child lived from 1939 until his death.[20] It was perhaps characteristic of him that he had his entry in the London telephone book as 131 Roseville Road, Cranford St John, using the long-defunct name of the feudal manor which covered the northern part of the parish and which he always used for the living.

Child was a man who, in Cranford as elsewhere, excited strong feelings either for or against. One of his most vigorous supporters was Arthur Alfred Sadler (1912–98), a market gardener in the village, whom he befriended and who married his housekeeper. Mr and Mrs Sadler then lived at 133 Roseville Road, next door to the rector, and Mrs Sadler acted as an intermediary and gatekeeper when callers arrived to see him. In 1946 Arthur Sadler became a churchwarden and remained so for over 50 years.

The church at Cranford is and was picturesque on its own account, even without the setting: it fulfilled perhaps a Betjemanesque fantasy of

---

20 See S. Reynolds, ed., *Victoria County History of Middlesex*, Volume 3 (University of London, 1962), pp. 184–5.

Middlesex and perhaps deserved a poem on that account. It was in size rather similar to Compton Beauchamp, its length being about 20 yards only, and it was aisleless. The chancel and lower part of the tower are of flint and rubble and were constructed in the fifteenth century. The nave was badly damaged by fire in 1710 and was reconstructed at the expense of the Berkeley family in red brick, and then in 1716 a belfry in the same material was added. There are a remarkable collection of seventeenth- and eighteenth-century monuments in the chancel, mainly to members of the Berkeley family and their associates.

In 1895 the church was extensively reordered under the direction of John Loughborough Pearson: the roof of the nave was renewed, the gallery was removed and a new east window, by Kempe, was installed. At the same time a small vestry was built out from the north wall of the tower.

The last rector who was treated principally as an adjunct to Cranford House seems to have been the Revd Heathfield Hickes (1837–81). He was followed after a short interval by the Revd Joseph Frederick Vincent Lee, who came as a young man in 1888 and stayed until 1925, and who appears to have instituted daily services during lent in the late nineteenth century and also to have involved himself in starting various parish activities and societies. He appears to have moved the churchmanship substantially upwards. Child's immediate predecessor was the Revd Edward Pilcher Lewis (1925–35), to whom there is a commemorative tablet in the chancel. Father Lewis had had a varied career, which included a period as a curate at St Matthias, Earl's Court Road (1891–98), well after Frank Kingdon had ceased his association with that church, and a spell in Lisbon as chaplain (1907–15). He was a keen Freemason, which would not have been appealing to his successor.

When Maurice Child moved to Cranford he was anxious to institute immediate changes to the liturgy so that the practice at Cranford conformed to that to which he was accustomed. His use was in general that followed by Father Humphrey Whitby at St Mary, Bourne Street, during the time that Child was a curate there, and indeed subsequently, namely the Book of Common Prayer disguised by a heavy covering of Roman ceremonial. It would also appear that he was influenced by the organization at Bourne Street of parochial guilds and the like to involve the laity in the life of the church. However, he was extremely cautious, and examination of the parish magazines shows that he did not use the term 'mass' when setting out the list of services, although he did so refer to it in his commentary on occasion: nor did he abandon matins immediately before the sung celebration on Sundays or even institute daily services. When his friends came to preach, and he was able to command the attendance of many well-known Anglo-Catholics, they were referred to in the magazine as 'Mr' rather than 'Father', even in the case of such as Father H.A. Wilson of Haggerston, the popular writer on East End life and his predecessor as secretary of the ACC, who had never been known by any other appellation.

As well as those matters, Child was faced with two immediate problems. One was that the parish church required extensive work on it, not only to make it suitable for the forms of worship which he wished to introduce, but also because there were structural problems which had not been attended to in earlier renovations. The other was that the population growth which was taking place in the south of the parish, around the main Bath Road, required the provision of a church building which was larger than St Dunstan and nearer the new houses. He dealt with both these matters with characteristic energy and application.

By the time that Child moved to Cranford, the Back to Baroque tendency in the Church of England had almost run its course. Most such schemes were completed by about 1930: Compton Beauchamp was a late exception. The work which was carried out at Cranford was almost the last such complete refurbishment, but it was one of the most successful, not least because the size of the church and the monuments which were already in place enhanced the effect of what was put in. Predictably, Maurice Child turned to Martin Travers, who in later years was to consider that Cranford was his most successful such commission: he appears not to have been as constrained by cash considerations as in many places and the work has lasted better than at Compton Beauchamp, as the church is not so badly affected by damp and the materials used were of better quality. In fact, Travers himself wrote to the parish magazine in June 1936 pointing out, before the work began, that elimination of damp was a prerequisite to anything else being done. An appeal was launched, of which Captain Geary-Hill RN, Father Child's brother-in-law, was treasurer.

The extent of the building work required necessitated the complete closure of St Dunstan for a time, from October to Christmas, 1936, while the nave was renovated. This was not least because the floors of the church were themselves unsafe as a result of excavations which had taken place beneath many years before to produce burial vaults for the Berkeley family and others. The four such vaults were opened and the bodies were reburied in the churchyard, thus enabling the floor to be strengthened. The chancel was renovated in the spring of 1937 and complete by 2 May of that year.

It was characteristic of Child, who was well known for his ability to acquire and reuse objets d'art from foreign convents and the like, that he rescued from the vaults a coronet which had belonged to Frederick Augustus, 5th Earl of Berkeley (1745–1810), and later had it remade as a sanctuary lamp by the distinguished silversmith Omar Ramsden. One of the monuments in the church itself, to Sir Roger Aston and his wife, dating from 1611–13, was reconstructed so that it did not project so far into the chancel and thus improved the sightlines to the altar, and by the repositioning a priest's door in the north-east corner of the chancel was unblocked and a new window inserted.

A new gallery designed by Travers was constructed over the west end, thus reverting to the situation before the 1895 renovation, and, more importantly, significantly increasing the seating capacity as well as providing room for a choir and for the organ. A mediaeval wall painting was also uncovered on the wall above the high altar, although this has never been fully renovated. The work continued into the early part of the war, and in about 1940 the old vestry was demolished and a new sacristy was erected in its place, made rather crudely in concrete: it is now cracked and showing its age. Electricity was not, however, installed at this time and the church remained dependent on atmospheric gas lighting until well into the 1950s: the approach to it was unlit and this made late services difficult in the winter.

This extensive building work was at least partly carried out in order to provide a stage for the introduction of the neo-Baroque furnishings, which tone in particularly well with the monuments, as they were intended to do.

Travers produced several designs for Father Child, one at least of which involved the removal of the Kempe window and its replacement by one designed by the artist himself, but this was not carried through. He did, however, install a new high altar with reredos of terracotta colour, designed to resemble leather, as was the double-sided frontal. The reredos had incorporated within it a large tabernacle, which could be converted to a throne for exposition of the Blessed Sacrament by sliding the roof forward over the doors, a typically ingenious solution by Travers which no doubt delighted his client also. The altar was provided with four Baroque candlesticks with a crucifix. Above the altar was hung an octagonal canopy, as similar to that which was proposed at one stage at Compton Beauchamp, with wooden pendant tassels: the whole ensemble is in scale with its surroundings.

Travers then remodelled the chancel arch and placed a cherub on each side with accompanying cartouche and a decorated keystone. He made new wooden communion rails and a pulpit and carried out many small improvements such as the provision of a new processional cross, gilded hymn boards and a tabor for exposition of the Sacrament in silver-gilded wood with a large painted angel or cherub's head on the face.

As late as 1941 Travers designed a statue and plinth of Our Lady with an extraordinarily tall light blue wooden canopy above, rising almost to the ceiling, which was originally to the north of the chancel arch but has since been moved to the south, exchanging places with the pulpit. In the chancel was placed a memorial tablet to Father Lewis, which uses much more modern lettering than the other items, and in the sanctuary is a small cartouche commemorating the renovation of the memorial to the Revd Thomas Fuller (rector 1658–61) and the contribution to it of Sidney Sussex College, Cambridge. Fuller was the author of *The History of the Worthies of England* and *The Church History of Britain*.

Maurice Child had relatively little time to enjoy the church when it was completed, particularly of course because the war was still raging during the first years after the work was finished. When Child stayed the night at the Bourne Street presbytery after a function in London, he was said to have retired to his campbed clad only in a silk dressing gown, on the basis that that was how he would like to appear either before the divine judge or to the vulgar gaze if he were bombed out.[21]

The second problem with which he was faced was further provision of accommodation for the growing parish. From the late nineteenth century a chapel at ease had functioned in the Church School, but by 1935 it was clear that a better solution had to be found.

The building and opening of the mission church of the Holy Angels shows just what an accomplished publicist Child was, and also what an able administrator. The church cost only £600, and was built in three weeks, opening in the late autumn of 1935. It was dedicated by the Bishop of Kensington on 12 October 1935.

Father Child encouraged the newspapers to refer to it as 'the most modern church in England' and himself compared it to a cinema. It was a corrugated iron Nissen hut, just south of the Bath Road, with a green cement floor and a concrete altar and font. The frontal was opaque and lit in different, liturgically correct, colours. The hymns were indicated by an electronic indicator and there was a siren or hooter in lieu of a bell to call the faithful: it thus provided something of a contrast to St Dunstan. The crucifix which was attached to the plain reredos looks like the work of Martin Travers, and a picture of the interior was among his papers, which would suggest that he provided that fitting. A vestry, pulpit and lectern were added in 1938.

Maurice Child was a most ingenious fundraiser, and he managed to persuade three local hostelries (one of which, fittingly, was the Berkeley Arms) to sponsor some of the furnishings. Many of his contemporaries would have regarded such a step as beyond the pale, but he saw the value of community relations and, of course, of the press.

It was that sort of gesture which made some regard Child as an embarrassment, whereas in fact he was making effective use of his talents. He would also have been criticized for using prize draws to raise money, as he regularly did. He attracted a great deal of controversy by commenting that every new housing estate should be provided with a public house

21 See N. Price, ed., *Streets of Heaven* (St Mary Bourne Street, 1999): article by the Revd David Powell, p. 23.

as a social centre. On the other side, he also attended the reopening of Cranford Baptist Church when it was forced to move because of the purchase of its site by the Air Ministry, and spoke at the ceremony, which was not a course that many of his contemporaries would have contemplated.

In 1940 the new church was taken over by the London Home Diocesan Mission, and they were able to pay for a priest for it. Although the parish was not heavily populated when Child arrived, for the first year he had an acting curate, the Revd Cecil Clark, who combined that post with the secretaryship of the London area for the Church Union: he left in 1936 for a parish of his own and he was replaced by the Revd Morgan Griffith. In 1938 the Revd A.E. Bloore arrived in Father Griffith's stead: he had been a priest for about five years and was curate of Cranford until 1940, at which time he took on the Missioner's post at Holy Angels. He stayed until 1942 and was then replaced by the Revd J.D. Dale, who had come to Cranford as curate in 1940 upon his ordination, working mostly at Holy Angels, and then in turn moved on to be Missioner. In 1944 the Revd A.A.M. Sandeman, who had been working in the West Indies and then in Canada, came, his arrival having been delayed by the need to wait for safe transport from North America. By the late 1940s the population of the parish was in excess of 4000 and was increasing rapidly.

In addition to this assistance, the Revd Montague Eyden, the founder and headmaster of Quainton Hall School, Harrow, acted as honorary curate after 1941: he had previously held such a position at St Mary, Somers Town.

On 17 January 1941 the Holy Angels was burned out (not as a result of enemy action) but was almost immediately replaced on the same site by a converted Rodney hut, which was a superior version of a Nissen. In the meantime a community hall and a temporary chapel in the High Street were used. Rebuilding began on 1 July 1941 and rededication was as early as 30 August. The interior was more elaborate on the rebuilding, with cherubs and the like: Martin Travers, who was very short of work during this period for obvious reasons, was asked for designs although rather oddly those which survive are dated 1943.[22] They show a sanctu-

---

22 A note in *The Times*, 23 May 1969, indicates that Travers had also designed the Nissen-like structure erected in 1941.

ary with a neo-Baroque altar with six candlesticks and a rood: behind was a screen, thus forming a vestry. On each side was a pillar topped by a cherub holding a candlestick. This was similar to that which was actually installed. The detail of the work was altered during the course of the life of the building, which in its turn was to be burned out in early 1969.

Interestingly, the presentation of the religion at Holy Angels was more forward than at St Dunstan, particularly after the arrival of Father Dale in 1940, when daily mass (so termed) was commenced in the new church and communions there increased from 715 in 1938 to 1715 the following year and then to 2219 in 1940.

Holy Angels was replaced in 1970, when a new, permanent church in modern style, designed by the Norman Haines Partnership, was erected off Cranford High Street, adjacent to an equally modern Roman Catholic church, a visible demonstration of disunity.

Father Child was anxious to develop the devotional life of the parish. His major contribution to that was the foundation in 1937 of the Livery of St Dunstan, which was given its charter by Bishop Winnington-Ingram in 1937, shortly before he finally relinquished his see. The purpose behind the Livery was to bring together the servers of the parish in a formal organization. Father Child took the view that young men, rather than children, should be given what he considered was the great privilege of serving at the altar. The Livery consisted of the rector and eleven serving brothers of whom one should be Master, a limitless number of Freemen who were aspirants to the brotherhood, and the Court, who were the former servers. They were given special short capes to wear over the cassock at meetings and their special days of devotion were St Dunstan's Day and the Feast of Christ the King. The Livery was initially extremely successful and has indeed continued to the present day, although the more recent photographs show that the members are somewhat older than was originally envisaged.

This organization has remained almost unique in the Diocese: the only other such body under charter is a similarly organized Confraternity at Quainton Hall School: the idea was imported there by Father Eyden, who had been enthused by it when assisting Maurice Child at Cranford. The

School had been transferred in 1945 to the ownership of the Guardians of the Shrine of Our Lady at Walsingham.

Maurice Child also interested himself in outside organizations: in 1938 he was appointed as an Officer (Brother) of the Order of St John of Jerusalem, with which Isabel Gurney had also been concerned, and in 1948 he became the assistant General Secretary of the Church of England Council of Foreign Relations, in which capacity he was able to use his unique personal knowledge of other countries. He was also Chaplain to the local Sea Cadets and, during the war, to Heston Airport, which involved informing relatives when a man stationed there had been killed. At such delicate tasks he excelled. He had been a Proctor in Convocation before the war, losing his seat in 1935 but regaining it in 1937. He continued travelling, and before 1939 he established a pattern of generally being away in February, on one occasion informing his no doubt bemused readers of the newsletter that he was off to the Cameroons.

By the late 1940s parish life at Cranford had changed completely from the time of Child's arrival in 1935. There was a great deal of activity and the new church of the Holy Angels, despite its unprepossessing exterior, was welcomed by those living around: by the end of the 1950s there were more than 250 on the electoral roll. The old church had been renovated and beautified: because the underlying need for structural work had been addressed as well, the décor has remained much as it was in Father Child's time.

Maurice Child's later years were coloured by his strong opposition to a book entitled *The Rise of Christianity* written by Bishop Barnes of Birmingham, who was by this time a great embarrassment to the rest of the episcopal bench. Canon Hood thought that had the Archbishops not repudiated the book in strong terms, which they did, Child might have resigned his living, but would never have gone over to Rome.

On 26 January 1950 Maurice Child died suddenly and unexpectedly in Charing Cross Hospital after falling down stairs after a dinner party and fracturing his skull. His last words before the fall indicated his unshakeable belief in a future life: even his will, dated 8 May 1940 but proved with a later handwritten codicil 27 January 1947, commences: 'I declare that I die in the Catholic Religion asking mercy of the Lord Christ.'

Maurice Child left £13,200 odd gross, £12,700 odd net, which by the standards of the time was a considerable amount albeit not redolent of real wealth. He had clearly invested in property in and around Cranford. The will and codicil included mention of 11 Berkeley Parade, Cranford, one of a parade on the Bath Road (left to the Dean brothers), 'Endyon', Bath Road, Cranford (left to his nephew), property at Cranford Church Close (left to the parish) and the semi-detached houses at 131/3 Roseville Road (also to the parish) and an interest in a house in Firs Drive, in which Father Clark had lived. He left many vestments and the like to the church, £500 to the Fidelity Trust founded by Athelstan Riley, and some shares to the Anglo-Catholic Ordination Fund. He also, with a characteristic touch, left £100 to provide beer at the annual Cranford parish feast. The main provision of the will was entirely conventional in that his residuary beneficiaries were his brother and sister and their families. The proving executors were Eric Dean, Roger Geary-Hill (Child's nephew) and Arthur Sadler.

The Anglo-Catholic tradition of the parish of Cranford has been maintained ever since Child's time, although there have been a number of priests who have occupied his position. His immediate successor was the Revd Christopher Byron, who remained until 1957 and whose parish magazines indicate that Father Child's caution over liturgical matters had been abandoned. He was replaced by the Revd Michael Dean, whose close connections with Father Child have already been outlined.

Father Dean was initially at All Saints, Clifton, Bristol, but from 1946 to 1952 was himself at Pusey House as a librarian and at the same time acted as college chaplain of Christ Church. He then took on the post of parish priest of St Stephen, Bournemouth, but when Cranford became vacant he decided to follow in the footsteps of his mentor. In the event he stayed only for seven years, and then went to St Mark, Regent's Park, but his entire career was heavily influenced by the patronage of Father Child, who saw his underlying talent at an early stage.

Maurice Child is one of those who are remembered for what he said in conversation or from the pulpit, rather than for what he wrote: his correspondence was frequent but often almost illegible. He was not a profound thinker who left volumes for future generations to digest. Since he died almost 60 years ago, the numbers of those who knew him are falling rapidly, but he undoubtedly made a deep impression on many whose path he crossed. It does seem that he was able by his regime at Cranford, which of course coincided with the very rapid increase in population of the area, to enthuse the congregation with his interpretation of Christianity and that tradition has continued. The parish of Cranford has been fractured by the motorway and is even in two separate London boroughs (Hillingdon and Hounslow), but unlike some of the other places discussed here it has not been absorbed into a larger unit.

There is perhaps one story which could be told only of Maurice Child. In 1930 Lord Stickland, the Prime Minister of Malta, came to England following a strong campaign against him by the Roman Catholic bishops of that island. Child was sympathetic to him and, with his tongue firmly in one cheek, rang John Kensit, a man not known for his ready wit, suggesting that the Church Union and the Protestant Truth Society organize a joint demonstration in favour of Stickland. Kensit on this occasion did see the joke.

6

St James, Marshland St James, St Matthew, Littleport, and other Fenland Shrines

Norfolk, as one of Noel Coward's characters so memorably remarked, is very flat. In fact, as with so many of Coward's witty aphorisms, that is misleading because much of Norfolk is pleasantly rolling. However, in the far south west of the county, and in the part of Cambridgeshire which used to be known administratively as the Isle of Ely, lies an almost forgotten area of archetypal fenland in which there is no hillock for miles, and across the dykes and fields there are views as far as one can see in every direction. Perhaps the best description of this area on the Norfolk/Cambridgeshire border is given by Dorothy L. Sayers in her murder mystery *The Nine Tailors*: she had good reason to know the landscape as her father, the Revd Henry Sayers, moved from the civilized surroundings of Oxford to be rector of Bluntisham with Earith, near St Ives, where he stayed from 1897 to 1917. Bluntisham was attractive as he had a number of relatives dependent on him, and the stipend was very substantial. However, he then exchanged livings with the vicar of Christchurch, a very isolated hamlet in the deepest of fen countryside south of Wisbech, as he was sorry for the incumbent, who had a large number of young children to support. Christchurch forms a model for Fenchurch St Paul in the novel: Henry Sayers remained there until his death in 1928.

In the centre of this district, on the Norfolk side of the boundary but still, as with most of far south-west Norfolk, since 1914 in the Diocese of Ely rather than in that of Norwich, is the scattered settlement of Marshland, in which is the tiny church, now closed and converted to residential accommodation, of St James.

On the face of it the Fens were an unattractive area for the growth of Anglo-Catholicism. Because of the difficulties with drainage, there was little population outside of the villages until the nineteenth century. As outlying areas were drained and long straight roads with right-angle bends were laid down across the landscape to lead to the new farms, the Nonconformists saw an opportunity to which the Church of England was slow to react. Small brick-built chapels of various sects, often Methodist, sprang up in the new settlements: many of them have now been adapted for other purposes.

It was not until the late nineteenth century that Anglicans began to build for themselves small churches, also brick built, in these outlying areas. Very often there was nothing much by way of a village centre, and a church was simply placed in a convenient spot where land was available, so that most of the farmers and their labourers would have to walk considerable distances to attend. This can be seen very clearly in places such as St James, Marshland and St Matthew, Littleport, both of which are now deconsecrated and used for other purposes. In other villages, the church has become unsafe because of subsidence and stands derelict and empty, with broken glass around, as at Holy Trinity, Nordelph, Norfolk and St Mary Magdalene, Guyhirn, Cambridgeshire (see Chapter 8).

However, just as some Anglo-Catholics were called to the East End of London by concern for the welfare of the poverty-stricken inhabitants, others may have found that it was only in an unpopular parish with a very small stipend that they could further their vocation: most fashionable and wealthy livings closed their door to those who were thought to be 'extreme' or Romanizers. So it was in some of the Fenland villages, which were neither pretty nor well remunerated, but offered opportunities for those denied their own incumbency elsewhere.

The village of Marshland St James (otherwise known as Marshland Smeeth) covers a very substantial area of fen, with one long main street, known as The Smeeth, running across it. In recent years a large number of new houses have been built along that road, because, as with other villages in the area, land has been cheap and, by virtue of very long days, commuting to London and other places is possible. It could not be described as an attractive spot by the most committed publicist, and it is the only civil parish in Norfolk which contains no listed building. There were stations in the parish at Smeeth Road and at Middle Drove, which reduced its remoteness somewhat.

The small brick-built church of St James is, however, not in or even near the main settlement, but about a mile further south on Middle Drove. In this remote spot, up a cul-de-sac by the drain (an artificial river), is a small group consisting of the church, a substantial vicarage (said to date from 1927 but looking older) and a former school dating from 1857. The church is hidden from view from the main road by the other two buildings. There was at one time an adjacent church hall, which has been demolished. There are no other buildings in the immediate vicinity.

In such an unlikely and windswept location there flourished for many years a lonely outpost of Anglo-Catholicism which was little known even when it was in existence, and now has almost completely disappeared from consciousness.

Marshland originally formed part of the parish of Walpole St Peter, but the splendid fifteenth-century parish church, one of the finest in East Anglia, was a very long distance from the houses which sprang up further south. Services in Marshland began in a converted barn in 1853, and then the school was built in 1857 and served a dual purpose until the construction of the church. The foundation stone of that was laid on 30 September 1896 and the building was opened and dedicated as a mission church on 1 July 1897. The church was given in memory of the Revd Philip Salisbury Bagge, who had been rector of Walpole St Peter for 37 years, and was a member of a prominent local family. His daughter Grace laid the foundation stone.

There could hardly be a greater contrast between this modest building and the magnificent parish church of which it was an offshoot. The architect of St James is unknown: it is only 40 feet by 20 feet with an apsidal chancel with a radius of 6 feet and a small porch to the south. A vestry was added on the south side in 1915 and enlarged in 1933. The walls are of red and yellow Fletton brick (originating from the Peterborough area, not far away), and the roof is slated.

The nave was rectangular and had four bays on each side between plain buttresses. In the three western bays on the north side were placed rectangular windows of a domestic nature and in the fourth was a curious three-light hipped dormer window. The pattern was similar on the south side but for the entrance and the vestry. On the west wall were three plain lancets within a relieving arch, above which was a small timber bell-cote and on the north side a brick chimney.

The total effect was far more akin to the many Nonconformist chapels which dot the landscape than to an Anglican parish church, which in due course it became. In 1922 it was assigned its own district and on 17 November 1933 it was consecrated and a new parish was created from parts of as many as ten adjoining parishes.

There is no evidence to suggest that prior to 1942 there was any Anglo-Catholic tradition in the church: in that year, however, the Revd C.N. Bales arrived to commence what was to be a very long incumbency.

Charles Noel Bales was born on 7 December 1907 in the small town of Wymondham, just west of Norwich: indeed his place of birth is very near to the famous Abbey. He came from an unusual background for a priest of his generation in that his father, Arthur William Bales (born 1878), was a manual and later an agricultural labourer. In 1905 he had married his next-door neighbour, Mildred Everitt (born 1870 in Norwich), who appears to have come from a slightly higher rung of society. Charles Bales' father died in 1908, so the boy grew up without any paternal figure. The only clue to any involvement in church affairs is that his grandfather, John Bales, was the sexton and caretaker at the Abbey and so the young Charles was no doubt taken there as a child. The great screen by Comper was not in existence when he was a small child; although designed in 1913, it was not erected until 1919–27.

The circumstances of Charles Bales' early education are not known, but in 1931, at the age of 23, he was admitted to the Dorchester Missionary College. It is clear that by then he had been imbued with the spirit of Anglican Papalism, which he was never to lose.

It would appear that Charles Bales had not undertaken any further education, and although that was not then a prerequisite to ordination there were some bishops, including Bishop Bertram Pollock of Norwich, who were strongly against permitting those who had no degree to go forward: this was one of his many complaints about Father Hope Patten, who had not been to university, and who then encouraged others, including his protégé Derrick Lingwood, to take orders when it was impossible for them to attend such an institution.

It was well understood at the time that missionary colleges, such as SS. Peter and Paul, Dorchester-on-Thames, Oxfordshire, St Paul at Burgh-le-Marsh, Lincolnshire, St Boniface at Warminster, Wiltshire and similar organizations, such as the Brotherhood of St Paul at Little Bardfield, Essex, all of which were designed to prepare men for foreign postings, had lower standards for entry than some of the more prestigious theological colleges. Thus young men of an Anglo-Catholic background but without higher education, who were often discriminated against by bishops but felt a call to the Church, were able to undertake such training more readily via that route.

There were, for example, a number of men associated with Walsingham who were encouraged by Hope Patten to apply to one of these establishments, or to seminaries in the West Indies, in order to by-pass an unfriendly diocesan. The Revd Moses Harbottle, another protégé of his, went to Dorchester in 1937 but could not complete the course then and was later ordained in the Windward Islands. Dorchester had a higher reputation than some other mission colleges and indeed the relentlessly academic Dr Darwell Stone had been principal there for a number of years prior to his move to Pusey House in 1904.

Charles Bales was ordained deacon in 1935 and priest in 1936 in the Diocese of Peterborough. He served his title at All Saints, Kettering, Northamptonshire, which is a substantial church in the centre of a town which has a notable tradition of Anglo-Catholicism and had hosted local Congress meetings during the inter-war period. In 1938 he moved to the very well-known Anglo-Catholic citadel of St Peter, Folkestone, where he had permission to officiate rather than being a regular curate, and from 1940 to 1942 he is simply listed as having permission to officiate in the Diocese of Norwich: it is unclear what exactly he was doing during that period although it appears that he was living in the City itself. However, in that latter year he was presented to Marshland St James, which objectively must have been one of the least desirable livings in the country. Even the vicarage, he said later, had been built by a London architect who knew nothing of the Fens and was unsuitable, although large.

Father Bales was to stay at Marshland St James for the remainder of his active ministry. He stayed looking after the church and celebrating his daily mass even after he reached retirement age, until eventually in May 1992 infirmity drove him to vacate the vicarage and move to the nearby town of Downham Market, where he died aged 88 in late 1996. He was thus in charge of the parish for almost exactly 50 years. After his departure services immediately ceased and the fabric began to deteriorate.

Father Bales' last few years were unhappy. On 22 August 1994 the Council for the Care of Churches prepared a thorough report on the church, which had been referred under the Pastoral Measure 1983 for possible redundancy. The report was passed to Father Bales, who wrote back in a crabbed and shaky hand, for by then arthritis had affected him badly, giving an explanation as to the provenance of various fittings but above all protesting against the proposed closure and conversion to residential accommodation. On 25 August 1994 he wrote: 'Is it all to end?' After digesting the report he wrote further on 2 March 1995: 'I had no idea when I left in 1992 that the church would no longer be used. The idea of turning it into a house fills me with horror. It is a consecrated building and in the past has been loved and treated with care and devotion.'

Unfortunately, these protestations had no effect. The church was declared redundant on 17 May 1995 and a redundancy scheme in relation to it took effect on 19 December 1996 with provisions for sale for residential use. These were followed through and the church is now a small house, although the outside is little altered save for a plaque above the south porch indicating that it was converted in 2002. The living was united with that of Emneth, the last parish in Norfolk on this boundary.

Other churches which have been discussed in this book show the impact on a small parish of a rich patron or a wealthy priest, well able to afford to transform the interior of a building with gold leaf, statuary and the best that Sir Ninian Comper or Martin Travers could devise. Marshland

St James was at the far end of the spectrum of financial resources: it is evident that the priest himself had no substantial funds and there were no outside parties prepared to pay for the embellishment of the somewhat bleak architecture.

The way in which Father Bales did alter and add to the furnishings is, however, very well documented, because not only was the report by the CCC clear and exact, it is supplemented by the vicar's own written recollections as to where he obtained the items concerned.[1]

When the redundancy enquiries were carried out the church remained internally intact, but when photographs were subsequently taken to record it some items had been removed. The report, however, commented that 'the simple chapel-like exterior does not prepare one for the devotional atmosphere of the interior'.

Father Bales made it clear in his letters that the church had significantly changed internally after his arrival, and it appears that many of the additions were made in his earlier years. However, he established the principle that when a member of the congregation died some item should be placed in the church in their memory.

Although Father Bales was not well known nationally, and appears to have kept himself to himself on the wider scene, he was quite prominent at Walsingham. He was clearly not only devoted to the Shrine, which of course was near his own place of birth, but was also persona grata to Father Hope Patten, who was not always the easiest man with whom to co-operate. Rather surprisingly he was given no official recognition there, but he led many pilgrimages from the Fens the relatively short distance to Walsingham, and he is also seen on a number of photographs in the archives, particularly at the twenty-first anniversary (in 1952) of the translation of the Image of Our Lady from the parish church to the new Shrine. He is a slim, bespectacled, somewhat donnish-looking figure in biretta, lace alb and vestments who walks on the right of Father Hope Patten and holds up the edge of his cope. On the far side of the parish priest of Walsingham walks the Revd L.H. Michael Smith, of South

---

1 The report was one of about 1500 written for the council by D.I. Findlay FSA (1950–98), and is characteristically lucid. He was the author of the history of the Council, *The Protection of our English Churches* (Council for the Care of Churches, 1996).

Creake, a well-known figure in the local area, who was particularly valued for his skill at flower arranging and is said to have referred to his colleague as 'great-aunt' because of his slightly austere manner, which was in vivid contrast to his own. Other contemporary pictures show Fathers Bales and Smith acting as deacons of honour for Bishop Gerald Vernon, the Bishop in Madagascar, who was a Guardian of the Shrine.

This close contact with Walsingham enabled Father Bales to make use of the artistic talent which Father Hope Patten encouraged there. The most striking features of the interior of Marshland St James church were the paintings on the apse walls and vault, depicting the Transfiguration and showing Jesus flanked by Moses and Aaron with Our Lady, St Peter, St James and St John: on the vault were sun and stars. They formed the background to the sanctuary, as there was no reredos and only oak panelling around the lower part of the apse. Father Bales explained that the original figures antedated his incumbency and were brown and white, 'a rather dull affair'. However, following Grace Bagge's death, after which he felt more able to alter what was in the church, a parishioner was commemorated by having the mural coloured and also completed on the end panels where it had not been finished.

This new work was carried out about 1955 by Lilian Frances ('Lily') Dagless (1902–94), who with her brother James came from Walsingham, and had had their talent fostered by Father Hope Patten. However, they were two of the very few locals who came under his influence who went over to Rome, and they then assisted with the redecoration of the Slipper Chapel: this did not preclude work being done by Lily for Father Bales.

The Daglesses also provided a reredos in 1934 for the church of St Peter, West Lynn (on the far bank of the Great Ouse from King's Lynn) when the chancel was reconstructed under the direction of the Revd Frank Arthur Haylock (vicar 1930–40): this church has retained its Anglo-Catholic tradition.

The better-known Walsingham artist was Enid Mary Chadwick (1902–87), who carried out a great deal of work for the Shrine Church and taught art at the associated School, but also for churches elsewhere, particularly Kettlebaston in deepest Suffolk. In about 1945 she took a plain wood Paschal candlestick, which Father Bales had purchased at auction,

and repainted it in her own idiosyncratic way in accordance with suggestions made by Father Hope Patten. At about the same time she painted a
small panel of St James as a war memorial and drew a number of scrolls
for the walls, one of which listed the clergy of the church.

The altar was of white marble and had a recess in it for a relic, and
a tabernacle on it. Even the tabernacle was purchased for the parish by
the Confraternity of the Blessed Sacrament and Father Bales was anxious
that it be returned to that body if no longer required. There were a crucifix and the obligatory six candlesticks, which had been removed before
the pictures were taken, and a processional cross which came from the
Continent and was then silver plated. There was a candelabra which had
been purchased second hand in King's Lynn for £8, and a seventeenth-
century wooden figure of St James which Father Bales had purchased
from a dealer in Scotland. Although there were various small shrines,
it was nothing like as cluttered as some churches of its persuasion, perhaps through lack of artistic talent by the incumbent and of funds by the
parishioners.

One item about which Father Bales was very anxious was an English
Missal, which had been presented in memory of another member of the
congregation who had been a schoolteacher and the organist. Father Bales
was clearly in the English, as opposed to Anglican, Missal party, which
indicates his greater acceptance of Roman liturgical importations than
those who followed the SSPP practices. There is an element of heroism,
or as detractors would put it, stubbornness in his attempt to re-establish
Catholicism in such a hostile environment, where there were no roots to
water and the ground was barren, at least metaphorically.

There is no doubt, however, that for a time Father Bales was able to
attract a reasonable congregation and he appears to have had little significant opposition. There is and was a Methodist church on The Smeeth,
which has recently, and unusually, been replaced by a striking modern
building and which provided a ready alternative to those who could not
countenance his presentation of Christianity. As time went by and his
congregation grew older, young people were not attracted to the church,
and its remoteness, which became more pronounced as the village grew
in other areas, was a hindrance. The school, which was next to the church,

closed and a new school was erected nearer to the centre of population. In earlier times Father Bales was regarded as somewhat eccentric but enthusiastic and friendly: one local child at least recorded much later her clear memories of his talks and the chart he drew himself to instruct the class about Lent, as well as preparation for confirmation.[2]

Essentially the church dropped out of the mainstream of life, caught in a time warp, and the ecclesiastical bureaucrats waited for Father Bales to resign or die. It was typical of the generation of priests in which he grew up that he did not leave Marshland until the last possible moment, when ill health finally prevented him continuing. The devotion to the altar and the daily mass shown by him and his colleagues was deeply ingrained and is now unfashionable. As a celibate, he was increasingly lonely as the years passed by and he found that most of the local clergy were out of step with his view of the Church of England: he was, however, friendly with Canon Mowbray Smith, the long-serving incumbent of nearby Wisbech St Mary (1914–51), and with his successor, the Revd William Henry Woodhouse, who was there from 1951 to 1961.[3]

There is, however, a memorial to Father Bales incorporating a small icon, in the secular village hall on The Smeeth, which serves to remind the present generation of his service to the area.

The story of Marshland St James is closely paralleled by that of St Matthew, Littleport, Cambridgeshire. Littleport is a substantial settlement about five miles to the north of Ely, which is best known for the eponymous riots in 1816, which were a result of the poor conditions for agriculture after the Napoleonic Wars.

Littleport has a substantial mediaeval church dedicated to St George, but, as with other Fenland areas, settlement in the nineteenth century took place over a wide area which had been drained and which was ideal for the production of crops. The main A1101 road to Wisbech from Littleport, which is as flat and as straight as one would expect, has leading from it many long dead ends with strange names such as Red Cow Drove: often the roadway of these is not made up. The main road leads on over the sus-

---

2 Audrey Getliffe, whose mother was the church cleaner in Marshland, on the Internet site of Fairfield Methodist Church, Buxton, 2006.

3 See Chapter 8.

pension bridge at Welney, which is still subject to flooding whenever there is heavy rainfall and leads to long diversions to avoid the inundations.

In the second half of the nineteenth century, attempts began to provide for the spiritual and educational needs of the inhabitants of these outlying areas.

In 1866 a new ecclesiastical parish of Little Ouse was formed, partly from Littleport and partly from Hilgay and Feltwell in Norfolk, and it also incorporated the entire extra-parochial districts of Feltwell Anchor and Redmore. The two parts of this new parish were joined directly only by a foot bridge over the river, which divides the two counties. A church in Early English style with tower was constructed in 1869 at the sole expense of Canon Edward B. Sparke, the rector of Feltwell and the son of Bishop B.E. Sparke of Ely, who was well known for his nepotistic appointments. The settlement is very isolated and is to the north east of Littleport.

In 1869 a school was provided at Littleport Fen and Dairy Houses, at the end of Hale Drove, almost six miles north west of the village and well off the A1101, and the school was used on Sundays as an Anglican mission hall.

However, the school was remote from many droves and it was decided to erect a new church in the area known as Westlands, about two miles from the centre of the village on the Wisbech Road, which had also been provided earlier with its own mission room, although the date of that is unclear. It was also resolved that the new church should have its own parish, which would include the Dairy Houses mission room and would largely be carved from Littleport St George, with some areas from Little Downham and from outlying parts of the Ely parishes. The population of the new parish at that time was thought to be about 625: this compares with St George, Littleport, which had about 3000 inhabitants.

The church is very similar to that at Marshland St James: it is of yellow local brick with red bricks used for decorative effect, and with a slate roof. The nave was 35 feet by 20 feet but there was a 16-feet-square chancel in addition with a Bath stone arch between the two, and transepts, with a north vestry and a south porch. Lancet windows were provided, two lights in the west wall and three behind the altar on the east wall of the chancel. The only stained glass was a coloured cross in the east chancel window. A small western turret held a bell.

The architect of this modest and undistinguished building was William Edward Bassett Smith, a reasonably prolific but neither much regarded nor original practitioner from London. He did what he was asked to do, namely to produce a small church (it held 230) at low cost (about £1600). There was no great benefactor and the money was collected locally. As at Marshland, the church is not near many other houses, but unlike St James it is on the main road, by the corner of Burnt Chimney Drove, and thus visible to passers by. Next to it was erected a very substantial vicarage. Bassett Smith had also earlier designed the much larger but otherwise similar church of St Augustine in Wisbech.

The foundation stone of St Matthew was laid at a ceremony on 20 July 1878, which was presided over by the Revd W. Burleigh, who was vicar-designate: he had been a curate at the old parish church for some years. The fact that there was a procession from the mission room to the church indicates that ultra-Protestantism was not the tone of the parish, as was the fact that when the building was completed and was consecrated by the Bishop of Ely, in April 1879, holy communion was then celebrated rather than matins being said. However, there was nothing to suggest then or in the next years that Anglo-Catholicism was acquiring a hold over the parish.

Although the population was relatively small and did not increase much, it was widely scattered and services continued to be held at the Dairy Houses school and after 1894 at a new mission room at the Littleport end of the hamlet of Ten Mile Bank, which as its name suggests is on the river, as well as in St Matthew: a school was then opened in Westlands in 1900 in the former mission room.

Various items of no particular interest were given over the years to enhance the interior of the church, and it appears that a fairly vigorous life continued, with special efforts being made for the Golden Jubilee in 1929, when an organ was purchased, and the Diamond Jubilee in 1938, when a wooden chancel screen was bought from Chevington in Suffolk, another rural church which had taken up Anglo-Catholicism: it had been installed there only in 1910.

The parish priest from 1923 to 1937 was the Revd Frank D'Ynza Brace, who had been trained at Warminster and had then served in the almost uniformly Anglo-Catholic Diocese of Nassau in the Bahamas. He was succeeded by the Revd A.A. Taylor, who moved from his first curacy at Beverley (1933–37). He had been trained at Ridley Hall, the Evangelical theological college in Cambridge. However, in 1942 a new vicar, the Revd W. Hum, arrived who was to change the churchmanship of the parish immediately and, as it turned out, irrevocably. It is odd that the Bishop of Ely, who held the advowson as he did those of Littleport St George and of Little Ouse, should successively present to the living of St Matthew three priests of such different outlooks, but it may be that it was not a very attractive post for which to find candidates.

Walter Hum was born in Colchester on 20 January 1908. He was a schoolmaster before he was ordained and was also married. He went to Bishops' College, Cheshunt in 1934 and was made deacon in 1935 and priest the following year in his home diocese of Chelmsford. Initially he was a curate at Barking, which was generally not a parish of his outlook, but from 1936 he was given charge of the daughter church of The Ascension, Eastbury. In 1938 he moved to the more congenial surroundings of All Saints at St Ives, Huntingdonshire, under the Revd H.S. Newill, from where he came to Littleport.

Father Hum was a member of the Catholic League (of which he was much later, from 1970 to 1974, Priest Director) and was also a frequent presence at Walsingham, where, as with Father Bales, he was captured on film several times in procession. His stay on the Fens was quite short, because in 1947 he exchanged livings with the Revd S.C. Chambers, parish priest of the large Victorian church of St Edmund, Holbeck, Leeds, and then in 1954 he moved on to another such church, All Souls, Blackman Lane, also in Leeds, where he stayed for many years. He died in Norfolk on 4 March 1993.

Father Hum's impact on the parish was immediate. He carried out many changes to the furnishings in the relatively short time he was there, and of course altered the tone of the services very considerably. He was an effective and clear preacher and an enthusiastic and pleasant man who appears to have related well to his various congregations.

In 1943, the year after Father Hum's arrival, the Dairy Houses School, and therefore mission hall, closed and so he could concentrate on the parish church. The altar table from the mission was brought to St Matthew and reused there: it was a constant theme in Anglo-Catholic worship at that time that there should be as many altars as physically possible in a church. In 1943 the south transept was formed into a lady chapel and a further altar with brass tabernacle was provided, subscribed to by the congregation. Father Hum saw also to the provision of a processional cross and a set of Stations of the Cross. In the following year a new oak high altar was purchased, again with funds collected, and was dedicated by the Bishop in memory of the Revd D'Ynza Brace, who had died.

Father Hum's successor, Father Chambers, continued with this change of direction. He was an older man, born in 1890, who had been ordained priest in 1919 in the Scottish Episcopal Church and had served for a time (1920–23) in the well-known Middlesbrough church of All Saints: he had moved to Holbeck in 1943, and obviously must have wanted a country parish instead. In 1955 he took on Little Ouse as well as St Matthew, so he became parish priest of a very substantial slice of some of the least attractive rural landscape in the country.

In 1948, shortly after his arrival, Father Chambers formed a new vestry by cutting off the north transept with a screen made by Faith Craft, which commemorated those lost in both wars and which incorporated a plaster statue of St Matthew. The former mission hall altar was placed in front of that. In 1954 a statue of Our Lady, also by Faith Craft, arrived: that body had a very substantial business at this time in providing furnishings produced by a number of artists and it is regrettable that nothing has yet been written on it. Statues of St Francis and Our Lady of Walsingham arrived at about the same time.

The last parish priest was the Revd Sydney George Cade, who was trained at St Stephen's House and arrived in 1965. He was a late vocation who had himself previously been a manual worker, an unusual route to the priesthood at that time. He continued the tradition established by Father Hum, and to the end of his time the Sunday morning service was termed 'parish mass'. In the July 1973 parish magazine, however, he announced that there was to be a special meeting to consider the future of the two outlying churches: such a meeting and other consultations took place and it was concluded that they should be run from St George and that there should be no resident priest any longer. Father Cade preached his last sermon in the church on 31 March 1974 and the parish came under the care of Canon Dennis Foulds of St George: interestingly, that church had acquired some Comper altar furnishings in 1960, the year after the artist's death, and had become perhaps further influenced by the Catholic Movement as time had gone by. Father Foulds had trained at Mirfield.

In 1978 a centenary service was held with a full church and the Bishop of Ely preached. There can have been no thought of closing the church at that time, as a chandelier was presented to it in memory of a deceased parishioner.

However, as time went on and congregations generally declined, and as travelling became easier with so many more people having access to personal transport, thoughts changed. Little Ouse church had already been declared redundant in that same year, 1978, and was sold for residential use in 1982. St Matthew lasted longer, but was declared redundant on 14 May 2001 and was sold for residential use on 17 December 2002.

Other local churches of similar vintage and in similar locations which have now closed include St Etheldreda, Queen Adelaide (built 1883) and another St Etheldreda (the patron saint of Ely) at Coldham, near March (1875). Father Claude Kingdon's old church of St Peter, Prickwillow (1868) hangs on only by a thread.

Both Marshland and Littleport show how Anglo-Catholics were able to 'capture' outlying churches which were deeply unattractive to most priests. In both cases it appears that limited success was achieved and that the eventual closure was not caused by flight from the religious teaching but rather by the retrenchment from the advances which had been made only about 100 years before.

Although the Fenlands are not normally considered to be hotbeds of Anglo-Catholicism, there were other churches in the area in which the Movement took hold. The particular example of Newborough, near Peterborough, is discussed in the next chapter and in Chapter 8 consideration is given to Wisbech St Mary and other surrounding places.

The first church in the Fens which was founded to promote Anglo-Catholicism seems to have been St Peter, Ely. Even a small place such as Ely had areas which were economically disadvantaged. The minute city of

Ely is on an island in the Fens, from which the cathedral dominates a large area. At the foot of the hill leading up to the cathedral was the River Ouse, which carried a considerable goods traffic well into the twentieth century, and the railway line: the city was an important junction. A number of streets of small houses sprang up to cater for those who worked on the railway and in the docks, and they had no church near. The area was in the parish of Holy Trinity, which is now the lady chapel of the cathedral, but that appeared somewhat distant: the other historic parish church was St Mary, which is itself near to the cathedral.

Canon Sparke, who had paid for the building of Little Ouse church, died in 1878. His widow Catherine Maria Sparke wished his life to be commemorated and decided to build a mission church in Broad Street, the main thoroughfare of the dock area. It was begun in 1889 and dedicated to St Peter and opened to worship on 30 June 1890. The church remained within the parish of Holy Trinity (after 1938 of Ely, following the union of the two city parishes) but is a proprietary chapel, an unusual survival. There are few if any such chapels which have a tradition of Anglo-Catholicism: most of those which remain are staunchly Evangelical.

Mrs Sparke provided a simple but appealing stone structure in an Early Decorated style with a chancel, nave, south-west porch and a small bell turret with a single bell. The cost was just over £4000 and it was designed by J.P. St Aubyn, who in 1881 had been the architect of the nearby Ely Theological College.

The interest in the church is, however, almost entirely in the interior: it was provided in 1893 with a magnificent screen, a very early work by Comper, at the expense of the Revd Salisbury Price, who had been a curate of Holy Trinity, Ely from 1884 to 1887.[4] The screen was prepared in London but then despatched to Ely in sections, erected, and painted on site. It has a very wide gallery with a rood above and with its exquisite decoration reflects exactly Comper's thinking at that time: it reproduces in late nineteenth-century form a mediaeval precedent. There is a Kempe window in the east wall, which was also paid for by Father Salisbury Price and is in memory of a friend of his. There are three clear panes at the

---

4 See Chapter 3.

foot of the window in its centre, which indicate where a reredos originally stood behind the altar. In the early 1950s, under the direction of the
then priest in charge, the Revd G.A. Field, the reredos was removed and
the altar extended to a length of ten feet. At the same time Father Field
took the former credence table, which would not fit into its former place
once the high altar had been lengthened, and moved it in front of the
screen, where, with the addition of a marble top and a statue of Our Lady,
it became a secondary altar. In the same era, Stations of the Cross were
installed, paid for by the congregation.

Among the notable priests to be associated with this little church, which
remains in use with a sung Eucharist every Sunday morning, have been
the Revd C.H. Scott (1926–28), who was later involved with Father Drew
in the Missal controversies, after he had moved on to Folkestone, and the
Revd Frank Harwood (1960–64). Father Harwood was a veteran Anglo-
Catholic who was a strong supporter of Walsingham and a good friend of
Father Hope Patten. In post-war years he had run the Society for Catholic
Reunion, one of a number of such bodies, but it had effectively become
moribund by the time he came to Ely. He introduced into the church
small statues on either side of the nave of St Thomas More and St John
Fisher, who are not generally commemorated in Anglican churches. They
have, however, remained in place.

A few miles to the west of Ely is the small village of Coveney. It was
originally very much larger, until the driving of the Old and New Bedford
Rivers in the seventeenth century separated it from the settlement of
Manea, which then became a separate parish. It was a very remote place
until quite recently, and indeed for many years there was only one metalled
road into it, from Wentworth to the south.

The patronage of the church of St Peter ad Vincula, Coveney, was purchased by Athelstan Riley in 1883, when he was only about 25 years of age
and it was the first of his collection of advowsons. The nave and chancel
of the church are of the early thirteenth century, and then about 100 years
later the chancel was extended and a porch and the lower part of a tower
were added. In the fifteenth century another stage was added to the tower.
When Riley first became involved with the church, the chancel and nave
were still thatched.

In 1896 Riley had the church thoroughly restored and the thatched roof was replaced by tiles. The front of the porch was reset and a vestry was added to the north of the chancel. It is of some interest that Comper was not called in to refurnish the church as he was to be at Little Petherick and had done at St Peter, Ely. Instead, a considerable number of furnishings of Continental origin were imported: these included a sixteenth-century carved reredos from Germany, which has been very heavily restored, a painted pulpit dated 1706 from Denmark, bought in a Continental antique shop, and an eighteenth-century brass chandelier from the Netherlands. Riley also added a rood screen, designed by an incumbent, which characteristically featured his initials and the gridiron of his patron, St Laurence.

There appear to have been a large number of incumbents at Coveney, with no priest staying for a long period. However, the tradition which Riley established has continued to this day and the main service remains a parish mass. Little Downham, the village next to Coveney, where the Bishops of Ely had a palace, also had a Catholic tradition but that has disappeared.

There are two other churches in this area which perhaps are worth more than a mention.

The next village north of Littleport on the route to King's Lynn is Southery, Norfolk, where a new church was built in 1858 to replace an existing building. It was designed by Higham and Robinson and constructed of thin tiles of carstone with Bath stone dressings: it has a square tower with a broach spire above.

The rector at the time of the rebuilding was the splendidly named Revd Archibald Aeneas Julius, who was in the parish from 1855 to 1895: there is nothing to suggest that he was particularly influenced by the Catholic Revival, but his successor, the Revd George C.M. Hall, who was there from 1895 to 1932, certainly was. The look of the interior dates from his incumbency, as he, his relations and his friends donated money to beautify the church. The chancel screen was erected in memory of his predecessor. The porch was added in 1904 and a plaque in it commemorates its construction. It was designed by the priest-architect, the Revd Ernest Geldart of Little Braxted in Essex, and names all the workmen involved. Immediately above it is another enamel plaque, also dating from Father Hall's time, which reads: 'Why do I belong to the Church of England? I belong to the Church of England because Jesus Christ founded One Catholic Church and the Church of England is a true and organized part of that One Church.'

The rector himself gave the tall but narrow high altar reredos and the stained-glass windows behind it in thanksgiving for the safe return of his son Basil from the First World War. It is redolent of an earlier age of Anglo-Catholic furnishings and owes nothing to the Back to Baroque tendencies which were so apparent elsewhere in the 1920s.

Unusual features of this church are the plaques erected in memory of deceased church members, which have been erected since the commencement of Father Hall's incumbency. From 1947 to 1951 the parish priest was Father William Woodhouse, Father Bales' friend, who later moved to Wisbech St Mary. During his time, a rood, probably by Faith Craft, was added to the screen in memory of a young parishioner who had died.

Although St Ives is on the very edge of the Fens, its church ought also to be discussed, not least because of its connections with a number of the personalities so far mentioned, particularly Dr Salisbury Price. St Ives is a market town which has expanded with many new estates for commuters in recent years, rather than a village. Its stately parish church, All Saints, with its graceful tower, dominates the centre of the settlement and the Ouse river bank.

St Ives parish church is largely fifteenth century: the earlier building was substantially rebuilt in 1470. Further significant repairs were required after an incident in 1918 when an aircraft hit the tower, much of which then collapsed on to the roof, which in turn required replacement. The work was not completed until 1924.

The interior of the church is illuminated by the work of Ninian Comper, which was carried out over a number of years and was added to by his son Sebastian. That work was illustrative of and guided by the churchmanship of the parish, which was established at least by the incumbency of the Revd Arthur Stapylton Barnes (1891–94), a considerable liturgical scholar, who had come to St Ives from St Agnes, Kennington

Park: he went over to Rome in later years. He presented to the church a spectacular rood screen surmounted by an organ case and rood, designed by Comper. Its painting was paid for by Father Barnes' successor, Father Salisbury Price, who stayed at St Ives only from 1894 to 1899. The organ itself was later removed from that position because of practical difficulties in keeping in touch with the choir in the chancel, and was rebuilt in the old north chapel, but the visible pipework was left over the screen so as not to compromise the integrity of the Comper design.

In 1897 Comper also provided figures depicting a variety of saints for the nave pillars on original stone brackets. This development is not without interest as at that date it was extremely unusual to see statues of saints in even the most advanced Anglican churches. He also produced a Gothic high altar with iron riddels in approved style.

Salisbury Price resigned in 1899 but in the same year he acquired the advowson from the trustees of the Ansley family: he then donated it to the Guild of All Souls, thus securing the continuance of the Anglo-Catholic tradition. He was replaced in 1899 by the perhaps unfortunately named Revd Oscar Wade Wilde, who had previously been a curate successively at St Barnabas, Pimlico, St Mary Magdalene, Munster Square and St Saviour, Pimlico. He was apparently proud of the family connection to his then notorious namesake.

In due course Father Wilde removed Comper's high altar to the south chapel and gave to the church the present high altar, which carried six candlesticks, according to Western rather than English Use precedent, and has a reredos which depicts Our Lord crowned with St Edward the Confessor, St Wilfred, St Augustine of Canterbury, and St Oswald. Father Wilde also provided the north or lady chapel reredos with its statue of Our Lady and the Holy Child.

The original high altar remains in the south chapel and is now devoted to the Sacred Heart of Jesus: it has later work, including Baroque embellishments, by Sebastian Comper. Ninian Comper also designed two windows for the church, one in 1895 in his early style and another in 1929 from his more developed years.

Wilde was a somewhat controversial figure. It was later said by an observer that: 'His religion was exotic, and he left St Ives rigidly, and even bitterly, divided.'[5] He was a man with a caustic tongue who was not anxious to open the vicarage to the local population.

Wilde retired in 1930 and was replaced in 1931 by the Revd William Strowan Amherst Robertson (known as Strowan to his family but as Algy to everyone else) (1894–1955), who had come back from India, where he had been involved in a multi-racial community named the Society of the Servants of Christ (Christa Seva Sangha). His return was caused by concerns about his health, which for the rest of his life gave him serious problems, mainly caused by colitis. His predecessor thought that he was selling the pass and is said to have remarked: 'I am very much afraid that my successor is jeopardising the Catholic religion. I am credibly informed that he has already abandoned the asperges.'[6] Father Robertson also removed such oddities as two very large Spanish spittoons from the sanctuary.

The new vicar remained interested in life in community, particularly on Franciscan models, and during his time at St Ives the vicarage was used by those preparing to go to India and by those on leave from the Servants of Christ. In 1934 the St Ives group severed their attachment to the Indian brotherhood, which itself had split, and they reconstituted themselves as the Brotherhood of the Servants of Jesus, a name later changed to the Brotherhood of the Love of Christ.

It was a curious interlude, as the parish was effectively run by members of the new community. There were two curates, the Revd Denis Marsh (Father Denis) and the Revd William Francis Tyndale-Biscoe (Father Francis). The Revd H.R.C. Lovell, a Franciscan tertiary, as was his wife, was at the daughter church in the adjoining village of Woodhurst.

Father Robertson was eccentric and often very difficult, but was esteemed for his obvious holiness. He also opened the vicarage and its grounds to the locals, especially young people: many of those who lived around were surprised by what was happening there, not least by the appearance of so many Indians, who were at that time very rarely seen in East Anglia. They may also have been surprised by the preaching of the aged and by then blind Socialist firebrand, the Revd Conrad Noel of

5 See Father Denis [Marsh] SSF, *Father Algy* (Hodder & Stoughton, 1964), p. 98.
6 Father Denis, *Father Algy*, p. 94.

Thaxted, who was one of those invited to St Ives, and by the signs erected
to welcome tramps to the vicarage, an extension of work being carried out
by another Franciscan group at Cerne Abbas in Dorset.

In 1936 Father Robertson was involved in bringing together his own
group with the nascent community at Cerne Abbas to form the Society
of St Francis, and took a year's absence to assist in its birth, leaving Father
Francis to run the parish. The following year the vicar left to join the new
Society. He had always been known since school as Algy and it was as
Father Algy SSF that he is best remembered. He made a substantial contribution thereafter to the Franciscans, in particular as novice master and
in his powerful preaching.

Following Father Robertson's departure, he was replaced by Father
Newill and then in 1946 by Father Alexander Cuthbert Lawson, who was
a protégé of the flamboyant and aristocratic Revd Roger Wodehouse.
Father Lawson had been ordained in 1932 and became a curate at St
Mary Magdalene, Oxford, but initially he lived in the vicarage of Father
Wodehouse's parish of St Paul, Walton Street. Wodehouse had turned the
small classical building into a passable replica of a French urban church
and the practices of the congregation were of a similar nature, featuring
outdoor processions of Our Lady and the like and benediction on the
outside terrace. The church is now a restaurant although traces of Father
Wodehouse's embellishments can still be seen inside.

Lawson himself was a great Mariolatrist and contributed articles on
shrines to the Walsingham newsletter. In due course his personal collection of books and articles on Our Lady were left to Walsingham, of which
he was a great devotee. Father Wodehouse was a Guardian of the Shrine
until he resigned for a period following a sexual indiscretion in 1936
which also meant that he had to leave Oxford. Lawson remained there in
a house in Park Town, where he had a private chapel with a fully dressed
statue of Our Lady which had been acquired in Munich, until he moved
to St Ives, where he stayed for 16 years. He then retired to the outskirts of
Cambridge.

Father Lawson was thought by some to be unduly rigid on certain
parochial matters and he certainly refused to alter opinions once he had
expressed them, which caused some local unhappiness. He laid down rigid

rules on baptism and marriage, which caused problems: he was never an easy man with whom to deal.

Colin Stephenson, Father Hope Patten's replacement at Walsingham, was somewhat unkind in his reminiscences, *Merrily on High*, about Father Lawson, suggesting he had burned himself out after 'a tough time in a Fenland parish'.[7] This comment is somewhat snide so far as it relates to the area: St Ives was a market town with strong support for the church and a well-established tradition, an ideal situation for an Anglo-Catholic vicar to take on. Lawson was a talented but difficult man who was always anxious to be in control.

Father Lawson's successors have continued to preserve the outlook he espoused, although not perhaps exactly as he did, and the church is one of the very few in the Diocese of Ely affiliated to Forward in Faith.

7 See C. Stephenson, *Merrily on High* (Darton, Longman & Todd, 1972, reissued by Canterbury Press, 2008), p. 94.

7

St Bartholomew, Newborough, Peterborough, and Father Clive Beresford

One of the most remarkable ministries in the recent history of the Church of England was that of the Revd Clive Robert Beresford (1897–1967), and the most interesting and illuminating period of his life was spent as vicar of the small village of Newborough, just north of Peterborough, from 1949 to 1967.

Newborough is not far away from the boundary of the City of Peterborough, which was until the mid-1960s a relatively small township, dependent largely on the railways and other heavy industries but also of course with its splendid cathedral and a number of fine surrounding buildings. After that time it has expanded enormously both in population and in area, with successive waves initially from London, when it was designated as a growth area, then from the Indian subcontinent, and more recently from all parts of Eastern Europe. Those changes have pushed Peterborough outwards so that it now nearly reaches Newborough: in addition, in the last few years the village itself has increased very considerably in population, with many new houses, as it has become a dormitory for the nearby city. It now has about 1300 residents, some of whom are in the oddly named hamlet of Milking Nook, with another 130 in the adjoining settlement of Borough Fen. There were far fewer when Father Beresford was there.

Newborough is now on the edge of the Fenlands, characterized here as elsewhere by straight roads and featureless landscape. It originally formed part of the Borough Great Fen, drainage of which began in the seventeenth century. It was then in the old administrative area of the Soke of Peterborough, then the County of Huntingdon and Peterborough, and is now within the Peterborough City unitary authority. It is near to the substantial ancient abbeys of Crowland in Lincolnshire and of Thorney in the Soke, and to the very pleasant market town of Stamford.

It would not be unfair to say that the church building of St Bartholomew, Newborough, is particularly unattractive. It lies in the centre of the village, and is thus conveniently situated, and it has an unusual date, 1830, well before the great rush of expansion in the High and Late Victorian years. The relevant edition of *Pevsner* fails even to mention the village, never mind the church.

Newborough was carved out of the adjoining parish of Eye in 1812 and the new parish was later held with the former extra-parochial area of Borough Fen, which is just to the north of the village.

Building work for a church was financed following the enclosure and sale of part of the Borough Fen Estate in 1822, but, however, construction did not actually commence until eight years later. A plain rather thin neo-Gothic church was built, which is approached by steps on every side, perhaps to guard against flooding. It was a church which prior to the Second World War had little internal visual stimulation: poverty had precluded fine stained glass or the like, although there was a three-light east window.

It appears that Newborough was a perfectly ordinary middle-of-the-road parish until the arrival of the Revd Cyril John Newman in 1939. He came from a curacy in Lowestoft and went on to be parish priest of the well-known church of St Lawrence, Northampton[1] in 1948: he died in 1960.

Father Newman was a definite Anglo-Catholic who was also an affable and inspiring man. He was able to relate to the local villagers and to enthuse them with his interpretation of the Faith. A picture of the interior of the church survives from 1949, at about the time when he left. It shows that he had introduced six candlesticks on the high altar, which had no reredos or other backing, and that in the south aisle was an English-type

---

1 The church is now used by the Polish community.

altar with riddels and curtains, next to which was a statue of Our Lady. On the walls were Stations of the Cross. The overall impression, however, was still quite bare. Within the confines of the war years, he ran various societies and the church was at the centre of the social life of the village.

The Lilley family were born and brought up in Newborough and all six of the children were confirmed after receiving instruction in the village church. Father Newman was able to perceive the reality of a religious vocation expressed by one of them, Ethel, and encouraged her to persist: she became, and remains, a member of the Community of the Sacred Passion, an offshoot of an order founded in East Africa by Bishop Frank Weston, the English branch of which was then in East Hanningfield in Essex.

Father Beresford came in 1949 to replace Father Newman. It was an odd appointment to a Crown living for it is fair to say that there are and were many who found Clive Beresford's attitude to the Church of England incomprehensible and somewhat strange, although his views were by no means unique. He considered that the Church of England was a true part of the Catholic Church, but that it had no right to devise or to prescribe forms of worship of its own, and that its priests and people should assimilate their liturgy and practice to those of Rome, with a view to visible reunion as soon as possible. It was his custom, certainly in later years, to remove his maniple whenever he was required to use a part of the 1662 Prayer Book or any other Anglican liturgical usage or even if he was present when these were said.

There is considerable mystery about Clive Beresford's origins. His birth certificate indicates that he was born at 55 Maida Vale, Paddington, on 17 April 1897. The name given to the child on the birth certificate was Clive Beresford Eunson Candy and the informant was his mother Ethel May Candy, née Woodland. The father named was Charles Harrison Candy.

The next official document which records the child is the 1901 census. In that he is shown under the name Clive Beresford, aged three and living at 33 Castletown Road, Fulham, which is near West Kensington Station. The head of that household was Alfred Jackson, aged 80, a retired merchant, and also living there were his wife, his two single daughters Alice (aged 38) and Agnes (aged 34), and his son Randolph (aged 32), with two servants. The three younger Jacksons were born in Sydney, Australia.

In that same 1901 census Clive's mother was shown as living in Dartford, Kent, with four of her older children.

The 1911 census is now available, and it appears that Clive Beresford (as he was now known) continued to live with the Jacksons in Fulham/West Kensington. Alfred Jackson died in 1905. The First World War service papers show that Clive Beresford was still living at the Castletown Road address in 1915/16, when he was described as working as a clerk. Agnes Jackson was named as his guardian, with no mention of his parents. His military service was very short and without incident: he was discharged because of mitral incompetence (heart valve problems) and described as 'physically unable to march or to carry pack and rifle'.

The Candy family were long established in Anglo-Indian Society. Charles Harrison Candy was born on 7 March 1851 in Mahabuleshawar, India. He came to school in England and then went up to Gonville and Caius College, Cambridge as an undergraduate. He proceeded into the elite Indian Civil Service and appears thereafter never to have lived in this country save for short periods: he died in Kolhapur, India, in 1925.

Ethel May Woodland, Clive Beresford's mother, was born at Bridgwater, Somerset, in 1862, the daughter of a banker, but the family thereafter moved to Minehead, on the North Somerset coast. She married Charles Harrison Candy in 1881 and had a number of children by him, some born in England and some in India. The last born to her before Clive was Harrison Rolfe Candy, born in London in 1892, who died in 1971. She clearly came and went reasonably frequently between England and India, sometimes leaving all or some of the children in the other country.

The bare facts set out above leave a great deal of room for speculation. It is not clear whether the Candys' marriage came to an end (in fact if not legally) at about the time the child was born, or indeed whether the person named was in truth his father or was entered on the certificate as a matter of form. It is extremely odd that by the time the child was three he was living away from the rest of the family on an apparently permanent basis, and even odder that he had by then adopted a new name based on his forenames. The middle name Robert appears to have been added even later. In written reminiscence when he was an adult,[2] Clive Beresford referred to his mother having brought him home a gift from shopping when he was small, but that may have involved some poetic licence, or even an unwillingness to explain a complicated set of circumstances.

It is also not clear what if any connection there was between the Candy and Jackson families. Earlier in the nineteenth century there had been a marriage between a Candy and a Jackson, and one of Alfred Jackson's sons is described in the 1891 census as being a student for the Indian Civil Service, but in neither case can any definite link be established.

Because Father Beresford did not die until 1967, there are a large number of people who can recall him: thus he is different from most of the other personalities described in this book. One priest who knew him recalls that he was absolutely indifferent to many of the problems which worry most people, particularly the state of the vicarage at Newborough, which was extremely decrepit and was also very untidy indeed. One day, it came out in conversation with him that he claimed he had slipped entirely through the net of bureaucracy and was unknown to the 'powers that be'. That little oddity is of course easily explicable on the grounds that he was not in fact registered officially under the name he always used.

It is clear that Clive Beresford did not initially undertake tertiary education, and instead went out to work. When he was about 11, he re-counted later,[3] he had attended St Andrew, Fulham Fields, in which parish Castletown Road fell, and there met the Revd Robert Ernest Young, who was a curate there and was to have a significant impact upon his later life. The following year he was prepared for confirmation by Father Young at the latter's house in Turnville Road, nearby, but he implies that at that time the priest had not adopted the Anglican Papalism for which he was later noted and, for example, he was not then taught the necessity of making his confession. Father Beresford said that when they met again, in 1927, 'we had both come by our devious paths to a fuller knowledge and appreciation of the Catholic Faith'.

It appears that the young Clive Beresford first came into contact with a more advanced form of Anglo-Catholicism through the church

2 See *Crux*, December 1963.
3 See *Crux*, October 1965.

of St Alban, Margravine Road, Fulham, which was not far away from Castletown Road.

St Alban was a year older than Clive Beresford, having been built by Sir Aston Webb and Ingress Bell in 1896. In 1911 the Revd G.G. Elliott became vicar and remained until 1918 when he moved on to the famous church of St Bartholomew, Brighton. Father Elliott was very well respected in the neighbourhood because he set up a series of initiatives to relieve poverty in the surrounding area, which was then entirely working class. The street where the Jacksons lived, in the next parish, was rather better housing and they were people of some considerable means.

In 1918 the Revd J.E. Watson arrived as the incumbent of St Alban. Father John Watson had been an undergraduate at Sidney Sussex College, Cambridge, and had served a number of curacies, the last two of which were under Father Deakin at Christ Church, South Hackney (1913–16) and then under Prebendary H.P. Denison at St Michael, Ladbroke Grove (1916–18). When he arrived in Fulham, he inherited as a curate the Revd C.C. Higgs, who had been there since 1916, immediately after his ordination. Father Higgs was to succeed Father Watson on the latter's death in 1934.

As soon as Father Watson took over at St Alban, he adopted an entirely Roman system of liturgical and devotional practice, which included the use of Latin for all masses. The local support which Father Elliott had built up dissipated, although in due course Father Higgs was to gain the respect of his parishioners by his willingness to help and by his devotion to duty in the face of the blitz. To Clive Beresford the new regime represented an exemplar of that which he thought the Church of England should become.

Father Watson was a man who would not deviate from his principles and kept to his decisions once made, which was another characteristic which Clive Beresford took on, although his mentor was in that respect very difficult. He discouraged many of the usual church-based organizations, which were flourishing elsewhere at that time, and refused to keep service registers, on the basis that God knew who had come for his sacraments.

It is possible that Clive Beresford had decided to proceed to ordination even before Father Watson came to St Alban, because it was shortly after that that he went to St Chad's College, Durham to study to that end. It may be that he was friendlier for rather longer with Father Higgs, who was nearer his own age. Certainly it appears that Clive Beresford had been taken up by Anglo-Catholicism before Father Watson's arrival, as he himself later wrote that in 1917 he attended a chapter meeting of the Catholic League, the most forthright of the organizations campaigning for reunion with the Holy See, at St Cuthbert, Philbeach Gardens (also near his home), and there attended and assisted at benediction for the first time.

He also says that at about the same time he was admitted to the League by, he thought, the Revd C.F. Hrauda.[4] Father Charles Frederick Hrauda (1881–1945), who was born in England but whose father was Austrian, was an extremely difficult and disputatious man who always used the Latin rite and was known to deliver harangues encouraging conversion to the Roman Church, while staying perhaps rather loosely within the Church of England himself.

In 1922 Clive Beresford graduated from Durham with a BA and a Diploma in Theology. In the same year he was ordained deacon in the Diocese of London, and the following year priest. His first curacy (1922–27) was at St Barnabas, Kentish Town, although he said his first mass, in 1923, in his spiritual home of St Alban, Fulham.[5] From the commencement of his ministry he continued to be involved with the Catholic League, and with its adjunct, the Sodality of the Precious Blood, membership of which was strictly restricted to celibate priests and generally numbered about 40. Its members were bound to a full recitation of the Latin breviary and to exclude any connection with Freemasonry: Father Beresford was permitted to join the Sodality on ordination as a deacon in 1922. The breviary and the daily mass became the cornerstones of his life and although there were those who doubted his mission, there were few who questioned his sincerity.

St Barnabas, Kentish Town, is a church built by Ewan Christian in 1884–85. It stands on the corner of Kentish Town Road and Rochester

---

4 See Father Beresford's introduction to B.J. Doolan, *The First Fifty Years* (Crux Press, 1966), pp. i–ii.

5 That church has now been stripped out and, although still open, is used only by an Evangelical Filipino group.

Road: it was closed in 1957 and passed to the Greek Orthodox, as have so many churches in that area, and is now known as the Cathedral of St Andrew. The parish was united on the closure of the church with that of Holy Trinity, Oseney Crescent, which in turn is now held with that of St Silas the Martyr, Kentish Town.

St Barnabas was never a well-known church either in the Anglo-Catholic Movement or in the Church of England generally, and it may well be that the young curate cast envious eyes on its near neighbour St Silas, where the teaching was always very advanced. The parish priest while Father Beresford was at St Barnabas was the Revd Geoffrey Snowden, who was ordained priest in 1904 and moved there in 1921 after a short spell in Australia before the First World War, followed by a succession of curacies in London in churches which were not in the front line of the Movement.

In 1927 Father Beresford moved to what would appear to have been a far more congenial position, as curate of St Thomas, Godolphin Road, Shepherd's Bush, which coincidentally is also now used as a Greek Orthodox cathedral. The parish priest at that church at that time was the same Father Young as had prepared him for confirmation before the First World War.

Father Beresford stayed for seven years at St Thomas, which he later described as being a very happy period. The parish church was designed by Blomfield. Construction began in 1882, when a nave and side aisles were built, and then in 1887 a chancel, transepts and choir vestry were added. There is no tower and so the church is not visible from far off: it stands in an area of terraced housing off the Uxbridge Road, well hidden from most passers by.

The first vicar of the parish was the Revd Henry Small, who stayed until 1919, when he resigned, shortly after celebrating the fortieth anniversary of his ordination. He was a middle-of-the-road churchman, but was replaced by the Revd P.M. Bartlett, who immediately replaced morning prayer with solemn Eucharist as the main Sunday service. He stayed only a very short time before being offered, and accepting, a parish in the East End, and Father Young arrived in his stead.

Father Young was ordained priest on 1 October 1905 and lived to see the sixtieth anniversary of that event. After his curacy at St Andrew,

Fulham Fields (1904–12) he spent three years as Railway Missioner in the Diocese of Qu'Appelle, Saskatchewan, Canada.[6] He then spent from 1915 to 1919 as a Temporary Chaplain to the Forces, before returning to London. By that time he had adopted the uncompromising Papalist position from which he never thereafter wavered during a long life: he did not die until 1966.

The *Jubilee Chronicle* of the parish, published in 1932, records that in October 1919, shortly before Father Young's induction, he held a meeting with the congregation: this was shortly before his induction. He displayed the mass vestments and explained that there should be six candlesticks and a crucifix on the high altar. The meeting resolved to give him their backing, and he soon reorganized the parish along the lines he wanted, with guilds for servers and others and also troops of scouts and guides and such bodies.

In 1924 a large rood was erected over the high altar, incidentally blocking much of the light from the east window, and Bishop A.C. Chandler, formerly of Bloemfontein, came to dedicate it. Once Father Beresford arrived, the impetus to refurnish the church grew, not least because as well as his desire to incorporate items of a Continental provenance or style into the church, he was himself artistically gifted and able to sew and to manufacture such features, talents which he was later to put to great use at Newborough.

In 1928 a pulpit and altar rails were acquired from Belgium, and in 1932 a new high altar was constructed for the golden jubilee of the church. It again foreshadowed what was to be installed at Newborough, for although the well-known firm of Louis Grossé designed the altar, Father Beresford assisted with the plans and was himself responsible for the construction of the screens on either side. The main part of the altar and reredos were of classical design, incorporating a very large central tabernacle between six lofty candlesticks. The reredos had a picture of the Assumption, above which were the words of St Thomas, 'Dominus Meus et Deus Meus'. The congregation in what was still a poor area contributed to the cost of the

---

6 He wrote in *Crux,* June 1960, of the efforts made in building new churches on the Prairies of Western Canada and the contrast between that and the proposed demolition of St Thomas (which did not in fact take place).

new altar and the guild system was used to raise money for specific items. Father Beresford arranged, for example, that the Sodality of the Sacred Heart collect for a lace antependium.

It was while Father Beresford was in the parish that the controversy over the new Prayer Book occurred, followed by Bishop Winnington-Ingram's clampdown on churches which would not agree to his regulations designed to prevent the service of benediction of the Blessed Sacrament. Father Young was one of the Twenty One who would not comply with the Bishop's requests, and he was naturally strongly supported by his curate. It is typical of Winnington-Ingram that despite that serious falling out, he then came to the church to dedicate the new altar.

Many of the themes of Father Beresford's later ministry were established during his time at Shepherd's Bush, such as the need to focus at all times on reunion with Rome. Along with some other Papalists, Father Young was somewhat sceptical about some of the celebrations in 1933 for the Oxford Movement Centenary, writing in June that year that the ideals behind it 'visualized the return of the Church of England to the Faith and practice of historic Christendom; they visualized the reunion of the Church of England with the rest of Catholic Christendom'.

In 1934 Father Beresford left St Thomas and was given a cheque for £8, which does not seem overgenerous even by the standards of the time. Father Young stayed until 1942 and then served in two country parishes before commencing what turned out to be a very long retirement in 1950. The church was declared redundant in 1972 and handed over to the Greeks, but some of the furnishings introduced during Father Young's incumbency were retained and adapted for the Eastern rites.

Father Beresford's next port of call was Worcester. He became curate to the Revd William Beattie Monahan, who had been rector of St Swithun with Old St Martin since 1902. Father Monahan was of Irish stock but was born in Camberwell in 1866. He was the older brother of the better-known Revd Alfred Edwin Monahan, who was Bishop of Monmouth from 1940 to 1945.

Father William Monahan was a convinced Anglican Papalist. St Swithun is a particularly complete example of the Georgian churches of which there are a number in the City of Worcester and which reflect the prosperity of the area at that time. He does not appear to have added significantly to the furnishings. It was closed for worship in 1976 and vested in the Churches Conservation Trust. Old St Martin is also an eighteenth-century church, but remains open for worship.

Father Monahan was a substantial scholar who published a number of books on St Thomas Aquinas and his theology in the 1940s.[7] However, as well as those somewhat rarefied publications, he also issued a large number of short tracts, usually foreseeing imminent doom for the Church of England, under the pseudonym 'The Voice from Worcester'. This use of short, topical but sometimes melodramatic material was something which Father Beresford himself was to take up in later years.

Father Monahan was married, as indeed were a number of Papalist priests: one criticism made of Anglo-Catholics was that they advanced the cause of union with Rome but on the other hand took advantage of the ability provided by the Church of England to marry. Father Monahan's wife played the organ and ran the choir in the church and his daughter Bridget (born 1910) was also a prominent musical presence in the city. After her father's death she remained in contact with Father Beresford and continued to sell the books of Thomist theology, advertising them in his publications, but she also ran for more than 50 years an orchestra in Worcester, which she conducted until she was 97. It was only disbanded in early 2008 when she went into a care home.

Clive Beresford had two spells at Worcester: he left in 1936 to take charge of St Luke, Swindon, a daughter church in the parish of St Mark, but he returned in 1937 and only left finally when he at last obtained his own church, in 1939. Worcester was congenial to him because he approved of his rector's theological position, but as he approached his own fortieth birthday he wanted a parish or at least a church of his own.

The church of St Luke, Broad Street, Swindon, already mentioned in connection with Samuel Gurney, is one of those backstreet churches in what was originally an entirely working class area of a town. Sir John

---

7 These were *St Thomas Aquinas on the Eucharist* (1940); *on the Incarnation* (1940); *on the Sacraments* (1943); *on the Life of Christ* (1946); *Moral Theology of St Thomas Aquinas* (3 volumes) (1942) and *Psychology of St Thomas Aquinas and Divine Revelation* (1946).

Betjeman was particularly fond of this unobtrusive building, and wrote that except for the Railway Works, which he thought were awe-inspiring inside, St Luke's was the only fine interior, architecturally, in Swindon.

Its mother church, St Mark, was built in 1845 to serve Swindon New Town, which grew up around the works of the Great Western Railway, on which virtually the whole local population was dependent directly or indirectly. St Luke, like its progenitor, had a strong Anglo-Catholic tradition, which has continued to this day. There can be few churches in the Anglican Communion which possess within the altar authenticated relics of St Pius X and St Thérèse of Lisieux, although these were not present when Father Beresford went and indeed perpetual reservation was not commenced in the parish church until 1937 and in St Luke until 1938, a measure of the careful and measured way in which teaching had developed.[8]

The Revd Trevor G. Jalland was in charge of St Luke, from 1925. He commissioned Martin Travers to carry out some work to the interior, but it was not a wealthy area and money was scarce. Although a sound teacher and a distinguished theologian who had come from being Vice-Principal of St Stephen's House, Oxford and eventually was to become a Professor at the University of Exeter, the priest in charge was an eccentric and often divisive man who was prone to be publicly rude to members of the congregation. He left in 1933 to take on the living of St Thomas, Oxford, and was replaced after an interval by the Revd W.H. Stuart Tayler, who tried to reunite the people after the difficulties caused by his abrasive predecessor. He gave many gifts to the church to enhance it, but in September 1936 he left to become vicar of St John the Baptist, Tuebrook, Liverpool.

St Luke would appear on the face of it to have been an ideal situation for Father Beresford, as it was part of a well-run system in which the Catholic Faith had been instilled for many years. However, his stay was very short: he cannot have arrived until after Father Tayler's departure in September 1936, and he had left before the end of 1937: he does not feature on the staff photograph for that year. The history of the church says rather coyly

---

8 See *S. Mark's Swindon 1845–1945: A Record of a Hundred Years' Work Written by Priests and People* (St Mark's Parochial Church Council, 1945).

that he 'came ... to a church still experiencing some frictions amongst its congregation ... Perhaps because of this, [he] did not stay long ... '[9] One of Father Beresford's colleagues on the staff in Swindon was the Revd E.U.T. Huddleston, later better known as Bishop Trevor Huddleston CR, who was equally strong-minded and inflexible.

In 1939, however, and after a further stay in Worcester, Father Beresford finally acquired his own church. He became parish priest of St Michael, Hill Square, Edinburgh, in that year and remained there until 1947.

The small but influential Episcopal Church of Scotland had of course a completely different history from the Church of England, and the Catholic Revival within it ran parallel to and separate from the Oxford Movement rather than as an integral part of it. The leader was the Revd Alexander Penrose Forbes, Bishop of Brechin from 1847 to 1875, who is sometimes termed 'the Scottish Pusey'. The best-known Anglo-Catholic church in Scotland was Old St Paul, Edinburgh, but St Michael was by this time far and away the most Papalist in tone. Peter Anson (whom Beresford knew quite well and with whom he corresponded in later years) referred to the church in characteristic prose as 'a lonely northern outpost of the most Tridentine variety of Anglo-Catholicism'[10] and also commented in another book that by the 1960s it was 'almost a museum of now faded Baroque furnishings'.[11]

The foundation of St Michael was the work of the Community of St Andrew of Scotland, a small order of sisters indigenous to the Episcopal Church. Mission work commenced in 1865 and a chapel of St Andrew was opened in 1868. In 1882 this was renamed St Michael and then in 1888 the former Roxburgh Free Church of Scotland in Hill Square, in the University area of Edinburgh, was purchased and adapted for use. At that time the priest in charge was the Revd T.I. Ball, who later became Provost of Cumbrae. The sisters in due course declined in number and the last of them died in 1949.

---

9 F.W.T. Fuller, *St Luke's Church in Broad Street, Swindon* (Red Brick Publishing, 1987), p. 19.

10 P.F. Anson, *Call of the Cloister* (SPCK, 1964), p. 413.

11 P.F. Anson, *Fashions in Church Furnishings 1840–1940* (Studio Vista, 1965), p. 323.

Initially the fittings of the former Protestant tabernacle were Gothic, such as the richly coloured and delicately coloured carved altarpiece of St Michael, designed by Hamilton More-Nisbet in 1901, but as time went by it was re-equipped with furnishings which were either of Continental origin (such as a seventeenth-century Spanish pulpit) or were intended to look as if they were. That tendency was accelerated during the incumbencies of Father Beresford and that of his immediate predecessor, the Revd Basil Edward Joblin (1932–39), who was his closest friend among the clergy and whose career ran alongside his. The exact sequence of events is not now clear, but in 1936, during Father Joblin's time, a painting of Our Lord after being taken down from the cross was hung above the high altar and was surrounded by extraordinary lofty Baroque embellishments including a large cherub on either side. This was in memory of two deceased members of the congregation and was described in a wall tablet with equally ornate surrounding. There was also a very tall throne for exposition on the high altar. Later four large reliquaries of Austrian origin in Rococo style were attached to the east wall on either side of the high altar. It seems likely in the light of his other activities that Father Beresford was responsible for the acquisition of these.

St Michael was closed in 1965 and united with All Saints, Tollcross (now known as St Michael and All Saints), to which a number of the furnishings were taken, and in which they remain to this day. They include the painting formerly above the high altar of St Michael, now hung on the west wall of All Saints albeit without its enormous surround, the tablet commemorating the original ensemble, and the altar and reredos by More-Nisbet. The wall-mounted reliquaries were removed by at latest 1961 by the Revd John Milburn, probably the Church of England's greatest collector of his age in relation to vestments and furnishings, and taken by him to his then church of St Stephen, Grove Street, Liverpool. Father Millburn later moved to St Paul, Brighton, where he installed the altar rails from St Michael, which dated from the nineteenth century and were reinstalled there with other rails of French origin constructed in about 1700.

The last rector of St Michael was Father C.H. Scott, whom we have already met in these pages both in connection with his time at St Peter, Ely and in his negotiations with Father Drew over the Missals.

Liturgically, Father Beresford would have had no need to make any significant changes when he moved to Edinburgh as he and Father Joblin were in accord about such matters.

Basil Edward Joblin was born in 1895 in Blackheath. His father, Francis Edward Joblin, was a solicitor who had been born in the Isle of Wight but practised in Durham, and his mother came from that latter area: as was quite frequently the case in the Victorian era, she was older than her husband, and in consequence Basil was an only child. It is not now clear how he took up Anglo-Catholicism, but like Clive Beresford he was a life-long member of both the Catholic League and the Sodality of the Precious Blood, which he joined in 1921 and of which in 1953 he became the director upon Father Fynes-Clinton relinquishing that position.

Basil Joblin was educated at Corpus Christi College, Oxford (BA 1916) and was then in the Labour Corps during the First World War. He was trained at Cuddesdon and ordained deacon in 1920, priest in 1921. His first curacy was in the archetypal backstreet Anglo-Catholic church of St Alphege, Southwark (1920–22), which was followed by a spell at St Bartholomew, Whitworth, near Rochdale. The effect of his Papalist views on the local mill workers is not recorded, and in 1924 he returned to London, firstly to St Augustine, Victoria Park (arriving shortly after Father Drew had left) and next at the then notorious St Saviour, Hoxton (1928–32). Father Bloxam[12] died early in 1928, and the vicar once Father Joblin arrived in Hoxton was the Revd D.A. Ross, who had had to promise to Bishop Winnington-Ingram that he would reintroduce the vernacular to the liturgy.

In 1929 Father Joblin was appointed as the English Secretary of the Confraternity of Unity, which had been founded in New York by several priests of the American Episcopal Church, and was explicitly ultramontane in its declarations: the secretariat in this country was centred on St Saviour. Father Milburn also served a curacy at that church. It was from Hoxton that Father Joblin moved to become rector of St Michael, Edinburgh.

When Father Joblin left Scotland, to be replaced by Father Beresford, he took up a position as chaplain to the Community of St Peter the Apostle,

---

12 See Chapter 5.

Westminster, at Laleham Abbey, Surrey, then under the leadership of the formidable Mother Sarah. He remained there until 1956, when he returned to parochial work for a time as curate to the strongly Papalist Revd W. Robert Corbould at Carshalton and was placed in charge of the daughter church of The Good Shepherd, Carshalton Beeches. He later assisted elsewhere and he died in 1971.

Edinburgh was a congenial place for priests of Father Joblin and Father Beresford's outlook because the Episcopal Church was not established and the complaints often made about the Church of England being subject to secular directions were not applicable. Also it would seem that control exercised over teaching was perhaps more lax than in England. It also happened of course that during the Second World War Father Beresford was away from the bombing which so badly affected many urban centres. The parish was mixed and the congregation eclectic.

One of Father Beresford's traits was that he would give room in his rectories to any young men who were in difficult circumstances and without anywhere to live. This would no doubt nowadays cause some eyebrows to be raised, but at that time it was regarded as quite acceptable: women in the clergy house would have been a different state of affairs altogether. Further, after he moved to Edinburgh he had no clerical colleague in the parish and was no doubt lonely. One young man whom he helped in this way was Alexander J. (Alec) Dunn, who was in the St Michael's choir and then went to live in the rectory because of family housing difficulties: he was to play a significant part in future events.

In 1947 Father Beresford left Edinburgh and moved to be the parish priest of SS. Peter and Paul at Tickencote, which is just outside Stamford but is in fact in the County of Rutland. The village is very small and is in a cul-de-sac off the Great North Road. Tickencote church is architecturally stunning, with an original and unique Norman chancel arch with six bands of carving around it: further substantial renovations and additions took place elsewhere in the church in 1792, an unusual date for such work. However, it is not now clear what it was that drew Father Beresford to it: there appears not to have been any tradition of Anglo-Catholicism in the parish and the only clue today is a disused aumbry on the north side of the chancel. His stay there was not long lived (November 1947 to March

1949) and it may be that he encountered difficulties with the parishioners or the patron. Certainly it is apparent from all we know of him that he would not have changed any of his own firmly held views on the liturgy and on teaching. It was, however, the second occasion on which he had moved and then moved on again very quickly.

Alec Dunn went with Father Beresford from Scotland and lived in the vicarage in Rutland.

It was from there that Clive Beresford moved the short distance to Newborough. The situation there was different, because Father Newman had carefully laid the ground for Anglo-Catholic worship. The late 1940s and early 1950s were fruitful days for the Church of England as the population, wearied by the privations of the war, turned to social outlets, many of which, especially in small villages, were centred around the church. Also the boom in births at that time meant that children were being brought for baptism in large numbers.

Father Beresford initially tapped this post-war enthusiasm. He continued with the archetypically Anglican Mothers' Union, but added to it a Guild of St Hugh for servers and threw himself into village activities such as the vicarage fête and the like. He took parties to Walsingham, and was popular with the boys who served, whom he used to take camping on the Norfolk coast. Alec Dunn moved with him from Tickencote and lived in the somewhat dilapidated vicarage while working locally. He then met and courted Rose Lilley, sister of Ethel who had joined the Community of the Sacred Passion, and they were married by Father Beresford in 1952 and lived in the village.

Thereafter the Dunns became great supporters of the parish priest and Alec Dunn became churchwarden. Father Beresford often went to their house on Sundays for his evening meal and relaxed by playing dominoes. Other young men stayed at the vicarage for varying periods of time after Alec left.

Father Beresford decided to refurnish the interior of what was an unpromising building in accordance with his own outlook. His initial scheme, which was circulated around the village with a request for voluntary labour to assist, was for the provision of two parclose screens projecting each side from the chancel arch, which thus provided two recesses for new altars. However, this did not proceed and in fact Father Beresford himself designed, constructed and fitted out three altars, including carrying out much of the carpentry and sewing, but without the making of any screens. He made the reredos for the high altar, which was itself then extended by screwing on whitewood projections, a replacement altar of Our Lady for the south aisle and an altar of the Sacred Heart for the north aisle. In order to accommodate the last, he threw out the organ which had previously been in that position and replaced it with a harmonium with electric blower.

It could be said that those three altars were in a sub-Travers style, or in other words that they were in a pastiche of a pastiche Baroque. They were also made very much later than most imitation Baroque fittings, although Travers' pupil Douglas Purnell made a series of such fittings for St Augustine, Tonge Moor, Bolton, in the 1950s and later still, in about 1963, for the Roman Catholic Church of the Assumption, Warwick Street. While Father Beresford was installing his elaborate creations, most other churches were simplifying and stripping out the interior of their churches.

The high altar as rebuilt blocked out a considerable part of the east window. It had a large central domed tabernacle and behind it an exposition throne of the same general pattern as in Edinburgh. Six candlesticks stood on the gradine and another four on the altar itself. On the altar linen was written 'Dominus Meus et Deus Meus', just as at St Thomas, Shepherd's Bush. The altar of Mary also held a tabernacle and was built up behind to a great height, with a central niche for a robed figure of Our Lady. It appears to have been loosely based on Martin Travers' design at St Magnus, London Bridge, where he had adapted an old door frame to make a side altar and even the inscription 'Mater Misericordiae' on the frontal is in similar type. The Sacred Heart altar was similar, but the composition was even more elaborate, with six pilasters and yet another tabernacle. Hardboard was used extensively in the construction of all the new altars.

The taste underlying these works is perhaps open to question and it may even be that this was appreciated by their creator's friends and contemporaries: Father Joblin apparently referred to them as 'Berry's

174

fretwork', Berry being the name by which his closest friends referred to Father Beresford.

The high altar appeared on a line drawing on the cover of the parish magazine which Father Beresford started, which was entitled *The Flail* after the symbol of St Bartholomew. There were a number of idiosyncrasies in relation to the way in which he ran the parish: in particular, the magazine for July 1957 showed Sunday services as being holy mass at 8 a.m., Holy Communion at 9.30, solemn mass at 10.30 and evening service at 6.30 p.m. The initiated would understand that in the evening there would be benediction, but many even of the knowledgeable would not immediately grasp that the service at 9.30 was not another celebration, but rather communion from the tabernacle for those who could not otherwise receive. He had a mass stipend book, such as possessed by Roman clergy in England, although he was never paid any such sums.

It would appear that there was a change in Father Beresford's relationship with the parish which can be dated from about 1959–60. Up to that time, his views may not always have been accepted, but he clearly devoted a considerable amount of time to the parish activities and his eccentricities were tolerated. After that time, the population of the village began to grow with newcomers who were not used to his way of worship, and also, more importantly, he began to take on more external work.

On 4 December 1959 Father Fynes-Clinton, co-founder of the Catholic League and its Priest Director for many years, died at the age of 84 and Clive Beresford was elected to replace him. This involved him in a great deal of extra work and in particular of travel, because he was attempting to widen the geographical scope of the League, which had always been somewhat London based. In 1961 the first Northern Festival took place, at Father Hum's church of All Souls, Leeds, and these continued thereafter. In 1963 the Golden Jubilee of the League was marked with the traditional pilgrimage to Walsingham and annual festa at St Michael's School, Otford, Kent, which had been founded by the so-called 'ritualist martyr', the Revd Arthur Tooth, and by regional events at Leeds, at St Agatha, Sparkbrook, Birmingham and at St Winwalloe, Poundstock.

The other new development was that Father Beresford became interested in printing and publishing. In 1958–59 a new publication entitled

The Dome had appeared to represent the views of Catholic-minded Anglicans, but it lasted only about 18 months after which a combination of financial problems and the secession of the editor to Rome saw its demise. Father Beresford determined to fill the gap and acquired a Gestetner duplicator. One room at the vicarage was turned into a printing press and he began production from April 1960 of *Crux*,[13] which he edited, largely wrote, printed, folded, addressed and distributed, with assistance only from those who lived in the house from time to time. In these times of digital printing it is easy to produce high-quality work within tight time frames, but then it was difficult to reach acceptable standards, and the end result now looks amateurish. It improved significantly after 1963 when he replaced the duplicator with a printing machine. This still, however, required him to type out the contents and it was almost impossible to correct the frequent mistakes which were made. The circulation he recorded in various editions as being in the 3000–4000 range.

Crux ran from 1960 until Father Beresford's sudden death in 1967. It thus covered an interesting period in which there were great changes being made in Rome and in which the scheme for union with the Methodist Church was very much to the fore. The tone of the news sheet was very combative and there were those who thought its motto of 'Charity to All' was inappropriate.

It was predictable that the Methodist scheme should be the subject of somewhat hysterical hostile propaganda, which was often expressed in separate sheets such as had been issued by Father Monahan in Worcester. There were a series of such efforts, some unnamed and some under various titles. *St John's Tracts* were produced by Fathers Beresford and Hum and P.J. Hodges, Father Hum's churchwarden, but after two had been issued the sequence came to an end, perhaps because of the latter's untimely death in 1964. There were also *Crux Papers*, *Carshalton Tracts* (named after the 1958 Carshalton episode in which the veteran Revd R.A.E. Harris was barred from his church by Bishop Mervyn Stockwood and described as published by St Joseph's Press, Newborough) and others. The style was short and direct: Number 2 of the *Carshalton Tracts* was en-

---

13 Father Beresford was clear that this should be pronounced as if it were 'crooks'.

titled *'Broken Vows': My Aunt Fanny!* and another unnamed commentary on the Methodist scheme was simply headed *Betrayal!*

Perhaps less predictably, and in contradistinction to some of his brethren, Father Beresford was moderately enthusiastic about the new liturgical changes emanating from Rome and was anxious to disseminate information about them, which he did. The Crux Press dealt with that, as it did with the various tracts and the production of mass books. In 1955 a duplicated parish mass book was produced and in October 1965 a new edition, printed by the press, was published, which sold out almost immediately and was reprinted with corrections the following month. However, it could still be said that Father Beresford and his associates in the Catholic League were not generally absorbing and reflecting Vatican II, but rather simply passing on the authorized changes. The mood was inward-looking and also perhaps preoccupation with the Methodist union scheme deflected attention.[14]

In addition to these other matters, the Press printed the quarterly *Messenger* of the Catholic League, and some parish magazines for other churches, including those for Father Hum. It also produced *The First Fifty Years*, which was a history of the Catholic League from 1913 to 1966: the odd period covered by the book is explained by Father Beresford in the introduction, as he intended to write it himself to commemorate the Jubilee in 1963, but was unable to do so and it was then done by Brian J. Doolan. The typography and spelling in the book was so bad that Father Beresford added a postscript apologizing for it, but it does contain some interesting information not available elsewhere.

In the early 1960s Father Beresford also published a short book, and a later supplement, by G. O'Halloran of Ipswich, which was entitled *Some Churches outside London where Full Catholic Privileges are Available.* It was typical that the supplement contained a notice that 'Those less demanding of Catholic practice are referred to the *Church Traveller's Directory* by the Revd P.E. Blagdon-Gamlen'.

Father Blagdon-Gamlen's book was published in 1965 and was indeed more comprehensive, but despite the put-down it appears that Father

---

14 See R. Farmer, *The Catholic League 1913–1988* (Catholic League, 1988), p. 13.

Beresford was quite friendly with him and invited him to preach at Newborough on occasion. Peter Eugene Blagdon-Gamlen (born Gamlen, but he hyphenated his last two names) (1920–2004) was during the 1960s parish priest of St Bartholomew, Derby and then of Harrold, Bedfordshire and was involved with virtually all the Anglo-Catholic societies save the Sodality, for which he was ineligible because he was married, although his personal life was somewhat idiosyncratic. Although born into the Plymouth Brethren, he enthusiastically embraced the higher echelons of the Church of England, without ever being as Papalist as Father Beresford, who, for example, was very opposed to the cult of King Charles the Martyr on the grounds that he was not recognized as a saint in Rome.

It does appear also at this time that Father Beresford lacked many neighbouring clergy of his outlook. He never seems to have been very close to Father Bales at Marshland St James, and although he was very happy when the Revd Francis Ogden went to SS. Peter and Paul, Great Casterton, near to his own former parish of Tickencote, in December 1962 he stayed there only a year, the historian of the church saying enigmatically that 'neither his health nor his disposition were suited to the climate'.[15]

On 2 May 1962 there occurred one of the high points of Father Beresford's life and ministry. He went to Rome with a small group of priests from the Society of the Holy Cross (SSC), including Father Colin Stephenson, by then Administrator of the Shrine of our Lady of Walsingham, and they were received in private audience by Pope John XXIII. He was clear that that represented a proper step forward to reunion and was a contradistinction it to the proposals for Anglican–Methodist coming together. Although the views expressed by those of that viewpoint were unfashionable then, time has shown that they were correct in their assessment of the deep flaws in that scheme and of the ambiguities inherent in it.

In June 1962 Father Beresford edited a new edition of *The Flail*, which had failed to appear for two years because of the work involved with *Crux*. In it he appealed for attenders at the weekday mass as he made it clear he could not say mass without another being present, a point which had been the subject of much discussion in *Crux*.

---

15 H.L. Young, *The Key to Casterton Magna* (parish, 2000).

At that time he was saying mass in the church daily save for Monday and Wednesday, but on Monday he said mass at the Hermitage of the sisters of the Community of the Holy Family at Peakirk, which was very near Newborough.

In August 1962 Philip Gray, then a layman but later to be ordained and for some years himself Priest Director of the Catholic League, visited Father Beresford and stayed for a few days in the somewhat chaotic conditions of the vicarage. There were then two other young men who were long-term residents, one of whom was one of the Lilley children, and a boy of about 15 who had moved in to the vicarage, although his parents lived elsewhere in the village. The cats were given great privileges and on one occasion when there was a misunderstanding as to when he was coming back, he returned to find that they had been fed with his dinner. One of the cats featured in a picture in the *Peterborough Standard* the next year when the national papers, and later the local, discovered that the vicar of Newborough was able to sew and to design altars, and ran articles on him.

The congregation by this time was fading away somewhat, although Father Beresford, as we shall see with Father Butler of Kettlebaston, did not keep service registers so it is not possible to see exactly what the attendance was. He was very careless about paperwork generally, and in effect he had opted out of the diocese. Newborough did not, for example, pay its parish quota during these years. At the main Sunday mass when Philip Gray was in the village there were about 15 adults and a number of children, all of whom crossed themselves devoutly as they were aspersed, but on the Feast of the Immaculate Heart of Mary, which was celebrated with a weekday sung mass, the congregation was only three.

There were a number of distinctive features about the liturgy at Newborough, which was also overlain by the celebrant's inability properly to pronounce the letter 'R': rosary is a difficult word to say for one with that problem, as is St Rosa of Lima, whose feast was piously celebrated in Newborough church. Philip Gray was also surprised to observe that water was placed in the chalice using a spoon, and that the vicar told him that he did not participate in any Anglican liturgy, so that while evensong was sung he anticipated matins of the next day from his breviary. He did not

Outposts of the Faith

in any event approve of solemn evensong on the basis that it was 'dressed-up Cranmer' but did hold sung evensong, followed, as was solemn mass in the morning, by benediction.

On 11 April 1964 the Catholic League had a pilgrimage in honour of St Guthlac, a Fenland saint, which began with high mass at Newborough followed by benediction and the litany of the Sacred Heart: they then moved on to Peakirk and then Crowland, where the saint is commemorated. Philip Gray was again present and was surprised to notice that in the heat of the sun some of the homemade decorations stuck on to Father Beresford's vestment began curling off as the glue which had been holding them melted.

It is difficult to resist the conclusion that by the 1960s Clive Beresford was finding his parish difficult to manage, not least because of all the publishing in which he was involved. In July 1963 he said that a proper new office was required for *Crux*, and that a limited company should be set up to run it. In March 1964 he floated the idea of a home for retired priests (which would include himself) with an attached production centre for the newsletter. By late 1966 it seems clear that the congregation had largely disappeared and the local newspaper carried a rather sad article on the priest without a flock, who nevertheless tried to bring carols to the village since they would not come to him.

In October 1966 Father Beresford himself wrote in *Crux* of the problems he faced in these terms:

As some of our readers know this vicarage, which houses the press, the editor, three cats and quite a lot else, is ever more and more rapidly going the way of all buildings erected years ago on this shifting fenland. The ground floor falls away from the walls at various interesting angles, steps occur where no steps were ever intended, and the mere jumping of one of the cats from table to floor in one of the rooms occasions all the symptoms of a minor earthquake throughout the building. This happens quite often. A trip upstairs (carefully, please, the stairs are not very firm) displays ten gaping holes in the various ceilings and when it happens to rain we are in the position of the widow in the Old Testament whose sons had to report that 'there is not one vessel

180

left' – though in our case they are needed to catch rain water rather than to hold oil. The building is condemned and so the Authorities will do nothing. Perhaps that is not quite fair, for they have promised a new house several times. I expect they have forgotten . . . as your editor approaches the ripe old age of 70, he finds that it is not so easy to endure such things without considerable protests from the flesh by way of rheumatism and bronchitis and, sadly and reluctantly, the inevitable conclusion has now been reached that he must very soon be compelled to relinquish his home and his benefice and find somewhere to live and continue the work of *Crux*.

He then went on to ask if any readers had a house which he could use, but he never appears to have had a satisfactory reply. Philip Gray tried unsuccessfully to get him to set up a community in Kettlebaston, but Father Beresford thought it too remote. It was said later that the vicar himself owned three houses elsewhere, but they were all heavily mortgaged and he was falling into some financial difficulties: previously he had paid some of the parish expenses himself when funds were low.

Early in the morning of 30 July 1967 Father Beresford died peacefully while asleep. The heart problem which had been identified as long before as 1916 finally caught up with him. One of the lodgers was able to alert those who required telling, and the requiem was arranged for the next week: in so far as the service register was completed at Newborough, it was compiled in Latin, and it was recorded that he had died *in somno suo* – in his own sleep. High mass was celebrated by the Revd Peter Etchells, parish priest of Ashby Magna, Leicestershire, who had been ordained in 1953 and was almost immediately inducted into the Sodality by Fathers Beresford and Joblin. Father Joblin was the deacon and preached the panegyric. The church was packed, a contrast to attendances at regular services over the past few years. Canon Taylor, the Roman Catholic parish priest in Peterborough, vested the body for burial and bought at his own expense the coffin – an act of charity which was also far-seeing for its time.

Clive Beresford was buried just outside the church he had served so faithfully and a headstone was erected to him. It transpired that his only

will had been made some years before and he had left his property principally to a former lodger in Scotland with whom he had lost touch. His
vestments were taken by the last residents of the vicarage, who both went
over to Rome and presented them to a church of their new persuasion.

The death of the vicar left the diocesan authorities with some immediate
problems. The vicarage was not fit for human habitation and the services
which had been held in the church bore little resemblance to those held
in other parishes under the jurisdiction of the Diocese of Peterborough.
A solution was found by Bishop Cyril Eastaugh, whereby the Revd F.E.
Pickard, the Master of Divinity at King's School, Peterborough, who was
licensed as the second minor canon of the cathedral, was very speedily
appointed as priest in charge of the parish. It was thought that because
Father Pickard had been a Roman Catholic for a short time (1960–63), he
would be able to take over the preparation of Father Beresford's confirmation class without the difficulties which others would have faced.

There was an immediate change in the liturgy and also in the appearance
of the church, although Father Pickard was a committed Anglo-Catholic
and joined, and is still, a member of the Catholic League. It transpired
that the altars which Father Beresford had constructed were riddled with
woodworm, and becoming less stable, and were also a fire hazard since
the candle stocks were made of rolled paper: over the next month they
were swept away and burnt in the churchyard. The reredos of the high
altar was removed and the screwed-on additions taken away. A new lady
chapel altar was constructed in the north aisle, where the Sacred Heart
altar had stood, but it incorporated a mensa containing a relic, which was
on long-term loan from Father Joblin and had been used in the former
altar. The statue of the Sacred Heart was given a cloak and crook and
became the Good Shepherd, standing over the font. More prosaically, the
registers of marriages and the like were brought up to date with the aid
of the Registrar. There was a great deal of very good quality linen, which
was in a filthy state.

In the autumn of 1969 Canon Pickard dedicated a memorial clock to
Father Beresford, saying of him: 'The presses are still and the church is
poorer for the silence. We can do nothing about that. In placing a clock
in his church we make a gesture. He loved clocks and such a memorial

is wholly congruous. But the real memorial to Father Beresford is one that can properly be made by all here, whether they approved of Father Beresford and his ministry or (let us be frank) looked askance at it. Clive Beresford was a man of God. "He lived for the altar" one of his penitents told me, and this is obviously true. No one could doubt his integrity, even if they questioned his judgment. He fulfilled his ministry as he understood it, and he gave to this church the best he had to give all of the time ... '[16] Some time later, a complaint was made to the *Catholic Standard* that the clock was not to be seen: in fact it was undergoing a temporary repair.

Father (now Canon) Pickard was made vicar of the parish in 1968 and stayed until 1972: the letter of appointment to the living from the Crown Appointment Office to him expressed the wish that lawful services return to the parish.

The church newsletter for November 1968 makes it clear that the main Sunday service was by then termed 'Eucharist' and was Series 1, evensong was with a sermon rather than followed by benediction, and the high altar had been moved forward to become freestanding. It was said that the 'keynote of the sanctuary is now austerity': nothing could be a more radical *volte face* after the previous furnishings. The village began to reconnect to the church, congregations increased, and the PCC urged the adoption of Series II. The vicarage was thought not to be usable and the Pickard family were accommodated in a very small bungalow.

The Diocese did, later, finally build a new vicarage, which Clive Beresford had thought they never would, even though a proper survey of the house he had used showed that it was actually possible to save it, but he had written to Philip Gray on 4 October 1966 that '[the church] will meet the fate of so many Catholic churches and be swamped in the neighbouring High-Churchism ...'. To call someone 'High Church' was a profound insult from one of Father Beresford's outlook: to him it denoted one who did not accept the discipline of Catholicism and the need for reunion with the Papacy, while using ritual and wearing vestments, which was somewhat unfair on his two immediate successors. When Father Pickard left,

---

16 Reported in the *Catholic Standard,* February 1970.

the priest who followed him was a more old-fashioned Anglo-Catholic, who restored the high altar to its traditional place but with the credence table in front of it in order to celebrate facing the people: he also reversed the use of the statue of the Good Shepherd so that it once again became the Sacred Heart.

However, the next appointment was of an Evangelical, who introduced guitars and the like and at some point the statue of Our Lord which had had two guises disappeared, probably to the local tip.

Newborough is now held with the adjoining parishes of Eye and Thorney and of course the interior of the church is unrecognizable from Father Beresford's day. The main service on Sunday, however, remains a sung Eucharist. His prophecy has perhaps come true.

Father Beresford was succeeded as Priest Director of the Catholic League by his old friend Father Joblin, but he was in poor health and resigned in 1970. He was replaced by Father Hum, who himself then became seriously ill and resigned in 1974. It was only at that time, with the election of the Revd Raymond Avent as Priest Director, that the League began to grapple with the changes which Vatican II had introduced in perspective as well as in detail.

There can be no doubting Father Beresford's personal integrity or his devotion. His problem was that the age changed while he stood firm in the position which he had always taken, and in the process the congregation, and particularly the potential congregation, slipped away from him.

8

St Mary, Wisbech St Mary, Cambridgeshire, and places around, and Canon Mowbray Smith

Wisbech St Mary (a village entirely separate from the nearby town of Wisbech, the so-called 'Queen of the Fens') has an interesting and ancient parish church which in the middle years of the twentieth century was the subject of a fascinating and unusual programme of beautification brought about by the long-serving parish priest, the Revd Mowbray Smith (1879–1976), a moderate and long-lived Anglo-Catholic of charismatic personality, who is still well remembered in and around the area.

The original parish of Wisbech St Mary covered an area of 10,000 acres on the north bank of the River Nene and included the villages of Murrow and Guyhirn as well as many outlying hamlets, on the typical Fenland pattern. Many of the farms in the parish grow soft fruit, as do others in the Wisbech area. It appears that the area was separated from the town in 1109 and was given to the monks, as opposed to the Bishop, of Ely. The monks built a chapel in the new settlement, which was then reconstructed in the fourteenth century to result in the basis of the church we see today, with nave and aisles on either side, which was completed despite the Black Death ravaging the local population. Further work was carried out in the fifteenth century, including the construction of a tower, a clerestory, and a three-light window over the chancel arch, and the chancel itself was reconstructed. A porch was also added.

Wisbech St Mary then had a substantial early Perpendicular church some 120 feet in length, of which 80 feet was the nave and the balance the chancel, and at the west end was a four-stage tower some 63 feet in height. However, after the Reformation it had no resident priest: it was under the jurisdiction of the incumbent of the church of St Peter in Wisbech itself, who used to send out a curate on Sundays to conduct services. This was an increasingly unsatisfactory situation and was a long-standing example of the abuses which are always set out in elementary histories of the Oxford Movement and which were in due course remedied, not least because of the increased social responsibility and clerical professionalism arising from the new ideas which came to the fore after 1833.

In Wisbech St Mary, however, it was not until an Order in Council dated 11 August 1854 that a separate parish was established and the Revd Henry Jackson was appointed as first vicar. There were strenuous conditions attached to the appointment: not only was the new vicar to take the services at the church, he was also to restore it and the school, and to build a chapel at Murrow, and a parsonage house for himself. He accomplished a considerable part of this extensive brief before his premature death in 1863, building both a house for the vicar, which was, unusually, not near to the church but rather on the fringes of the village, and a chapel of Corpus Christi at Murrow, an unusual dedication but one which followed a mediaeval precedent. In addition the new vicar farmed a considerable acreage.

Extensive work was done to the fabric of the church in 1872, when the chancel was rebuilt, and then in 1894 and 1901, when restoration took place. One important consequence of the nineteenth-century work was that in 1872 the chancel roof was raised, so that the window above the chancel arch became internal rather than external as it had been previously. The village became less isolated after the construction in 1866 of the Peterborough to Sutton Bridge branch of the Midland and Great Northern Joint Railway, which had a station named Wisbech St Mary and one also at Murrow, and in 1867 of the March to Spalding line of the Great Northern and Great Eastern Railways, which also had a station at Murrow and one at Guyhirn.

Following Mr Jackson's death, a number of other priests followed. The patron was the Bishop of Ely. In 1882 the Revd Richard Devereux Jones was appointed, and it was during his incumbency that the two restorations were carried out. Although the fabric was restored in that way, there was little visual stimulation within the church and all the windows had either plain or yellow glass within. The vestry was at that time to the north of the chancel and the organ was in the chancel itself.

Although it seems that Father Jones had begun to teach along moderate Catholic lines, progress was very slow and measured and was handicapped in any event by his increasing ill health, and in particular by the loss of his eyesight. By 1910 he was for all practical purposes blind, and he handed over the running of the parish to his curate, the Revd A.C. Harper, in something of a reversion to that which had prevailed 50 years before.

It was in 1914 that Father Mowbray Smith arrived. The parish was more appealing than many in the area, because it had a noble, if somewhat under-furnished, church rather than the brick chapel like structures which had been erected in many Fenland villages, and also had a substantial vicarage.

There can scarcely have been a family more steeped in the Church of England than that of Mowbray Smith. His maternal great-grandfather, Robert Gray, had been Bishop of Bristol at the time of the Great Reform Bill in 1832, when his palace had been burned out by the mob. Both his grandfathers were priests, as were his father and all three of his brothers.

Mowbray Smith's paternal grandfather, the Revd Charles Smith, the author of a two-volume work entitled *An Inquiry into Catholic Truths Hidden in the Creed of Rome,* had been a fellow of Peterhouse, Cambridge and was for a time curate of St Mary the Less, next door to the College. In 1833 he was appointed to the college living of Newton, near Sudbury in Suffolk, then still in the Diocese of Ely, and he remained there for some 60 years.

Charles Smith's son, the Revd Reginald Smith, Mowbray's father, was born in the rectory in 1844 and having in his turn been ordained he became curate to his father at Newton in 1868 and remained there until 1883.

In 1871 Reginald Smith married Augusta Gray, who was herself the daughter of a priest and had been born in Godmanchester, but was then living in Brighton. They rapidly had a large family, all of whom, unusually, had only one forename. Constance was born in 1873, Bernard in 1876,

Violet in 1877, Mowbray in 1879, Douglas in 1881 and Agnes in 1882. In 1883 the family moved to Tretower, near Crickhowell in the Brecon Beacons, an area of which Mowbray Smith was to remain fond for the whole of his life, when Reginald Smith became vicar of the parish, and where he and his wife had two more children, twins Stella and Lancelot, in 1886. Reginald Smith then served for a time as a curate in Bristol, at St Paul, Clifton (1889–95), before moving to Walpole St Andrew, Norfolk, very near Marshland St James and on the other side of Wisbech from Wisbech St Mary. He became the Rural Dean of Lynn Marshland and a local magistrate.

Bernard Smith, as the oldest son, continued the family tradition by attending Peterhouse and later serving as vicar of Newton (from 1917). Douglas became vicar of St Peter, West Lynn from 1923 to 1930, so being the immediate predecessor of Father Haylock, who has already been mentioned, and then became vicar of Old Hunstanton with Ringstead, also in Norfolk. Lancelot in due course became the incumbent of St John the Baptist, Spalding, not far from Wisbech but in South Lincolnshire, and a Canon of Lincoln Cathedral.

Mowbray Smith was an undergraduate at Queens' College, Cambridge (BA 1901, MA 1905) and was ordained deacon in 1902, priest in 1903. His first appointment was as curate of the lofty church of St Wulfram, Grantham, Lincolnshire, but in 1905 he moved to the Diocese of Ely, where he was to remain until 1951. In that year he became domestic chaplain to the Bishop of Ely, the Rt Revd F.H. Chase, a post which he combined after 1907 with being curate in charge of the church of the Holy Cross at Stuntney, just south of Ely. While assisting the Bishop, he visited for the first time Wisbech St Mary, which was at that time labouring under the difficulties arising from Father Jones' failing sight, for a confirmation.

In 1914 Mowbray Smith moved to become vicar of Wisbech St Mary. He was inducted on Advent Sunday, just as the Great War was beginning. His gift for easy communication is well displayed by a letter he wrote to the parishioners, which was distributed in the Deanery Magazine, introducing himself and saying how much he was looking forward to meeting every-body, and, most appealingly, what a splendid village he thought it was.

From the beginning of his ministry in the village, Father Smith was anxious to ensure that his parishioners were given access to proper housing, health and education and he was also prepared to assist in any reasonable way that he could, with lifts and the like. He always had a car at a time when they were few and far between. He was clearly reasonably well off and he never married, so had no dependants. His attitude would nowadays perhaps be categorized as paternalistic, but he was a man of his time: also, he was a pleasant, compassionate and affable man who did not generally make enemies, rather like Father Gambier Lowe in Throwleigh, and these aspects of his personality attracted men and women to him.

Of all the characters described in this book, Father Mowbray Smith was probably most directly affected by the First World War. He had been at Wisbech St Mary for only about nine months when he decided that his duty was to volunteer as an Army Chaplain. In February 1916, probably when he was having a holiday in Tretower, where his father had been parish priest and which he continued to love, he was asked to go to France. The difficulties which were often placed in the way of those who had too clearly adopted Anglo-Catholicism do not appear to have held him back, no doubt because of his extensive clerical connections and relatively moderate teaching. He left the Revd H. Frew Simpson to run the parish in his absence.

Father Smith was allocated to the 26th Battalion of the Royal Fusiliers and first of all was sent to Aldershot. By June 1916 he was just behind the front line, and by August on it, with gas, shells and rifle fire to contend with as he attempted both to hold services and to comfort those who had been wounded, often horribly. In September 1916 he wrote to his flock, commending the example of the French population who thronged the roads on Sunday morning on their way to mass in the Roman churches. His thinking was, in this as in most other matters, conventional for the time, namely that England needed the war to bring it back on to the proper road, and he continued: 'One can see England purged and cleansed by the sacrifices of war, pure, clean, moral and sober.'

His battlefield experience was in fact relatively short, because on 15 September 1916, during the Battle of the Somme, he went forward to assist stretcher-bearers under fire. At Deauville Wood he was administering a dose of morphine to a badly wounded German soldier when a shell burst nearby, killing the man he was attempting to assist. A large piece of shrapnel hit Father Smith's tin helmet, leaving a small hole and a large dent in it: the head covering undoubtedly saved his life, and he kept it thereafter as a reminder of what had occurred and of how near he had come to death.

Although Father Smith's life was saved, he did suffer head injuries and was in hospital for some time. He came back to England and after convalescing he was given the post of chaplain to the school at Woolwich Garrison for a time. He returned to Wisbech St Mary in the spring of 1918 as a Captain in the Chaplains' Division and having been mentioned in dispatches. Although he rarely spoke in specific terms of his experiences, it is clear that he felt deeply what had happened and the tin helmet was placed in the church as if a relic: it remains there to this day. In particular, he did not say in the account which he sent back to his parishioners that it was a German soldier whom he was tending at the moment of impact: no doubt he thought that would not go down too well.

Over the next 30 years and more, Father Mowbray Smith's contributions to the village and to the church were very extensive.

The vicar's involvement in the wider affairs of the community was far reaching. He was chairman of the managers of the Church primary school for the whole of the 33-year period after he came back from the war, and encouraged the children to attend the church, especially on feast days which fell in the week, but in addition he supported such far-sighted initiatives as a playing field, separate rooms for arts, crafts and domestic science and a new dining hall. The extension of the school took place in 1926 and the playing field was acquired in 1930.

Father Smith campaigned with the local authority for the removal of a number of the stagnant ditches which ran around the village, carrying disease. He procured a resident nurse for the village in 1919 through the Church Army, with the aid of a mutual assistance subscription scheme, although some of the residents thought that it was strange that he then allowed her to live for a time in the large vicarage, which had been built for substantial clergy families. In 1924 the Church Army enforced their general rule that nurses so provided should live other than in vicarages.

The first child he baptized when he came to Wisbech St Mary, the later Mrs Beryl Burrows, went into service with him and she too lived in from the age of 15, which does not seem to have attracted any adverse comment. The vicarage was commodious enough for the vicar to be able to adapt a space within it for a private chapel, in which he used to hold daily prayers for the domestic staff and any visitors. Unlike many bachelors, he seems to have been fond of the company of children and given to spontaneous acts of generosity, such as anonymously providing footwear for three children of one family who came to school ill-shod, and, in 1921, assisting by providing accommodation for the children of some Russian refugees who appeared in the neighbourhood and began attending the church.

The gardens of the vicarage were of a sufficient size to permit the holding of fêtes and other events in them. Father Smith also had erected in the grounds in 1920 a substantial wooden building which he named St Mary's Hall, and which thereafter was used as a community centre. He later handed it over to the PCC and it remains in use as a Scout hut.

This led indirectly to one of his rare reverses, as in due course a number of residents decided that the village required a hall which was not under the control of the church, and so could be used for other activities which may not have been countenanced by Father Smith. The vicar thought this was quite unnecessary, but land was found and a brick-built building erected.

The experience of seeing the Roman clergy in action in the First World War may well have encouraged Father Smith to adopt a similar position towards his parishioners to that which he had observed. In particular, he was sometimes to be found on a doorstep on Monday morning if someone had not attended church the day before, a practice which was thought to be more typical of the discipline exerted in rural France by the priests.

After returning from his war-time duties, the vicar decided to beautify both the fabric of the church and the services held in it. The interesting aspect of life at Wisbech St Mary was that the adornment of the interior was planned and carried out by Father Smith himself, without any professional assistance. Although he seems not to have been short of finance, he did not call in Comper or Eden to produce a comprehensive plan for refurbishment, but rather added items which he collected on his travels at home and abroad in a somewhat magpie fashion. His intention was that the church, as the House of God, should and would be 'the most beautiful house in the parish'.

Unfortunately, no comprehensive record appears ever to have been made, or certainly to have been kept, as to the provenance of the objects which came to the church. They were manifold. It does appear that two carpets which were introduced for the chancel came from an auction house in London, and three copy Raphael paintings dating from the nineteenth century bear labels indicating that they came from the Uffizi in Florence.

The list of items which was procured is very extensive. Six brass candlesticks for the long high altar were found in Constantinople. A wooden dove dating from about the fifteenth century and of English origin was attached to gilt candelabra over the font, in order to represent the Holy Spirit. The traditional brass eagle lectern was removed and replaced by perhaps the most extraordinary addition, a carved ship's figurehead which was of Spanish origin and said to be from the Armada but had been purchased in Suffolk. It was then transformed into a lectern: the Virgin and her Child are depicted on the item, and beneath them is the motto SMDP (*Santa Maria Domini Progenitor*), which of course fits well with the dedication of the church. The sanctuary was furnished with three Italian gilt chairs of the early eighteenth century (about 1730) and the matching sofa was given to Peckover House, a National Trust property in Wisbech: these apparently came from Culford Hall, near Bury St Edmunds.[1]

In addition to these additions, Father Smith brought in a number of statues and the like, including a fine sixteenth-century statue of St Nicholas restoring life to small children who had been placed in a tub of brine, and a very large number of fragments of stained glass of various periods, some of it secular in origin, which were inserted in the windows. Other oddments were also installed, such as a late seventeenth-century bracket displaying two cherubs, and a late eighteenth-century mahogany

1 See C. Tracy, *Continental Church Furniture in England: A Traffic in Piety* (Antique Collectors' Club, Woodbridge, 2001), pp. 86–7.

holy water stoup, which was fitted with a hinged lid and used as a money box.

An interesting reflection on Mowbray Smith's attitude towards the embellishment of the church building is revealed by an article which he wrote in the *Wisbech Deanery Magazine* in February 1932 to this effect: 'You ought to notice and be able to admire the fine piece of old material that we have secured and hung to cover a bare piece of chancel wall. You have never seen a more beautiful piece of cloth. I came across it when it was in a very poor and dirty condition. [It has now been cleaned]. The experts ... were entirely mystified by it and could give me no definite opinion. But now, an authority of East Anglian repute has examined and reported that it is Chinese work, all hand made of "top-notch" material and some two hundred years old. The gold worked into the material is gold and has been tested by the chemists. Our expert thinks it is probable that the material formed the state dress of some high official in the old Chinese Empire; one can almost trace the position of the sleeves. How much we would like to know its history. It could not, of course, be put to any utilitarian purpose anywhere. It is now just a thing of beauty and adds its quota of beauty to our parish church, which is indeed a building both precious and beautiful.'

The tapestry in question is one of the few additions made to the church by the incumbent which have not survived and its present whereabouts are unknown. However, the concept that objects of artistic merit should be placed in the church, regardless of their utility and even if of no religious significance, was an unusual one, particularly coming from a man who was in most respects entirely bound by the conventions of the time.

Father Smith also instituted some more radical changes to the layout of the interior of the church, as well as persuading the parishioners and others to contribute towards the cost of providing four stained-glass windows, all of which were designed by Percy Bacon & Brothers. The first of these was the east window, depicting St Michael and St George on either side of the crucifixion, which was the village war memorial, and in the usual way the names of those who had been killed were set out on it. This window was installed in September 1920 and required the removal of the organ from the chancel to the west end in order to accommodate it.

In January 1922 a window depicting the Nativity was placed at the east end of the north aisle, in memory of Father Jones. In 1924 the window in the equivalent position in the south aisle was unblocked and a new window depicting the resurrection morning was given in memory of the parents of the donor. In 1928 the vestry was moved from its previous position in the south aisle to the west end, thus enabling the font to be moved and a baptistery formed. In 1930, after the completion of that work, a window was installed in the baptistery in memory of a local farmer who had been a churchwarden.

It is noteworthy that in the case of all these changes, faculties were obtained and senior church dignitaries were invited to the dedications. Father Smith was a representative of what those in authority thought of as the acceptable face of Anglo-Catholicism: in other words, a presentation of Christianity which was entirely faithful to the Established Church and which promised to bring dedication from the congregation and reverence to the services. There was no crypto-Romanism in this strand of the Oxford Movement and it was to prove an influential tendency, especially in cathedrals and large civic churches. In 1935 he was appointed as an honorary canon of Ely Cathedral, another sign of his acceptance in general ecclesiastical circles.

The services at Wisbech St Mary in Father Smith's time were in accordance with the Book of Common Prayer and by 1920 were established on Sundays as 7.30 a.m. Holy Communion, 10 a.m. sung Eucharist and sermon, followed by matins for those who wanted it, and then evensong in the evening. The absence both of the word 'mass' and of benediction after evensong are obviously indicative of the tone. Father Smith was also rather conservative in his teaching and, by the end of his incumbency, had perhaps fallen behind many of his colleagues. One elderly lady, still alive, who was instructed by him, is clear that his view was that the Blessed Sacrament should only be received on the first Sunday of each month, although of course attendance each week was compulsory. His social outlook also now appears somewhat dated, but that may be said of many priests between the wars. He had a simple but firm belief in decency and team sports, particularly those which involved Cambridge University, which was of course combined with a friendly and helpful nature.

In 1951 Father Mowbray Smith decided to resign the benefice. He was then over 70 and had been vicar of the parish for 37 years. There was a sense that he had perhaps lost his way in the later period: however, although he was elderly by some standards he was not yet ready to retire.

After leaving the village, Father Smith lived initially at Peckover House in Wisbech, and later in a little house in Hunstanton, where he had two housekeepers and 13 clocks, which were carefully co-ordinated to chime simultaneously. However, he had one last service to give: upon leaving Wisbech St Mary he became chaplain of Queen Anne's, Caversham, Berkshire, a boarding school for girls. He was given the use of a cottage in the grounds and soon became a much-loved figure to whom the girls felt able to turn for advice in moments of need.

When Brian Payne was researching his short life of Canon Mowbray Smith, *The Saint of St Mary's*,[2] he had a remarkable response to a request for memories of the chaplain from old girls of the school, who recalled him with great fondness, especially because he brought them large quantities of strawberries from Wisbech back to Reading. His only regret at being in a girls' school was that they did not originally play cricket, a sport to which he was especially attached, so he arranged games for the younger ones. He often invited the girls to stay either at Wisbech or later at Hunstanton and again they appreciated the attention they were given. At that time boarding schools, even for girls, were far grimmer and less humane places than they have become and the presence of a wise counsellor outside of the teaching staff was much welcomed.

Canon Mowbray Smith died at the age of 96 in 1976. His funeral, fittingly, was in the church to which he had devoted so much of his life and mass was said by the Revd Hugh Barker, assisted by the Revd Bill Woodhouse, his successors. The panegyric was delivered by none other than Father Charles Bales, who referred to his devotion both to his 'dear people' (as he had always called them) and to the church itself. A watch was kept throughout the night and following his cremation the ashes were spread outside the baptistery window, near the grave of his predecessor.

A few years before his death, Canon Smith had planned his final addi-

---

2 Published by the author in 2006.

tion to Wisbech St Mary church. He had secretly commissioned a brass depicting himself vested for the Eucharist, which was placed inside the entrance and dedicated in April 1977. It was indeed an anachronistic, but appropriate, gift and after many pecuniary legacies the vicar and church-wardens of the parish were named as residuary beneficiaries of his estate.

The 1950s are an understated and underwritten age in Anglo-Catholicism, and have now been overshadowed by the turmoil which followed Vatican II and the simultaneous intellectual doubts which affected all the churches in England. However, in the post-war period, up to about 1960, the Church of England was moving forward generally in numerical terms and the supply of ordinands was plentiful. Although the Liturgical Movement was beginning to be influential, there was still plenty of space for the flourishing of traditional Anglo-Catholicism, which required substantial attendances to provide the servers and choirs which were needed for proper performance of the liturgy. The choir at Wisbech St Mary in the 1950s often consisted of 20 people.

Father William (known as 'Bill') Woodhouse was born in Kettering in 1912 and like his predecessor lived to be a great age: he died at 90. His father was the Revd Francis Cyprian Woodhouse, vicar of Welford with Sulby, Northamptonshire, from 1914 to 1946, who sometimes came to assist his son and had the reputation of a 'hunting shooting fishing' parson.

Father Bill Woodhouse came to Wisbech St Mary in 1951 from Southery. He had been ordained just before the war and was then curate of All Souls, St Margaret-on-Thames, until he moved to Norfolk, but had combined that with being a chaplain to the RNVR, an organization with which he retained links.

Brian Payne, who lived in the village, was Father Woodhouse's godson, having been brought up in a Nonconformist household and then attracted to the more aggressive Anglo-Catholicism which began to emerge from the parish church, in which he was baptized.

Father Woodhouse had less to do with village politics and the facilities which were required for the parishioners, but of course by the post-war period local government was better organized and the National Health Service had been established, so basic needs were met. On the other hand, he was extremely keen on disciplined liturgical services and ensured that all those available were given particular functions and trained in them, perhaps an example of the application of naval ideals. A calendar was always displayed so that the forthcoming Holy Days were notified in advance.

In the 1950s the average attendance at the Sunday sung mass was about 60, and there were regular attendees from Wisbech town and other places outside the parish, drawn by the well-regulated liturgy. The villagers, who had been so devoted to Father Smith, although perhaps a little intimidated by his presence, took to Father Woodhouse, who was a strong personality who could lose his temper if the circumstances demanded it, and they had the novelty of a married priest with young children in the village to whom they could relate more easily. He continued to pay close attention to the church school.

There were a number of particular innovations during the Woodhouse years. He was close to the Society of St Francis in Plaistow and in about 1958 a mission was run in the village with the assistance of the SSF, one of the brothers of which surprised the parish by tearing about from house to house on a moped in his brown cassock. Another new feature was the centrality in the devotions of Corpus Christi Day, which was celebrated with considerable solemnity and involved an outdoor procession of the Blessed Sacrament around the church, at which other parishes were invited to attend. Father Bales and some of his small flock from Marshland St James were regular attendees at this event.

These activities did not alienate the vicar from his neighbours and in 1957 he became Rural Dean.

Father Woodhouse left in 1961 for Yate in Gloucestershire, then a relatively small village but which was transformed into a small new town, and then moved on in 1974 to North Cerney, near Cirencester but in the same county: he retired in 1982. His successor, Canon Hugh Barker, came from the very different surroundings of inner South London and stayed for 15 years (1961–76), continuing the same traditions: he too has been long lived, and at the time of writing is still alive at a great age.

After Canon Barker's departure, the tradition which had by then had 60 years behind it was, perhaps inevitably, diluted somewhat, not least because in the changing circumstances a village as small as this can no longer have its own priest, but very recently there has been a revival. The church, however, remains internally much as Canon Mowbray Smith left it.

The parish of Wisbech St Mary is now joined to that of St Mary Magdalene at Guyhirn.

Guyhirn had a mediaeval church, which was demolished at some point, and still has a small but interesting chapel, which was erected in 1660, at the end of the Puritan era and was connected thereafter with a local Anabaptist sect. It fell into disuse save as a mortuary chapel when, in the nineteenth-century extension of Anglican activities in the region, a substantial new church designed by George Gilbert Scott, whose brother was vicar of Wisbech, was erected and was consecrated in 1878, at which date the separate parish was formed: in addition a mission chapel was built at Rings End, and another at Thorney Toll, both within the parish. The new church is not like much of Scott's work, being Early English with a rose east window. The old chapel was declared redundant in 1973.

Guyhirn has generally had a moderate tradition, but that changed somewhat during the incumbency of the Revd Douglas Charles Freeman (1959–63), who in 1961 even received the imprimatur of Father Beresford, as he was invited that year to preach at Newborough on Corpus Christi. At some point statues of Our Lady of Walsingham and of St Mary Magdalene were installed. Father Freeman had first been curate of Christ Church, Isle of Dogs (the next parish to that of Father Reginald Kingdon) from 1955 to 1959, and later went on to be vicar of St Ives, Cornwall.

That change in the churchmanship was not maintained but, more radically, the building itself began to sink as have done so many others in the area. On 16 December 2004 it was declared redundant because it was unsafe and the contents were removed: it stands now waiting demolition. Ironically, one of the consequences of a recent increase in the population of the village with some new commuter houses being built has been that the old chapel has been reopened on an experimental basis for eight services a year.

The chapel at Murrow dedicated to Corpus Christi after its mediaeval forebear was of course constructed by the vicar of Wisbech St Mary, in which parish it then lay. However, there was a significant reorganiza-tion of the local parish boundaries which was effected by the Leverington Rectory Act 1870: this established new ecclesiastical parishes of Parson Drove and of Southea with Murrow and the latter took in the chapel, which thence became the responsibility of the vicar of that area.

Southea (pronounced as if it were 'Suthee') is an area to the west of the ancient settlement of Parson Drove and the need for a new church re-flected the fact that the population had moved to that point, only about a mile from the old church of St John the Baptist, which had been erected in the thirteenth to fifteenth centuries. In due course that church was made redundant (in 1974) and vested in the Redundant Churches Fund.

As part of the general expansion of the Church of England into the newly settled fen areas, a large new church of Emmanuel was erected at Southea in 1872. It was designed in the Early English style and has a substantial apse, a north aisle and a turret with bell. A large vicarage was constructed next to it.

Emmanuel Church is a prominent landmark on the long straight road west from Wisbech St Mary. It would appear that its churchman-ship was uneventful until the arrival of the Revd Walter Leslie Jonathan Dunkin (who used his second Christian name) in 1949. Father Dunkin was ordained during the war and had then been curate of Warsop, Nottinghamshire and then of St Giles, Cambridge, before migrating to the Fenlands.

There is an unusual window into church life in the early 1950s in this parish. Aelfrida Catherine Wetenhall Graham (née Tillyard) (1883–1959) was a novelist and also a writer on religious matters. She was born into a strongly Nonconformist family in Cambridge and married a diplomat, Constantine Graham, in 1907, by whom she had two daughters, Alethea, born 1908, and Agatha, born 1910. The marriage ended in divorce in 1921 and during the 1930s her thoughts turned towards mysticism and the religious life. After about 1925 she was strongly drawn towards Anglo-Catholicism, although she attended many different churches of various denominations.

In 1933 Aelfrida Tillyard's daughter Alethea joined the community of Benedictines at West Malling as a postulant. She later went to South Africa to work in a leper colony but never took life vows and eventually left the religious life. Her mother became an oblate of West Malling herself in 1934 and then lived for two years under rule at Oxford, during which time her other daughter Agatha committed suicide.

From 1936 to 1946 Aelfrida Tillyard lived at the Convent of the Sacred Cross at Tymawr, Monmouthshire, entering as an oblate but then being admitted as a tertiary in 1937. In 1939 she made life vows as a tertiary and was known as Sister Placida, under which name she published several books. Her desire was for increasing solitude and silence and she coupled this with use of a discipline and of a hair girdle. However, her stay there was marked by increasing ill health of many types and by personality clashes with the Mother of the community and eventually she was dismissed, although remaining a tertiary. She was an extremely difficult person with whom to live in close proximity.

In 1946 Aelfrida Tillyard moved to live at the Rectory at Lolworth, just north of Cambridge, to undertake parish work and the like under the direction of the rector, the Revd H.R.C. Lovell. Father Lovell and his wife were both themselves Franciscan tertiaries and their unusual pastoral assistant was able to continue with meditation and writing as well as helping in what was a very small rural village. Father Lovell was vicar of the parish from 1937 to 1957 and had moved there from his curacy at Woodhurst, a daughter church of St Ives, under Father Algy (1933–37). Although very much attuned to the religious side of life in Lolworth, Aelfrida Tillyard became exasperated by Father Lovell and looked for another place to live.

In July 1952 she moved from Lolworth to a similar position at Southea under Father Dunkin. She was, however, continuing to suffer from ill health and in July 1953, almost exactly one year after she moved to the fens, she left for St John's Home at Oxford, where she was allowed to follow a contemplative life so far as she was able: she recorded that her Guardian Angel had told her that she would not stay long in Parson Drove. She died in Oxford in 1959.

In the meantime Alethea had also been dismissed from the religious life and she then became the General Secretary of a support group entitled the Cowley, Wantage and All Saints Association, which obviously related to those communities: she shared a flat in London for a time with Professor Margaret Deanesley, a distinguished scholar and prominent Anglo-Catholic.

During the time she was at Southea, Aelfrida Tillyard continued to keep her manuscript diaries, as she had done for many years.[3] She lived in the very large vicarage with Father Dunkin, his wife and their four children, and another lodger. She was somewhat disappointed by the lack of ceremony, but the vicar explained to her that he thought he should progress slowly: certainly she records that the congregation at evensong was about twice that at mass. There was a daily mass, but on occasion the vicar overslept and she recorded in her diary her discontent with him. She also noted that the church was 'hideous inside' with 'bright red brick and pitch pine seats of the most uncomfortable kind' and the village was 'dreary'.

Father Dunkin left Southea in 1958 to become vicar of Downham Market, Norfolk, also in the Diocese of Ely, another church which had a Catholic tradition and has maintained it.

In due course Southea with Murrow absorbed the old parish of Parson Drove and then came to be held in plurality with Wisbech St Mary. The chapel at Murrow was closed and has now been converted to residential accommodation. Emmanuel Church at Southea is still in use and shares services once a month with the adjoining Methodists in their much smaller building.

There was one other nearby Fenland parish which shows, if nothing else, the variety of those who were permitted to minister to their flocks in out of the way places and paints a clear contrast to the respectability of Canon Smith and his successors.

Nordelph lies between Wisbech and Downham Market but is just in Norfolk. It has existed as a settlement only since the drainages of the seventeenth century and the name itself is Dutch. The parish church of Holy Trinity was built with the aid of a legacy from the Revd William G. Townley, rector of nearby Upwell, who died in 1862. The building was opened in 1865 and was designed by an architect named John Giles in an

---

3 They are held by Girton College, Cambridge: GBR/0271/GCPP.

early English style using red bricks and a small iron fleche at the junction of nave and chancel. The east window depicted the conversion of St Paul and the martyrdom of St Stephen, by Heaton, Butler and Bayne, and the reredos in front of it (later covered with curtains) had a marble wheel cross. It is therefore, although of reasonable size (110 feet by 22 feet), a church of remarkable simplicity.

Nordelph is on a main road, but the church is set back from that and is near a tributary of the River Nene. The area is subject to subsidence as there are soft clay and peat deposits beneath.

In 1909 the Revd Edwin Emmanuel Bradford was appointed to the living and he remained there until his death in 1944. Bradford was born in Torquay in 1860, the son of a jeweller. He went up to Exeter College, Oxford and took his BA in 1884. In the same year he was ordained deacon and the following year priest, and was successively curate of High Ongar in Essex (1884–86), Walthamstow (1886–87), at the Anglican church in St Petersburg (1887–89), and at St George, Paris (1890–97). He then came back to England, with further curacies at Eton (1899–1905) and Upwell (1905–09) before becoming vicar of Nordelph. Father Bradford was not as committed to hard-line Anglo-Catholicism as some of his neighbours in the area, and when visited by John Betjeman in 1935 he was described by him rather as a modernist who liked ritual, although both Walthamstow and St George, Paris were places where the Revival had taken strong root.

One of Bradford's close friends was the Revd Samuel Elsworth Cottam, who was born in Upper Broughton, Salford in 1863, the son of an accountant. He was at Exeter College with Bradford, and was also with him as a curate in Paris. He later became the parish priest of Wootton, Oxfordshire and appears to have been more overtly committed to Anglo-Catholicism in his later years than was Bradford, who moved somewhat away from his earlier beliefs.

Both Bradford and Cottam were members of a small loose group known as the Uranian poets,[4] who celebrated the love of the mature male for adolescent boys. The love was described as fleeting and often unobtainable. Bradford was the most prolific member of the group, pub-

---

4 See Timothy d'Arch Smith, *Love in Earnest* (Routledge & Kegan Paul, 1970).

lishing 12 volumes of verse, the first in 1908 shortly before he moved to Nordelph, and was also involved in a publication entitled *The Quorum: A Magazine of Friendship*, in 1920. Cottam published only one collection of poems, *Cameos of Boyhood,* in 1930, which is regarded as the last Uranian piece. It was said that Bradford was working on a poem about the love of a Modernist boy for an Anglo-Catholic boy, in which the former triumphed, thus reflecting his own change of stance.

Bradford's work is not all explicit although some of the poems are clearly erotically inspired. He was also nationalistic and an exponent of what he called 'the New Chivalry'. The chronicler of the group says: 'Bradford's poetry urges a return to the rural probity of England, a reversion from the feminine influences which have strangled civilisation for so long, and the cultivation of a healthy celibacy recognizing masculine beauty's pre-eminence.'[5]

One feature of the work of the group was that they were particularly interested in the sight of boys bathing. It was therefore predictable that Bradford had the village boys dig out a swimming pool next to the customarily substantial vicarage, and had them pile the soil removed to make it around in the form of small mountains, to recreate what he had seen on a visit to Switzerland. He then allowed his goats to graze around, and erected statues of lions around the pool: he was able to watch the young men swimming in it from his house, to his delight.

Betjeman described Bradford as a 'saintly and sweet little man', who was 75 years of age when he met him. He had also obtained a doctorate in Divinity, in 1912, soon after he arrived at Nordelph, for a thesis on St Paul and free will. Bradford told Betjeman that the laws governing sexual matters were outdated and should be abolished: he was in favour of birth control and thought masturbation should be permitted in public schools. Although Betjeman was ostensibly friendly to Bradford, and the latter no doubt appreciated the attention he received since there were few more lonely places than Nordelph in which to live, in fact the circle of friends in which the future Poet Laureate moved made fun of him and of Cottam behind their backs.[6] Betjeman always enjoyed eccentrics, particularly

---

5 Arch-Smith, *Love*, p. 124.
6 See B. Hillier, *Young Betjeman* (John Murray, 2003 edition), p. 177.

those who did not accept that they were out of step with most of the rest of the world. The villagers appear to have accepted Bradford's oddities and to have been rather fond of him: it was noted by Betjeman that there was a reasonable congregation and that he gave the children pennies for attending.

One of the features of life in the village was the constant problem of subsidence. Betjeman was somewhat surprised to be told by his host that the vicarage was propped up so he would be quite safe, particularly on the side where they were eating their dinner. However, there was a considerable irony in the fact that the *coup de grâce* was delivered to the building by the construction of the swimming pool, and eventually, at about the time of Bradford's death, it had to be demolished.

Bradford's immediate successor at Nordelph was the Revd John Harold Hardy, who arrived in Norfolk after 24 years in the very different surroundings of the Isle of Dogs, where he had been vicar of Christ Church, which had been bombed and rendered temporarily unusable. He was a committed Anglo-Catholic and had been a member of the Twenty One, but he stayed at Nordelph only about a year, possibly because of the difficulties with the vicarage. He then moved on to another rural parish in Lincolnshire.

The church itself lasted somewhat longer than the vicarage, although in 1996 the south porch was demolished after very large cracks appeared. By 1999 the whole building was displaying very considerable movement and the floor of the chancel was uneven, so it was closed as unsafe. It was declared redundant on 26 June 2002 and a scheme for its demolition was approved on 8 May 2003.

However, in early 2008 it still stands, now a dangerous eyesore with broken windows and loose masonry: it is said that the presence of large numbers of protected bats are holding up the demolition. In the meantime the villagers have to share accommodation with the Methodists.

9

St Mary, Buxted, Sussex, and Father Charles Roe

The attractive village of Buxted in Sussex lies on the railway line between London and Uckfield, which originally ran on to Brighton. It may be that it was the ease of access to the coast which attracted the Revd Arthur Douglas Wagner, the legendary church builder, to acquire a country retreat there. In due course he had built in the village the only one of the so-called Wagner churches which was not in Brighton itself. That church, St Mary, had from its institution a strong Anglo-Catholic tradition, which has been maintained. It has also become better known than many country churches because of its association with Walsingham.

In nearly every town there were a large number of new churches built during the Victorian era, and Brighton was no exception to that. The rising population and the spreading of built-up areas outside their ancient centres both required extensive new provision to be made. Brighton, however, was almost unique in that much of that expansion was controlled and financed by two generations of the Wagner family. The story is well known and need only be summarized here.[1] The Revd Henry Michell Wagner (1792–1870) was the vicar of Brighton from 1824 to 1870: his own maternal grandfather, the Revd Henry Michell had held that appointment from 1744 to 1789.

The parish church of Brighton was St Nicholas. In the fashionable Regency heyday of the town, a number of proprietary chapels had been

---

1 It is set out in considerable detail in, for example, A. Wagner and A. Dale, *The Wagners of Brighton* (Phillimore, 1983).

opened, but they were small and in any event were not welcoming to the mass of the population in the densely packed streets which were being thrown up. Henry Wagner began to remedy the situation, but he did not split the parish as occurred in most other places. Thus the new churches which were built during his lifetime were all dependent upon St Nicholas and were under the control of the vicar. The Revd H.M. Wagner was a pugnacious man of pronounced Tory views, but belonged to no particular ecclesiastical party.

The need to increase the church accommodation in the town had been recognized even before Henry Wagner was appointed as the vicar of Brighton and in the year of his arrival a competition was held in relation to the design of a chapel of ease. This was St Peter, Valley Gardens, which was built in 1824–28 and which in 1873 became the parish church.

Over the next years, Henry Wagner was instrumental in the construction of All Souls, Eastern Road (opened 1834 and now demolished), Christ Church, Montpelier Road (opened 1838 and also demolished), St John the Evangelist, Carlton Hill (opened in 1840 in a very poor area and now Greek Orthodox), and then, more controversially, St Paul, West Street (opened 1848). Even after that the pace continued, with All Saints, Compton Avenue (opened 1852, now demolished), and St Anne, Burlington Street (opened 1863). Henry Wagner provided some money towards the construction of all of these churches, but in no case did he provide the whole amount or anything near it. Other churches were also being put up during these years, including the ritualistic St Michael and All Angels, in the Montpelier area.

St Paul was a replacement of a chapel which was previously on the same site and was used by the fishermen who then lived in that area. In 1846 Henry Wagner purchased the site, demolished the chapel, and building commenced. He had always intended that the new church be the cure of his son Arthur Douglas Wagner, who had been born in 1824 and at this time was not even ordained.

Even at that time, the younger Wagner had taken up Tractarian ideas and he was able to influence his father in the construction of the new church. These ideas were reflected not only in the choice of architect for St

Paul, Richard Cromwell Carpenter, but in the construction and furnishing of the new building, which was one of the first anywhere in the country which reflected the new ideas. It was consecrated on 23 October 1849 and in 1850 Arthur Douglas Wagner was ordained and was appointed as perpetual curate of the church by his father. Unlike his father, Father Wagner was a retiring and diffident man who lived in some austerity, looked after by his cousin. He never married. He took little part in the secular affairs of the town but his ecclesiastical views were pronounced and well in advance of many of his contemporaries.

Over the next 20 years, St Paul became a fashionable and well-attended church, although there was considerable opposition to the ritual of the services, which would later have been regarded as very restrained. In 1855, when he was still only 30, Father Wagner founded the Community of the Blessed Virgin Mary (CBVM). Initially the purpose of the order was to assist in the St Paul's district, but in 1857 Father Wagner's cousin, the Revd George Wagner, who had been perpetual curate of St Stephen, Montpelier Place, died. He had been running a small home for the reclamation of penitents (that is prostitutes) in Lewes Road, and this was taken over by the sisters of the CBVM. The order adapted a number of houses in Queen Square and the adjoining Wyndham Terrace, Brighton, for their work, which was heavily subsidised by the founder.

The many opponents of these various developments seized on events in 1865 to launch a vicious attack on Father Wagner and his teaching, which led to a stormy and violent public meeting and even rioting. Father Wagner himself was assaulted in the street but later, with perhaps commendable but typical charity, assisted financially with the support of the dependants of those who were sent to prison in consequence.

The cause of this public disorder was that a girl called Constance Kent confessed to Father Wagner both under seal and out of the confessional that in 1860 she had murdered her half-brother at Rode, near Trowbridge in Wiltshire. No one had ever been convicted of the crime, which had become a cause célèbre: she had been charged at the time, but not committed for trial. It appears that her decision to unburden herself of what she had done came about as a result of her contact with the sisterhood: she had been a paying guest at the convent for about three years prior to her confession. She then gave herself up to the authorities: Wagner accompanied her to Bow Street police station for that purpose.[2]

There was no trial, because the defendant subsequently pleaded guilty to murder, but Father Wagner gave oral evidence at the committal proceedings about what had been said to him outside of the seal, and the publicity surrounding the case made overt and direct that confession was taught and practised in St Paul's Church and raised vehement protests, which were accentuated when it emerged that Miss Kent had wished to present the then substantial sum of £1000 to Father Wagner for the benefit of the sisterhood and the charitable work of his church. He had, however, refused to accept the gift.

In due course the immediate storm reduced and the Bishop of Chichester refused to accept Father Wagner's proffered resignation. Miss Kent was sentenced to death, but this was almost immediately commuted to life imprisonment, because of her youth at the time of the murder and her guilty plea.

Even before the death of Henry Michell Wagner in 1870, upon which his son inherited a very large amount of money, Father A.D. Wagner had himself begun to finance the building of new churches in the town. In 1862 a small church was constructed very near the by now rather grand St Paul: this was St Mary and St Mary Magdalene, Bread Street, which is now demolished. In 1864 he financed the building of the small but attractive Church of the Annunciation, Washington Street, in a poor and hilly area of Brighton, which from the very start had a strong Anglo-Catholic ethos, and this remains even today.

After receiving his inheritance in 1870, Father Wagner began to spend colossal, as opposed to very large, sums on new churches. The other substantial development at that time was that in 1873 the parishes in Brighton were revised and in particular the ancient parish was subdivided, so that the position of power which Henry Wagner had enjoyed was not to be held by his successor, the Revd John Hannah. Father Arthur Wagner became vicar of St Paul, a position he held until his death in 1902,

---

2 The story has recently been retold in Kate Summerscale, *The Suspicions of Mr Whicher* (Bloomsbury Publishing, 2008), which has been properly praised for its insights but is somewhat shaky on Anglo-Catholicism.

although for the last few years of his life he was mentally incapable of carrying out his duties. For that church he engaged a number of curates whose views were then regarded as extreme, particularly the Revd R.W. Enraght, who was later incarcerated for failing to comply with the Public Worship Regulation Act 1874.

Two very substantial new churches were built in the years immediately following the death of the Revd H.M. Wagner. The first was the startling St Bartholomew, Ann Street, near the railway station, which towered over the small terraced houses around. In 1868 Father Wagner had had built a school and a temporary church in the area, but he now decided to have constructed a grand edifice, for which he instructed Edmund Scott, a local architect: Carpenter had died in 1855, shortly after St Paul had been opened. Work began in 1871 and the immense building, 135 feet high to the ridge of the roof, arose. It cost Father Wagner some £18,000. It was the subject of substantial controversy and criticism, but it soon became a popular church and there were no pew rents, a subject upon which the vicar of St Paul had very firm views. The next church was St Martin, Lewes Road, which was constructed by Father Wagner and his two younger half-brothers as a memorial to their father, who had himself set aside £3000 to build a new church in a deprived area which was also used for this: most of the cost was, however, born by Arthur Douglas Wagner. The very large church was built between 1872 and 1875 and was designed by Somers Clarke, the son of the clerk to the Brighton Vestry, who had been a great friend of the deceased. The cost of this building was about £12,000.

The final church built in Brighton by Father Wagner was The Transfiguration (later The Resurrection) in Russell Street, which was intended for the use of the fishermen, who had never been attracted by the increasingly fashionable St Paul. Unlike St Bartholomew, it was constructed partly underground, which increased the cost to another £12,000. It was completed in 1877, but was never a success, was closed as early as 1911, and after many years as a meat store was demolished in 1966.

Father Wagner's activities in Buxted can only be understood against the background of what had occurred in Brighton. In 1873 Wagner acquired an early nineteenth-century property in the village named Totease House, which he used as a retreat, particularly in the summer months and when he was subject to too much controversy in the town. At that time the village was growing fast, not least because of the existence of the railway and also its picturesque location, and the only religious provision was in the mediaeval church of St Margaret, which was in the grounds of Buxted Park, well outside the burgeoning settlement. He therefore determined in due course to have built a church for the village at his own expense.

When Father Wagner was not himself at Totease House, he allowed the sisters of his community to use it as a place of respite, rather as he did so himself. In 1878, however, he had premises constructed especially for their use in what is now Church Road, and named them St Margaret's Cottage. In 1883 he left Totease House and had built for himself a new house called St Mary's, which was adjacent to St Margaret's Cottage, and which had a private chapel which he and the sisters shared. Father Wagner was a great devotee of Marian festivals well before this was common in the Church of England, and the chapel was opened on the Feast of the Assumption. It was thereafter also made available to other visitors and to locals.

It was to Buxted that Constance Kent was taken when, in 1885, she was finally released, after serving a much longer period than did most who were subject to life imprisonment at that time. Father Wagner took her himself from prison in London to Sussex, where she was cared for by the sisters. She then emigrated to Australia, qualified as a nurse, and died in 1944 aged 100.

There were already sisters in Buxted even before Father Wagner moved in his order. The Society of St Margaret at East Grinstead, not far away, had been founded in 1855 and had rapidly set up a number of branches, including St Saviour's Orchard, in what is now Gordon Road, Buxted, which was used as a rest home for church workers and was always a small establishment: it was in fact a dependant of the Priory of St Saviour in Haggerston, which was itself a daughter of the mother house.

It was a further connection with matters in Brighton that the building of the new church in Buxted, which was to be dedicated to St Mary the Virgin, should be entrusted to Edmund Evan Scott and his partner Frank Thomas Cawthorn. Scott's architecture is little known, apart from St Bartholomew, and was mostly carried out in and around Sussex. He had carried out work to remodel the early Wagner church of All Souls, Eastern

Road, and also St James, St James' Place, which is not a Wagner church but is well known in Anglo-Catholic history because of the judgement on the liturgical practices of its priest, the Revd John Purchas. Scott also built St Botolph, Worthing, St Andrew, Portslade, and St Saviour, Ditchling Road, Brighton, and in 1881 extended Wagner's Church of the Annunciation, Washington Street, with side aisles. In 1892 Cawthorn added a tower and vestry to that church. The partnership also carried out work locally to Christ Church, Eastbourne, and SS. Cosmas and Damian, Keymer.

In Buxted, a site was acquired near to the centre of the village and to Wagner's houses, and on 15 October 1884 there was a procession to and then a service on the designated area, in which the rector of St Margaret, Buxted, the Revd J.P. Gell, actively participated. The foundation stone was laid on 27 January 1885 and on 12 March 1885 a schoolroom, also provided by Wagner, was opened which was intended to serve as a temporary church until the new building was completed. On that day Father Wagner celebrated himself at a 7 a.m. mass and an hour later there was a further celebration by the Revd Edmund Francis Mackreth, who had been designated the first priest in charge of the new church.

The work of construction proceeded with expedition, and the new building was used for the first time on Thursday 10 June 1886 and was consecrated by the Bishop of Chichester on 11 June 1887. The poster for the opening indicates that the Sunday services initially were an early communion at 8 a.m., morning prayer, litany and sermon at 10.30 and evening prayer and sermon at 6.30 p.m., so the practices were not originally as forward as in Brighton.

The architects did not attempt to reproduce in the country the grandeur which had been displayed by St Bartholomew in its urban setting. Rather St Mary was an attempt to reproduce, using modern materials, a mediaeval Sussex church in a simple form of Perpendicular Gothic. It was built well back from the road and into a hillside, with a parish hall on one side and the vicarage on the other. The walls were faced with flints, which gives them a distinctive appearance: they are not naturally found in Buxted but were frequently used in churches on the South Downs. At the west end of the south chapel there is a tower and spire and inside a barrel vaulted roof runs right through with no distinction between chancel and nave. The east wall was plain, with no window or decoration, and behind it was an area which was left free for a further expansion of the church.

Father Wagner had some very strong ideas. He was never concerned about orientation and the Brighton churches were almost without exception set in an unorthodox manner. At Buxted he clearly wanted a church in which the altar was elevated and visible to the entire congregation. However, within that conventional framework he insisted upon two particular features of the new building, to demonstrate links with the Old and New Testaments respectively.

The Old Testament was reflected in the dimensions of the sanctuary. The specifications of the ark, which are set out in Exodus 25.10 were adapted for the sanctuary. The biblical information is that the ark was two and a half cubits long, one and a half cubits wide and one and a half cubits high, or on the assumption that a cubit was two feet, five feet by three feet by three feet. Those numbers were then multiplied by seven, a number with particular resonance to the Jews, to make 35 feet by 21 feet by 21 feet: however, because the church was never built out to the full extent planned, the sanctuary in fact is a 21-foot cube. The number seven was further utilized in the provision of seven lights in the west window and of seven lancet windows in the north wall. Further, the length of the nave and chancel together was 63, or seven times nine, feet.

The New Testament was reflected in an interesting way, in that the south aisle was enclosed by a screen to reflect the supposed dimensions of the Holy House at Nazareth, 25 feet 6 inches by 13 feet 2 inches, which had also been used in the mediaeval shrine of Our Lady of Walsingham. Father Wagner was well ahead of any other priest in the Church of England in this train of thought, although it is not apparent that he particularly promoted the cult of Our Lady of Walsingham.

When initially built, the church was not lavishly furnished: the decoration and embellishment appeared later. The first priest was Father Mackreth (1856–1907), who came from a curacy at The Annunciation, Brighton. He married when he was at Buxted and stayed only five years, moving to become parish priest of the first Wagner church, All Souls, Brighton, where he seems also to have taken in pupils. His successor was an older man, the Revd John Baghot de la Bere, whose father was also ordained and who came from Prestbury, Gloucestershire, his birthplace, where he was vicar. He was a married man with a number of children.

When Father Wagner died, on 14 January 1902, there were requiems in all his churches and he was buried at Lewes Road Cemetery, where the service was taken by Father Baghot de la Bere.

It has been reckoned that Father Wagner spent something like £70,000 in the building of churches alone: in addition to that he maintained the sisters' home almost entirely and spent considerable sums on providing, at his own expense, curates for the various churches. He also bought, and let out at cheap rents, several hundred houses for working-class tenants in Brighton.

Father Baghot de la Bere left Buxted in 1908 and was replaced by the Revd Charles Herbert Griffith, who had served a number of curacies, including at St Stephen, Lewisham (1888–92) and St John, Clevedon (1892–1900), a church which as we have already seen provided two priests for Little Petherick. He came to Buxted from Holy Trinity, Hastings, and left to be vicar of St Michael, Folkestone (1916–28), after which he retired to St Leonard's-on-Sea. His stay in Buxted was only from 1908 to 1916, but he was replaced by the Revd C.E. Roe, a priest of considerable talent who transformed the interior of the church.

It was during Father Griffith's incumbency that the sisters of the Community of the Blessed Virgin Mary left Buxted. Their mother house in the centre of Brighton was cramped and inconvenient, and they decided to move most of their work out of the town. There were also financial difficulties after the death of Father Wagner turned off what had been a steady stream of income to support the community. In 1912 a substantial new convent, designed by Cawthorn, was opened in Rottingdean, within convenient reach of Brighton, but then somewhat isolated. A small number of sisters was initially left in Queen Square in order to carry on parochial work, but the Buxted house was no longer needed. The community remained at their new home for many years, but eventually, as elsewhere, numbers (which in any event never exceeded 30) declined and the order is now defunct. The Rottingdean convent has been converted to residential accommodation.

St Mary's (Wagner's own Buxted house) was passed to the Community of St Mary the Virgin, which was founded at Wantage in 1848 and used it as a home, initially for training for domestic service as had the CBVM, and then for women and girls who, as we would say now, had learning disabilities. It was one of the smaller houses of what was one of the largest orders for women in the Church of England. St Margaret's Cottage became a secular private school.

Charles Edward Roe (1862–1940) is perhaps one of the forgotten men of the later Anglo-Catholic Movement, known if at all because he is commemorated by a brass at Walsingham. He had an unusual background and considerable artistic gifts, which are reflected in what he did at Buxted and indeed elsewhere.

Charles Roe was born in Cambridge and as a child lived at 14 King's Parade, opposite King's College. His father, Robert Roe, had been born in about 1792 in Needham Market, Suffolk, and was still fathering children when well past his seventieth birthday: he had had one family and been widowed before marrying Charles's mother Maria. He was a print-seller and engraver, who provided material for the Cambridge University Press and is mentioned in the history of that establishment. He died in 1880 and the business of print-selling and gilding was continued by his widow. In 1881 Charles Roe appears have been working with her in that enterprise and is described in the census return as an artist, as was his older brother Robert Gordon Roe, who was born in 1860: a younger brother is said to have been an art student.

Over the next decade, however, the course of Father Roe's future was set. In the late 1880s he went to St Edmund Hall, Oxford, as a mature student. This was an unusual course as there were at that time very few undergraduates who were not of the conventional age: the hall was not then a full College of the University. It is also interesting, with his Cambridge connections, that he avoided that city for his further education.

In 1890 he married Alice Mary Cookson in Ipswich: she was herself the daughter of an Anglican priest working in Suffolk. By the following year the newly married couple were themselves living in Ipswich, with the widowed Mrs Maria Roe and her sister. Father and Mrs Roe had no children.

Father Charles Roe was ordained deacon in 1892 and priest the following year in the Diocese of Winchester. His older brother, who was known as Gordon, was also ordained, in his case in 1886.

Charles Roe's first appointment was as curate of All Saints, Portsea (1892–95), following which he moved within the Wagner purview by becoming curate of St Mary and St Mary Magdalene, Brighton. However, after only two years he and his wife moved to Essex, where he became the chaplain to the House of Mercy (that is, home for the reclamation of prostitutes and those who had given birth to illegitimate children) at Great Maplestead, well out in the country. That establishment appears to have been set up about 1870, when it was built by Henry Woodyer, but was taken over in 1881 by one of the lesser-known women's orders, the Community of the Name of Jesus, which was founded at that time. In 1891 those sisters moved to South Wales and the home was then taken over by the very much larger Community of St John the Baptist, whose headquarters was at Clewer, Berkshire.[3] It was also somewhat unconventional for a married priest to take on the chaplaincy of a convent.

In 1902, after only five years in Essex, Father Roe left and returned to Brighton. After Father Wagner's death he was replaced as vicar of St Paul by the Revd J.E. Halliwell, and Father Roe went to be his curate. He stayed there until 1916. It is clear that Father Roe's artistic talent was notable. It is certainly unusual for a priest to exhibit at the Royal Academy, as he did in both 1913, with a painting of Ballachulish, Loch Leven, and in 1916 when he showed two further paintings of Scotland, both of Glencoe, one from Loch Lomond. In addition, he assisted in the beautification of the interior of the church of St Paul in a number of respects. He painted a picture of St Paul for the north aisle altar and a further picture of Our Lady for the south aisle. He is also said to have toned down the colours in the Pugin window of the crucifixion, behind the lady altar. The church had always had a screen, but in due course a rood was added and the screen was reconstructed: Father Roe assisted with this work and collaborated in its artistic presentation.

It was while he was at St Paul that Father Roe first encountered Alfred Hope Patten, then a somewhat neurotic and highly strung youth with an almost obsessive interest in the minutiae of worship. Although Hope

---

3 The Community of the Name of Jesus came to an end at about the outbreak of the Second World War, although the last sister did not die until 1959. The House of Mercy in Maplestead was largely demolished in about 1960.

Patten generally worshipped at St Michael, he undoubtedly frequented
the other incense-laden shrines of Brighton, and, for example, regularly
attended weekday benediction at the Church of the Annunciation. His
confessor was originally the Revd F.F. Smallpiece of St Bartholomew, but
later he turned to Father Roe, and the two remained on close terms thereafter: after Hope Patten's ordination in 1914, his former confessor certainly visited and stayed with him during his own second curacy, at St
Alban, Teddington (1915–18).

In 1917 Father Roe moved to be vicar of Buxted. From 1919 to 1920
Hope Patten served a short curacy at Buxted under him, moving on to
Carshalton in Surrey. It was Father Roe who rediscovered, or perhaps
reappreciated, the connection between the chapel at Buxted and the
former Holy House at Walsingham, and it is impossible to believe that
Hope Patten did not himself understand that association and research the
history of the mediaeval shrine while he was in Sussex: his later pretence
that he had scarcely heard of Walsingham before being offered the living there in 1921 was a characteristic half-truth. It is interesting that in
his book *Some Brighton Churches,* published in 1922,[4] the Revd Herbert
Hamilton Maughan, an author of extreme and often unintentionally
amusing partisanship, mentions specifically in his chapter on Buxted the
fact that the dimensions of the chapel were exactly the same as that at
Walsingham. The book was published in the same year that the devotion
was re-established in Norfolk. It is indeed sometimes said that the Revd
Gordon Roe, who was by this time Rural Dean of Walsingham, contacted
his brother in Buxted and by that route Father Hope Patten was suggested
as a possible parish priest for that village, but there is at least one other
plausible explanation for the introduction.[5]

The interior of Buxted church has changed in various ways very ma-
terially over the last 100 years. There can be little doubt that Father Roe
vitalized the parish and moved it in a distinctive direction which equated
with the path then being followed by other advanced Anglo-Catholics

---

4 H. Hamilton Maughan, *Some Brighton Churches* (Faith Press, 1922).

5 That is that his name was put forward to the outgoing vicar of Walsingham, the
Revd E.L. Reeves, by Hope Patten's former vicar at Holy Cross, Cromer Street, the Revd
F.E. Baverstock.

and that this was reflected in the décor. Later incumbents have removed much of what he did.

Extant pictures of the high altar prior to Father Roe's arrival show that it had a wooden reredos behind with a depiction of Our Lord. Hamilton Maughan is typically dismissive of the earlier work and contrastingly enthusiastic about that which had then just been done:

> The altar piece has recently been greatly improved and beautified. It was formerly painted white and had at the top a singularly inartistic white plaque bearing some kind of gilt explosion in the centre, while the picture beneath it was anything but a work of art. Small panels at the side contained the familiar reproductions of Fra Angelico's angels. The Revd C.E. Roe removed the plaque with its gilt firework and added a canopy with hangings, made by Watts to Bodley's design. The additional height thus given to the altar-piece has added greatly to its dignity. The angels and the cresting which now crown the altarpiece were carved and gilded by the vicar himself; the framework was relieved of its white paint, and stained. The Fra Angelico angels were retained. The worse than mediocre picture was removed, and its place taken by the really exquisite copy of Murillo's *Immaculate Conception,* one of the treasures of the Prado in Madrid, painted by the Revd C.E. Roe. From an artist vicar, whose pictures have often attracted no little attention and admiration, no doubt a good deal was expected; but the new picture which he has given to the altar piece of St Mary's has far exceeded all the expectations ... and its execution cannot be described as anything less than masterly.[6]

Father Roe also attached hangings to each side of the altar: the total effect was not exactly Back to Baroque, despite the copy of the Murillo, which was indeed very well carried out, but was a considerable move in that direction.

The sanctuary had at that time mural paintings of Saints Wilfrid, Richard, Augustine and Gregory, the first two of whom had Sussex associations: these ante-dated Father Roe's arrival. There were other wall

---

6 Hamilton Maughan, *Some Brighton Churches,* p. 88.

paintings elsewhere in the church. On the south sanctuary wall was hung a Spanish painting of St Francis of Assisi in a Florentine frame with a silver votive heart, which had previously been hung in St Paul, Brighton, but had fallen from its mounting there and been damaged. Father Wagner then presented it to St Mary together with a reproduction of the 'St Luke' Madonna, which hangs in Santa Maria Maggiore in Rome: he gave a copy of this to all the churches he had built. Father Wagner had given to St Paul an Italian painting of Our Lady of Sorrows, which was then passed on to St Mary by Father Halliwell and hung on the wall near the lectern. Father Halliwell also gave the church a copy of a Spanish painting of Christ being scourged. Finally, a nephew of Father Roe donated a Flemish picture on copper of a nun with rosary before Our Lady.

Father Roe also designed and painted the figure for the hanging rood, which was carved in Brighton. Glass by C.E. Kempe, who lived relatively near, in Lindfield, was introduced to the north wall of the nave and to the Walsingham chapel, in about 1921. Above the altar in the chapel was inserted a two-light scene of the Annunciation, and then in the south wall is a Nativity window in memory of Father Mackreth, a window of St Elizabeth and St John the Baptist, in memory of Father Baghot de la Bere's wife, and a Good Shepherd window in memory of her husband. In the nave was inserted a St Agnes window in memory of a parishioner with that forename and a window of St John the Evangelist, again in memory of the Baghot de la Beres. Stations of the Cross were hung, which are said to have come from a church in Brighton where they were no longer required.[7]

As well as these additions to the interior, a large rood under a penthouse was erected as a war memorial under the west window, and thus visible to passers by. This was installed in 1921 and was made by the Art and Book Company in Westminster. An American visitor then asked to donate a processional cross to one of the Wagner churches and St Mary was chosen for the gift.

It was not only the furnishings of the church which were altered at this time. Father Roe's incumbency lasted until his retirement in 1935,

---

7 Possibly Wagner's Church of the Resurrection.

during which time Buxted became a centre for Anglo-Catholic worship, which, as in other places, drew well-off devotees to the village both for residence and to stay for the summer. The statue of Our Lady was decorated with lace drapes and lights burned before it. The Angelus was said in the Walsingham chapel at noon each day and the pious ladies who had been attracted to the village attended. On Corpus Christi Day, Father Roe had erected a temporary outside altar against the east wall of the church, in the area which had been left free for possible extension, and a procession was held to it, followed by mass or benediction. Surviving photographs show that the girls from St Mary's Home were arrayed in white veils for the celebrations and the outside altar was banked with flowers.

In 1932 a meeting was held to consider future devotion to Our Lady of Walsingham at Buxted in the light of what was by then taking place in Norfolk, where the new shrine church had recently been opened. The outcome of this was that an image in the form used for the Walsingham devotion was carved at Oberammergau and erected in the south chapel. It was dedicated on 18 December 1932 and thereafter the rosary was said in the shrine at 6 p.m., as it was at Walsingham. It was also agreed that there should be an annual pilgrimage or 'Visit of Honour' to the church and these began, albeit on a relatively small scale. It is recorded that in 1934 there were over 100 at the devotion. Much of the organization was borne by three village spinster ladies, Miss Freda Treherne, who was later commemorated by a plinth for a statue of the Sacred Heart, and the Mesdemoiselles Hastings, who later moved to Walsingham: one of them wrote a pamphlet on Buxted church, entitled 'Nazareth in Sussex', which was published in 1934.

Father Roe retired in 1935 but continued to live in the village, in a house named 'Cortina' which he had had built. He died on 4 August 1940 and his association with Father Hope Patten and the latter's debt to him is reflected in the fact that a memorial brass was set in the floor of the shrine church at Walsingham (which by then had been extended), depicting him in mass vestments. Were it not for that, he would be an entirely forgotten figure, but in fact he had a striking artistic background and training and brought those considerable gifts to bear both in Brighton and in Buxted and he deserves to be better known.

His brother, Father Gordon Roe, was married in 1884 and had a substantial family. His career was spent mainly in East Anglia, and he too used his artistic gifts in the decoration of various churches. While vicar of St Margaret, Leiston, Suffolk, from 1909 to 1915 he designed for the church a rood beam, a side chapel, and new choir stalls. In 1927 he designed a reredos for the stately church of St Peter, Kirkley, Lowestoft, based on the mediaeval precedent of Ranworth in Norfolk, although he never served that particular church.[8]

Father Charles Roe's successor at Buxted was the Revd George Helier Duhamel Lovell, who stayed until 1946. He came from a curacy at St Saviour in nearby Eastbourne, but had previously been chaplain to two conventual establishments. During his incumbency, however, the sisters vacated St Saviour's Orchard and left for Haggerston, ironically after a bomb fell near to Buxted in 1940: the blitz was of course to be much worse in the East End. Their property is now known as Random Cottage.

The next vicar was the Revd Cyril Charles Barclay, a sometime Bush Brother who came immediately from Helmsley, Yorkshire, and who was in the village only until 1950.

It would appear that during those two incumbencies the furnishings remained in the same condition as under Father Roe, although the devotions were somewhat less exotic in tone and the pilgrimages became sporadic and occasional.

In 1951, after a short interregnum, Canon Robert Mortimer Gibbons arrived and stayed for 20 years. He had served as a missionary in the Diocese of Zanzibar and was then principal of St Andrew's Training College there (1926–51), before returning to this country. He determined shortly after his arrival that the interior of the church should be modernized in accordance with the new liturgical fashions which were just beginning to emerge. He took the view that the screen around the Walsingham chapel encouraged exclusivity, whereas the tradition of the organizations connected to Father Wagner had always been that all were welcome. He thus removed it in 1952 and placed it in the church hall where, fortunately, it did not deteriorate: he left the oak panelling on the two outside walls of

---

8 See R. Tricker, *Anglicans on High* (published by the author, 1988).

the chapel. He also had cleared out the choir stalls, significantly increasing the spaciousness of the sanctuary in what is a relatively small church.

The most important development, however, was that in 1956 Canon Gibbons dismantled the reredos as constructed by Father Roe only about 35 years previously, and had the wall paintings obliterated by white paint. In place of the reredos he erected a tall dossal curtain with tester above, against which was hung a large altar crucifix which the vicar had brought back from Zanzibar. An undeniably positive step taken at that time was the silvering of the six brass candlesticks, which had always stood on the altar and which had been criticized in 1922 by Father Hamilton Maughan as 'of a conventional and undistinguished design': he then had expressed the view that they 'will, no doubt, eventually be replaced by ornaments less suggestive of the warehouses of the purveyors of "ecclesiastical furniture"'.[9] Although the changes reduced the rather typical clutter of the chancel, the atmosphere of the church was significantly altered and it would be very difficult to say that what was done represented an improvement. There were also minor building works done to extend the vestry, which required alterations to one of the north wall windows.

The sisters of CSMV did not leave when the Haggerston community went and remained for many years: eventually contracting numbers meant that the work in Buxted was handed over to a secular organization, the Gilthalion Trust, but the sisters retained the gardener's cottage, known as Maryland, as a retreat house until finally ceasing their connection with the village in 1982. They donated to the church a processional cross which they had used and also a statue of Our Lady carved by one of the sisters.

Canon Gibbons remained until 1971, following which there were a number of short incumbencies. The first was that of the Revd Lewis William Rye Hollowood, who was in Buxted only from 1972 to 1974: during that time, however, he saw to the reinstallation of the Walsingham chapel screen, which for about 20 years had been stored in the church hall. Its historical interest and associations were such that it was entirely appropriate that it be restored to its previous place, and it has remained there ever since. Father Hollowood had a background in the Scottish Episcopal

---

9 Hamilton Maughan, *Some Brighton Churches*, p. 89.

Church. In 1967 he had been appointed to St Mark, Hadlow Down, which had been commended some years earlier by the usually unimpressed Father Hamilton Maughan as being one where 'the worship of the Church is . . . rendered with beauty and dignity'.[10] It was built in 1836 and enlarged and renovated by G.H. Fellowes Prynne in 1908: Hadlow Down is the next settlement out of Buxted on the road from Uckfield. From 1972 he took on Buxted as well, but in 1974 he moved to St Barnabas, Bexhill, where the parish priest for many years had been a well-known priest, the Revd H. Box.

After another short incumbency, that of Canon Henry Kilworth Maybury[11] (1975–79), who also held the living with the parish of Hadlow Down, Father Peter Sanderson, who was last mentioned in these pages in Chapter 2, when he was at Poundstock, Cornwall, arrived at Buxted and Hadlow Down. He left Poundstock in 1974 and then spent five years at St Patrick, Hove, and was at Buxted from 1979 to 1983, after which he retired.

Father Sanderson was a strong supporter of the Walsingham devotion and during his time in Buxted he revived the observances which had been instituted by Father Roe. In October 1982 a very well attended pilgrimage organized by the local Anglo-Catholic Societies took place, and others have followed thereafter. Father Sanderson was the last vicar of St Mary, Buxted: after he left the benefice was united to those of St Margaret the Queen, Buxted (the original parish church) and St Mark, Hadlow Down.

The tradition established by Fathers Wagner and Roe has been continued for over 120 years, an unusually long period of time for a country church. Today the church is internally far more bare than it was during Father Roe's time, but at least the screen around the chapel has been reinstated. It is interesting that while the church has obviously coloured the religious experiences of the village over the last century and more, its most active period was when it was being supported and patronized by the spinsters of the area, the 'rich ritualistic aunts' beloved of John

---

10 Hamilton Maughan, *Some Brighton Churches*, p. 92.

11 Father Kilworth Maybury had served much of his ministry (1948–74) in the United States and was a canon of the traditionally Anglo-Catholic Cathedral in Milwaukee.

Betjeman. That contrasts rather with the vision which Father Wagner had of his churches being open to all, and to the original conception, followed through to a degree, particularly in the early years, that St Mary, Buxted should appeal to the travelling and other lower classes.

Father Hamilton Maughan, who wrote the book on Brighton churches, was a parody of an Anglo-Catholic priest, never charitable about any of the institutions of the Church of England. He was born in Kent in 1884, the son of a priest. There were very few periods of his life in which he held appointments, although he had been curate of St Michael, Brighton (1910–12), and after a short period as Assistant Chaplain to Ellesmere School (1914–16) his only post was the somewhat incongruous one of London Home Diocesan Missioner for North Hillingdon (1930–31). In the post-Second World War period he ran the Coelian Press from an address in Hove: this produced biting literature lamenting any departure from Roman standards in the Anglican Communion, many pamphlets and books being written by him, including a life of Father Wagner (1950). In 1947 he left England to live in Loughlinstown, County Dublin, an unlikely destination bearing in mind he thus allied himself to the strongly anti-Ritualistic Church of Ireland, while living in a country in which the majority of the population adhered to the Roman Church. He established a chapel in the village for which he solicited donations in order to decorate it as if it were a product of the Counter-Reformation style which was, as he accepted, alien to the staunchly anti-ritualistic Church of Ireland. The chapel was in due course dedicated to St Gregory and in 1958 he celebrated there his sacerdotal jubilee. His last years were spent in writing letters to the Papalist newsletters complaining that birettas and lace cottas were going out of fashion.

The Coronation of Our Lady, Kettlebaston, Suffolk, and Father Harold Butler

Suffolk is not usually considered as a powerhouse of Anglo-Catholicism. However, there are and have been for many years some churches, both in the only major town, Ipswich, and in the countryside, which have been deeply influenced by the Oxford Movement and its further ramifications.

Perhaps the best known such country churches are St Mary, Mendlesham, and the Assumption of our Lady, Ufford. The former has had a Catholic tradition for many years, which has been strongly carried forward in the last 35 through the efforts of the Revd Philip Gray: the latter again had many years of devotion, particularly during the long incumbency of the Revd Herbert Drake (1919–48). For a short time in 1897 Father Drake, then known as Father Anselm OSB, had been the chaplain to Aelred Carlyle's community when it was at Lower Guiting, Gloucestershire, many years before the move to Caldey Island, but he then reverted to the secular clergy.

Another well-regarded church was All Saints, in the village of Hundon, near Clare. The mediaeval church was burned out in 1914 and rebuilt by the Arts and Crafts architect Detmar Blow. The interior was whitened in the same fashion as occurred at Conrad Noel's church at Thaxted in Essex, and the Revd A.F. Waskett exercised a notable ministry there from 1919 until he was forced to retire in 1981 after a fall, by which time he was 91. St Mary at Capel, near Ipswich, was restored and embellished by the

Revd A.C. Johnson during his long incumbency from 1878 to 1920. He was the father of Father Vernon of the Society of the Divine Compassion, a powerful preacher who went over to Rome in 1927 and later became Monsignor Vernon Johnson. At St Peter and St Paul in the small town of Eye, the interior of the majestic church was comprehensively refurnished by Comper in 1927, during the incumbency of the Revd J.R. Vincent. He was succeeded in 1934 by the Revd (later Canon) Donald Rea, who stayed for 32 years. Father Rea was one of the surprisingly large number of priests who came from a background in the stoutly Protestant Church of Ireland but who embraced Anglo-Catholicism. He was much concerned with the various societies which promoted reunion with Rome, and was presented by Pope John XXIII with his personal breviary when on pilgrimage in 1958. Despite these views, he was eventually regarded as being respectable enough to be offered a canonry of the cathedral of Bury St Edmunds.

A little-known centre of Anglo-Catholicism in Suffolk is the church of the Holy Trinity at Barsham, near Beccles, which retains a thatched roof. This was associated with the Suckling family, and the Revd Robert A.J. Suckling (vicar 1868–80 and a godson of John Keble) went on from this tiny settlement to be parish priest successively of St Peter, London Docks (1880–82) and of St Alban, Holborn (1882–1916), as well as being for a time Master of the Society of the Holy Cross. Following the design by Bodley for the new reredos for St Alban, in 1896, Father Suckling had brought to Barsham the original marble cross designed for that church by Butterfield, and it was re-erected here as a memorial to the 'Ritualist martyr' Father Mackonochie. The church at Barsham was at that time under the care of the Revd Allan Coates, whose incumbency ran from 1889 to 1921 and who was able to use his own artistic knowledge and flair and the generosity of Father Suckling to enhance the interior with both English and Continental furnishings, even refurnishing after lightening had struck the high altar in 1906.

However, the most remarkable country church in the county in terms of the influence of Anglo-Catholicism is undoubtedly that of the Coronation of Our Lady at Kettlebaston.

Kettlebaston (properly pronounced 'Kettlebarston') is a minute village, now hardly more than a hamlet, on side roads near to Lavenham. It was

recorded in the Domesday Book and in the Middle Ages was made prosperous, as were other villages around, by the wool trade. When that trade
disappeared it was left in a somewhat neglected state and as the numbers
employed in agriculture declined, the population shrank gradually away.
In the mid nineteenth century there were about 200 in the village, but by
1960 that had diminished to about 50, with many houses falling down
and abandoned. There was no mains electricity or water and the road
was little more than a track. From that low point, however, the village has
recovered, with old houses being renovated and new families moving in.

The church at Kettlebaston is mediaeval, but many of the furnishings
have been introduced during the last century, particularly during the incumbency of its best-known rector, the Revd Harold Clear Butler, from
1929 to 1964. However, the total effect is one of congruity: the combination of the various elements makes it a model for the restoration of village
churches.

There was undoubtedly a church on the present site in the Norman era,
and there is a Norman window of about AD 1000 in the north nave wall,
and a rather later Transitional south nave doorway of about 1200: the font
is of similar age. Much of what we now see was, however, comprehensively reconstructed in the fourteenth century, probably in about 1363,
a date referred to in a contemporary document. The tower was added
at that time and the chancel was completely rebuilt: it is disproportion-
ately long by comparison with the nave. In the fifteenth century several
Perpendicular-style windows were inserted and a staircase constructed to
lead to a rood loft above a new screen. That screen and many of the other
internal fittings were destroyed either after the reformation or following
the English Civil War. In the eighteenth century, rather unusually, a brick
south porch was erected and in the early nineteenth century a vestry was
added on the north side of the chancel.

A description of the interior was given in 1826 by David Elisha Davy,
who visited the church at that time. There was then a simple altar table,
dating from the seventeenth century, and above it, on either side of the
east window, were boards with the Lord's Prayer, Ten Commandments,
and Creed. The Royal Arms hung at the west end. The pulpit was in front
of the entrance to the rood loft stairs and had also been installed in the

seventeenth century as had the altar rails. There were deal pews in the nave. The tower was too dangerous to ascend: at that time it had been topped by a slender spirelet covered in lead, but when that was done is not clear.

Although Kettlebaston was something of a backwater in the nineteenth century, the long incumbency of the Revd John Robert Fiske (1839–91),[1] who succeeded his father Thomas Fiske (1805–39), did see some renovation. Unlike many other places, at Kettlebaston that renovation was incremental rather than comprehensive.

In 1864 work was done to the chancel, during which there were found the fragments of four exquisite alabaster panels, made during the late fourteenth or early fifteenth centuries and depicting the Annunciation, the Ascension, the Holy Trinity and the Coronation of Our Lady, the dedication of the church. They are probably the best of their type in the whole country. In 1883 they were presented to the British Museum by the rector of the neighbouring living of Bildeston, to whom J.R. Fiske had given them.

In 1879 there were repairs to the nave and it appears that the stonework of the windows was also renewed.

After the long incumbencies of the Fiskes, father and son, the Revd George Lloyd Jones came to the village, but after a very short time he died at the age of only 37.

It was in 1895 that the direction of ecclesiastical life in the village changed radically. In that year the Revd William Sellon arrived as the new rector.

William Storer Sellon was born in 1848 in Kentchurch, Herefordshire. His father, the Revd William Edward Sellon (1818–85), was the rector of that village and his mother, Margaret, née Storer, gave her son his second forename. Perhaps more importantly, his paternal aunt was Priscilla Lydia Sellon (1821–76), the founder of the Society of the Most Holy Trinity in Devonport in 1848 and a figure of heroic importance in the growth and development of Anglican religious communities in the nineteenth century. One of her brother's children received the same forenames as

---

1 J.R. Fiske married a woman over 40 years younger than himself and rapidly fathered two children by her.

her aunt: Priscilla Lydia Sellon the younger was born in 1851 and died in 1910.

Father W.S. Sellon was a convinced adherent of Anglo-Catholicism, as may perhaps be expected in the light of his family connections. He was ordained deacon in 1874, priest in 1875 and trained at Chichester Theological College, which had been founded as early as 1839. He served curacies at Forton, Hampshire (1874–76), then at the then new and 'advanced' church of St Michael and All Angels, Swanmore, Ryde, on the Isle of Wight (1876–77), and Kingsland, in his home county of Herefordshire (1877–78). He then became chaplain of St Saviour's Infirmary, Southwark (1881–83), and then moved back to Herefordshire to be vicar of Newton in Clodock (1885–87) and then of Llanfaino (1888–94), both of which he combined with being curate of Crasswall. Apart from his spell in London he therefore had a great deal of recent experience of rural ministry.

In 1889 Father Sellon married Margaret Turner, who although born in Staffordshire had lived most of her life in Herefordshire. She was the granddaughter of an Anglican priest. The couple had no children.

Almost the first step taken by the new rector of Kettlebaston was the commission by him of an architectural survey of the church to see which repairs were necessary. The consultant instructed to prepare the report was the Revd Ernest Geldart, then the rector of Little Braxted, near Witham in Essex. Father Geldart was himself a committed Anglo-Catholic as well as a talented designer and he had redecorated his own little church in accordance with his own book *The Art of Garnishing Churches*. He is best known for designing the enormous reredos at St Cuthbert, Philbeach Gardens, the church which so thrilled Father Frank Kingdon when he attended its opening in 1883. However, he also superintended the renovation of many churches and designed a completely rebuilt church at Rawreth, near Rayleigh in Essex.

In his hand-written report dated 16 November 1895, Father Geldart gave his preliminary views on the building. He reported that most of the walls were satisfactory but some underpinning was needed and some work was needed to some of the buttresses. He recommended the demolition of both the porch and the vestry and the complete renewal of the chancel roof and all the floors and steps throughout the church. He proposed that all that work be done, and a new vestry formed behind the altar. He also, interestingly, noted that the only fittings in the church at that time were a small altar table, a small prayer desk, the font and a few chairs. He suggested that a new screen be erected in the position where the original had stood and that there be a new reredos of oak with carved figure panels and a wooden font cover. The total cost of all the work, including the new additions, would be £1295.

Much of the work was not carried out immediately and some, such as the demolition of the porch and vestry, was never done. However, in 1902–03 Father Geldart did restore the chancel roof, although he left in place seventeenth-century cornices along the top of the walls, and he designed and installed both an elaborate carved reredos and a rood screen with three traceried openings on each side. Initially, neither the reredos nor the screen were coloured. At the same time, the altar rails were replaced and the originals were put in the nearby church at Rattlesden. At about the same time, Father Geldart also designed a rood screen for the nearby church of Preston St Mary, but that was never installed.

The alterations and additions to the fabric which Father Sellon commissioned were accompanied by significant changes to the liturgical practices in the church. He was a member of the Society of the Holy Cross and of the English Church Union, and a Priest Associate of the Confraternity of the Blessed Sacrament. The *Ritualistic Clergy List* of 1903, produced by those who were strongly opposed to such developments, reported that even at that early date he was wearing vestments, adopting the eastward position for mass, and using incense. It is not surprising that developments at Kettlebaston attracted the attention of Protestant protesters, particularly Nonconformists, who in fact had no interest at all in what occurred in a church on which they had turned their collective backs.

The main protagonist to Father Sellon was one Theodore Becket, the Baptist minister at Bildeston. He encouraged those villagers in Kettlebaston who were dissatisfied with the services provided by the new rector to attend his own chapel. In 1899 one of those who had defected to the chapel but who lived in Kettlebaston died, and Becket told the rector that he would himself carry out the burial service in the graveyard of the parish church – an echo of the better-known Akenham burial case, also in Suffolk, which had taken place in 1878. Father Sellon forbade any of his congregation to attend the interment but invited them to come to the 8 a.m. communion on the relevant day, 4 October 1899: he did nothing to prevent Becket from carrying out the burial. Becket, however, attended the service and was said to have behaved in an 'unseemly' way. Worse was, however, to follow because just as the congregation of about 15 were making their communion at the altar a small explosion was heard and a man ran from the church.

It transpired that he had lit the contents of a small bottle containing asafoetida, an Indian gum-like spice, which gave out a cloud which smelled extremely unpleasant and choked some of those present, just as incense was alleged to do. The man was later identified as one William Wakefield, a baker, who admitted when charged in the Hadleigh Magistrates' Court with indecent behaviour in church that he used a drain disinfector[2] to set off the asafoetida: he said he intended to merge its smell with that of the incense. Wakefield was convicted and fined £5, but Becket was acquitted of a similar charge on the grounds that the Bench was not convinced that he knew of the plan to let off the stink bomb in advance, although the Chairman said he was 'if not legally, to a great extent morally responsible for the unjustifiable and reprehensible act of Mr Wakefield'.[3]

The following year, 1900, Becket returned with the Revd R.C. Fillingham, an ultra-Protestant Anglican who was vicar of Hexton in Hertfordshire. He had preached at Becket's Baptist chapel in August 1899, in itself an unusual state of affairs in those pre-ecumenical days, and had incited the congregation to accompany him on a future occasion to disrupt the service at Kettlebaston. Father Sellon was forewarned on the day in question in January 1900 and the police were in attendance. Fillingham was escorted from the vestry by the churchwardens after attempting to serve a document of protest on the rector, but then interrupted the consecration by shouting 'Idolatry! Protestants leave this house of Baal!' before

2 In the first Sherlock Holmes short story, *A Scandal in Bohemia*, written before these events, Conan Doyle has Holmes procure for Dr Watson an 'ordinary plumber's smoke rocket', which he then throws into the house of the adventuress Irene Adler to cause a diversion. It would appear that this was a similar device.

3 See *The Times*, 28 October 1899.

leading out his followers and conducting an open-air service in the road. Unusually, he was prosecuted and convicted in Hadleigh Magistrates' Court: his defence, that there was no indecent behaviour because his protest was of a dignified nature, found no favour with the Bench although he was fined only £1.[4]

Mr Fillingham appealed to the Quarter Sessions at Bury St Edmunds but his appeal was dismissed with costs.[5] He was then brought before his Chancellor under the Clergy Discipline Act 1892 on the grounds that he had been convicted of a civil offence, and wrote a letter to *The Times* justifying his behaviour, with another letter from a supporter who said that all the vicar of Hexton had been doing was protesting against 'the adoration of bread in the Church of England'.[6] The Chancellor of the Diocese of St Albans upheld the complaint but remitted the matter to the Bishop to consider penalties.[7]

After those disturbances, protests died down and Father Sellon continued with his project to improve the furnishings. He left in 1911, having established the basis of a completely new way of worshipping in the church and retired to Carbis Bay, Cornwall, where he died in 1919. He is, however, buried at Kettlebaston and other members of his family, including his aunt, are also commemorated in the graveyard there.

Between 1911 and the arrival of Father Butler in 1929, there were four rectors, two of whom stayed for only very short periods. The first of these was the Revd Edward James Scarlett, who succeeded Father Sellon, but left the following year because of ill-health and almost immediately died. He was born in Manchester in 1847, the year before his predecessor, and married his first cousin Leonora in 1873, by whom he had a large family. He was ordained deacon in 1872 and priest the following year, and had been a curate at a number of well-known churches such as St Alban, Bordesley, Birmingham and lastly St Peter, Streatham, from 1904 onwards.

Father Scarlett's successor at Kettlebaston was the Revd James Frederick Todd, who was there from 1912 to 1921. He was born in Liskeard, Cornwall,

---

4 See *The Times,* 30 March 1900.
5 See *The Times,* 10 November 1900.
6 See *The Times,* 1 January 1901.
7 See *The Times,* 20 February 1901.

in 1853 and as with so many of the Anglo-Catholic clergy of the period was himself the son of a priest, although his father, the vicar of Liskeard whose name he shared, died when he was young. He was ordained in the Scottish Episcopal Church as deacon in 1881 and as priest the following year and served curacies at prominent Anglo-Catholic parishes: his first was in St Margaret, Aberdeen, the church founded by Comper's father, and later he was at St Chad, Haggerston and St Anne, Hoxton, both in the East End, and also acted as Assistant Chaplain to the sisters of St Mary in Shoreditch, before marrying in 1894 and moving to the country, although his final appointment before he went to Suffolk was at Dairycoates, Hull. Kettlebaston was his last parish and he retired from there. Under his care, it appears that services continued as before but that there were no great innovations to the fabric of the church and indeed by the end of his ministry the nave roof was near to collapse. At some point around this time the spirelet was taken down.

The next parish priest had considerably more impact than the preceding two, although his stay was quite short. The Revd Reginald Harry Nottage arrived in 1922 to find that he had no accommodation available to him, and he initially had to live and sleep in the vestry of the church: a temporary wooden bungalow was soon built for his occupation. He also found that the roof of the nave required immediate attention, and that services could only be held in the chancel. He raised money to pay for that and the church was reopened in September 1922 with a high mass celebrated by the Revd Claude T.G. Powell, parish priest of St Bartholomew, Ipswich from 1916 to 1946 and a well-loved man among all in the area. Prior to moving to Ipswich he had been for 12 years rector of St Bartholomew in the tiny hamlet of Shipmeadow, near Beccles, a rather similar place to Kettlebaston: in later years he was, like Father Deakin, one of the select few clerical Guardians of the Shrine of Our Lady of Walsingham who were married. The preacher was the Revd (later Canon) Dudley Symon, headmaster of Woodbridge School from 1921 to 1947, who strongly influenced the religious thinking of that establishment and who is also said, rather surprisingly, to have been a Socialist. He certainly employed as an assistant at the school the Revd George Chambers, one of Conrad Noel's followers and former curates, who was also a former member of the Caldey community and later became parish priest of Carbrooke, Norfolk.

In 1924 Father Nottage recorded on a grant application (which resulted in repair works to the east wall) that there were 82 adults in the parish, of whom 57 were Anglicans and the balance were Dissenters. Despite those small numbers, he attracted congregations of up to 70 on a Sunday, because people were drawn to his presentation of the Faith and to his easy social style. He had been born in Bermondsey in 1891, so was still young: his parents had taught at a church school in that area. He opened up the rectory for gatherings on Sunday evenings, where there were refreshments and other activities, rather as Hope Patten was doing at the same time in Walsingham. This was not then a usual way in which a country priest behaved, but it was very welcome to the congregation.

Father Nottage left in 1926 to move to Chevington, not far away. He decided to transfer for an unusual reason. He felt strongly attracted to a girl who used to play the organ at Kettlebaston, Florence Maud Foulsham, known as 'Peggy', but she had been born only in September 1909 and was thus very young, so he understandably thought it might lead to a possible scandal if he stayed. However, in 1928, when she was still only 19, he married her.

At Chevington he replaced the Revd A. Keble White, whose family had held the living, but who had died. It was during Keble White's ministry that the screen across the church was put in, which was later moved to St Matthew, Littleport.[8] His widow transferred the advowson to the Guild of All Souls and that body appointed Father Nottage: shortly afterwards, she went over to Rome.

The new priest immediately introduced more overt indicia of Anglo-Catholicism, such as the use of incense and of the term 'mass': these led to protests by Wickcliffe Preachers and others, similar to those at Kettlebaston 30 years earlier. However, they subsided and in 1930 he wrote a book, *The Village Eucharist*, based on his experience of working in Kettlebaston and in Chevington. In 1932 he moved to the very different surroundings of All Souls, Clapton in East London, and then to St

---

8 See Chapter 6.

Mary, Corringham in Essex. His last ministry was at the Geldart church at Rawreth.

Father Nottage's replacement was the curiously named Revd Richard de Bailleul Coussmaker, who stayed only for two years. He was born in 1887 in Staffordshire, yet again being the son of a priest, and was himself ordained deacon in 1910, priest in 1911. He had served a curacy at the well-known church of Our Most Holy Redeemer, Clerkenwell from 1912 to 1915 and again from 1920 to 1925, and after his short time in Suffolk he went on to other parishes in Staffordshire, becoming rector of St Chad, Lichfield, in 1933.

In 1929 Father Butler arrived to begin his long service in the area. Harold Clear Butler was born on 5 December 1888 in Ireland and attended Trinity College, Dublin, taking his BA in 1909 but his MA not until 1925: he was yet another Anglo-Catholic to come from that background. He was ordained in 1912 as a deacon and two years later as a priest and served two curacies at the backstreet church of St Agnes, in the St Paul's area of Bristol (1912–16 and again from 1919 to 1920), interrupted by a period in Falmouth, Cornwall (1916–18). He then moved to London, serving a curacy at the well-known church of St Michael and All Angels, Walthamstow, which has nurtured the careers of many Anglo-Catholic curates over the years. His final spell as a curate was at St John, Clerkenwell from 1923 to 1929: Kettlebaston was the first and only parish of which he was the incumbent. His last curacy, in the crowded urban setting of Clerkenwell, can hardly have been more different from the remote fastness of deepest rural Suffolk.[9]

It is absolutely clear that Father Butler, certainly by the time he moved to Suffolk, was a committed Anglican Papalist. His views were, in that regard, very similar to those of Father Clive Beresford. He believed that by providing his small flock with services on the Roman model and by imposing Roman standards of discipline in religious life, he would take another small step towards the reunion of the Anglican and Roman

---

9 The church in Clerkenwell served also as the chaplaincy of the Order of St John of Jerusalem, which we have already met in connection with both Isabel Gurney and Maurice Child, and the vicar served also as Chaplain to the Order. It was bombed in the Second World War and an ambitious rebuilding plan by Comper was not followed.

churches. Such a consequence could of course come about only if there were sufficient parishes where the same stance was adopted, and where the local population supported that position. In fact, there were over the country relatively few such churches and in many of those the parish priest did not carry the residents of the locale with him: the situation was rather different in London and other large urban centres where a congregation could be drawn from across a large area.

Father Butler was one of the signatories to the Papalist 1933 Oxford Movement Centenary Manifesto, which was organized by Father Fynes-Clinton and others who were concerned by what they saw as the betrayal of the original ideals of the Tractarians by creeping liberal thinking and by a lack of emphasis on organic unity with Rome. While it is not correct to say that every Papalist incumbent signed the manifesto, it is certainly true that all those who signed would have counted themselves as Papalists.

Father Butler said mass in Latin with the main service on Sunday being at 11 a.m., followed at 3 p.m. by vespers and benediction, and he held all the usual devotions throughout the year. At Kettlebaston the Feast of the Assumption of Our Lady was kept with particular solemnity: vespers and benediction was followed by a garden party. Evensong was too Cranmerian for his taste. Mariolatrous hymns were printed in a leaflet especially for the church.

A characteristic of some Anglican Papalists, which has already been mentioned in relation to Father Watson of St Alban, Fulham, was the refusal to keep registers of services. To Father Butler they were an unnecessary imposition and he was reinforced by the attitude of his own last vicar, the Revd T.C. Elsdon, of Clerkenwell, who also refused to keep such books. Father Butler said they were probably invented by those nineteenth-century High Churchmen who wanted to record all the new services which they were introducing. His attitude towards the rest of the Church of England could also be described as somewhat ambivalent. He disliked the fact that it was established, believing that its religious freedom was thereby compromised and refused to pin up in the porch any 'state' notices.

One of the better-known stories about him, which is confirmed by examination of the surviving documentary evidence, is that the only entry in his register is for 2 October 1933, when he wrote: 'Visitation of Archdeacon of Sudbury. Abortive. Archdeacon, finding no churchwarden present, rode off on his high horse.' As the years went by, the diocesan authorities simply ignored him and allowed Kettlebaston to go its own way: the congregation diminished over time as churchgoing in general did and as the population of the village declined. One elderly lady recalled him call out in Latin 'Tace, tace' to the children to make them keep quiet: of course they did not understand what he meant.

One of the features of Kettlebaston in the twentieth century was the presence of two small religious communities, no doubt attracted by the services at the church. The facts are not entirely clear, as they often are not in the case of less well established communities which have since died out, and the memory is kept alive today only by the pleasant guesthouse named The Old Convent, where the sisters once lived.

The first group to live in the village was the Sisterhood of the Holy Childhood, founded about 1881 and one of the many such communities which were extant at that time. There was another entirely separate community with a similar name which was founded in Oxford in 1895 to provide teachers for church schools, but the sisters in Kettlebaston had their headquarters at 19 Clapton Common, in East London, and their mission was to needy children. The Suffolk branch seems to have been established about 1912 and the sisters there looked after about 12 boys. It appears, although the dates are hazy, that the community ceased its presence in Suffolk in about 1930, or in other words at about the time Father Butler arrived, although the order itself may have continued in London until the outbreak of the Second World War.

The second group were rather more exotic. In 1913, when nearly all of the Caldey brothers seceded to Rome, there was a simultaneous move by the Benedictine sisters of St Bride's Abbey, Milford Haven. The loyal few brothers went on to Pershore and then Nashdom, but the two sisters who did not go over joined another community. However, some years before, another two sisters had left the community at about the time that Abbess Scholastica Ewart arrived at its then house at West Malling, Kent, to revitalize it in 1907.

These two, with others, lived an itinerant lifestyle for some years, calling themselves the Community of St Mary and St Scholastica. From 1913 to 1915 they were themselves at West Malling, after the main group of sisters had moved on to Milford Haven. By the post-First World War period the idea of a Benedictine sisterhood in the Church of England was no longer fanciful, and a new community at West Malling, which had no connection with either of those other two groups, was growing, and has persisted.

However, the few sisters of St Mary and St Scholastica continued in their independence and led a somewhat shadowy life on the edge of the Church of England. For a time they lived in Platt, also in Kent, and then in Plaxtol, in the same county, before moving to Kettlebaston in the early 1930s to take over the convent left vacant after the departure of the sisters of the Holy Childhood.

It appears that they were under the leadership at one time of Archbishop Bernard Mary Williams, a successor to Archbishop Arnold Harris Mathew in the tangled web of churches ministered to by *episcopi vagantes* at that time. In the late 1930s the *Anglo-Catholic Annual* lists the sisters as being at Kettlebaston, and names as their warden the Revd W. Noel Lambert, then rector of St Mary, Norwood, Hayes, who combined his living in the Church of England with an irregular episcopacy conferred on him by Mathew. These are deep waters and it is not clear how much Father Butler knew about these matters, or whether he was content simply to have a few more bodies in his church. It seems that this tiny group did not survive beyond about 1939.

One of Father Butler's very positive qualities was his artistic appreciation and, allied to it, practical ability. Over the years of his incumbency he gradually added to the beauty of the church without ever cluttering it in the way that some churches are. He also managed to improve the furnishings so that a non-expert would not appreciate that so many of them were modern.

The combination of the way in which the church was furnished and decorated with the exoticism of the services made Kettlebaston church a draw to others who were in the area or, as it was often described, a shrine.

The development of Father Butler's scheme for the improvement of the church is best described chronologically. It was done over a long period, with some of the most significant features being added after the Second

World War, at a time when the addition of colour and beauty to the interior of churches was deeply unfashionable: almost as unfashionable, perhaps, as the rector's adherence to his view of the priesthood.

The work was as follows:

1929   A new font lid was made and at the same time the lead lining of the bowl was pierced to allow the water to drain to the earth beneath.

1930   An original Norman window was discovered in the north wall of the nave, with wall paintings around it.

1930   A rood group was added above the screen.

1930   Father Butler purchased a tabernacle for the high altar.

1931   A sacristy area was formed behind the high altar and six baroque candlesticks and a crucifix were added on the altar.

1932   A statue of Sacred Heart was introduced.

1933   The chiming mechanism for the bells was replaced.

1934   Copies of the alabasters were presented to the church by the British Museum and placed in the nave.

1934   The floor beneath the former choirstalls was repaved.

1935   The Jacobean high altar was given a new base.

1936   Father Butler himself removed the brown paint which had previously covered the altar table. He also at some stage removed the paint from the main door, and from the sedilia.

1936   One of the many daughters of Father Claude Powell of Ipswich gave the statue of Our Lady with canopy. The votive lamp for the shrine came from Father Butler's previous church of St John, Clerkenwell. The lady chapel altar itself is of nineteenth century origin and came from another church.

1939   A wooden canopy for the Sacred Heart statue was given in memory of Featonby Jobson Smith by his daughter.

1939–40   Father Butler himself restored and repainted the seventeenth-century Jermyn monument in the chancel.

1941   A votive lamp of Indian silver was given for the Sacred Heart altar in memory of Peter Featonby Smith, who had been killed in action.

1946   A consecration cross on the north wall of the chancel was repainted.

1947   In a niche in the south-east buttress of the chancel wall was placed a carving by W.J. Drew of Ipswich. He extrapolated from the existing alabaster fragment of the Coronation of Our Lady to produce a replication of what the total original may have looked like. The sculpture was coloured by the distinguished Walsingham artist Enid Chadwick and small iron gates with a Marian monogram were made by H. Willmington of Thorngumland in the East Riding to cover the niche. This was in memory of the rector's older brother, the Revd H.C.D. Butler, parish priest of Holy Trinity, Kirton in Nottinghamshire, an area much influenced by the patronage of the Duke of Newcastle, and near to the Shrine of Our Lady of Egmanton. He had died in 1946.

1948   The lower entrance to the former rood staircase was fitted with an iron gate designed by Comper and again made by Willmington.

1948   Patrick Osborne of Maidstone coloured the reredos after restoration of the figures and pinnacles. It depicts the Annunciation, with on one side St Peter and St Edmund and on the other St Ethedreda and St Paul.

1949   Osborne coloured the Geldart screen in appropriate hues.

1950   A new high altar of York stone, to Father Butler's own design, was made by Saunders of Ipswich in memory of Eleanor Featonby Smith of nearby Preston St Mary, who had worshipped in the church for some years and who died in 1949. It was financed by her sister.

1953   The holy water stoup was renewed with Clipsham stone.

1954   Enid Chadwick added to the lower part of the screen vigorous depictions of six saints associated with England, two of whom, St Felix and St Fursey, have particular East Anglian connections. The depictions of St Alban and of St Thomas Beckett are conventional, but it is unusual in the Church of England to see St Thomas More and St John Fisher, although not unknown, as we have seen at St Peter, Ely.

1956   An inset altar stone for the high altar was consecrated by Bishop Gerald Vernon, Bishop in (not 'of') Madagascar and a Guardian of the Walsingham shrine.

In 1958 Father Butler was instrumental in the purchase of the former school, which had been closed as early as 1904, and an adjoining house, so that the school building could become the church hall and the house could be let out. This was to have important consequences for him later. One innovation which, however, he did not introduce to the church was electric light: its continued lack adds to the atmosphere of the interior.

Father Butler's ministry continued in the post-war period and, as shown by the catalogue of developments above, he was not complacent. However, the decay of the village and the decline in the population reduced the congregation. The Anglo-Catholic presentation of Christianity requires a more substantial attendance of the committed than do some other forms of worship, because of the need for servers and the like. In early 1963 Father Butler had a disabling attack of shingles and later that year he confronted the truth, writing in a letter that 'there is no congregation any more'.

However, the end of his long ministry in the village was marred by sensational developments which made national news and added an unpleasant postscript to his years at Kettlebaston.

The cottage attached to the former school was let to a self-employed printer in his mid 30s named Desmond Ernest Stanley Jeffery, who had a Spanish wife about ten years younger, named Libertad. When the rector had had his problem with shingles, Mrs Jeffery assisted him on two occasions at his request by applying a powder to the affected areas. It was alleged by Mr Jeffery that on the second occasion an act of indelicacy or indecency occurred, although Father Butler strongly denied it. Mr Jeffrey was indignant about this and was alleged to have said to another villager that he would like to 'shoot the old bastard'.

On 30 June 1963 Father Butler was stooping over his table when he felt something sharp on the right side of his head. He found he was bleeding and telephoned the doctor who observed a bullet hole in the window. When he was taken to the hospital it was found that a bullet had entered his head just above the right eyebrow and had then travelled through the head to the left side of the neck.

Desmond Jeffrey appeared at a special sitting of the Sudbury magistrates on the following day charged with unlawful and malicious wounding with intent to commit grievous bodily harm, contrary to s18 of the Offences against the Person Act, 1861. It was said that he had admitted he acted unlawfully but denied any malicious intention. He was remanded in custody.[10]

The defendant appeared further before the Hadleigh Magistrates on 2 August 1963 charged not only with malicious wounding with intent but also with attempted murder and was committed for trial in custody to Norwich Assizes. The prosecutor alleged that he had been out for a walk with his wife and had been carrying a 0.22 rifle which he used for shooting rabbits. He was also said to have drunk a bottle of rum and to have been ambivalent about whether the gun had gone off deliberately, on one occasion saying, 'I should have put the bullet between his eyes.'

On 7 October 1963 a jury at Norwich acquitted the defendant of both charges, which tends to suggest that they were sympathetic to his allegations against Father Butler, which others who knew him thought were far-fetched.[11] They must have had doubts about the assertion that the rifle was fired deliberately, although the chances of an accidental shot hitting the rector, a man he disliked, were very slight indeed.

The following year, 1964, the rector retired. Thereafter he lived an itinerant life in various hotels in the South of England. He died in Kent on 21 August 1969 and, perhaps appropriately, vespers of the dead were sung for him at St Barnabas, Tunbridge Wells, on 27 August 1969 at 7 p.m., followed the next morning at 11.30 a.m. by the requiem.

It was inevitable bearing in mind the number of people in the village that after Father Butler's death the church would not have its own priest. However, there was considerable concern among those who knew and loved the church that it would not be maintained and that all Father Butler's artistic endeavours would come to naught. Philip Gray was particularly concerned about the position and tried valiantly to interest a

---

10 See *The Times*, 1 July 1963.
11 See *The Times*, 7 October 1963.

number of people and organizations to set up a community or the like in the village and to run the church. Father Beresford thought it too remote: there were flickerings of interest, including one from a short-lived body called the Community of St Augustine of Canterbury, based in Petts Wood, Kent, but these came to nothing.

In the meantime the church had become neglected and dirty inside. It was then immediately cared for by the Revd A.C.W. Phillips, rector of Preston St Mary and Thorpe Morieux, who brought it back into the Anglican mainstream. From 1971 to 1991 it was under the rector of Hitcham, Canon Edward Wetherall, who ensured that it was internally maintained, although the circumstances dictated that services there could not be held every Sunday. The idiosyncrasies of the Butler regime ended, although the interior was left much as he had completed it and the name of Kettlebaston was known to some and kept alive by visits and occasional pilgrimages.

In more recent years there has been a renaissance of church life in the village in a number of ways. The increasing population after years of decline has made a considerable difference, and the parish is now held with Monks Eleigh and others and the parish priest, the Revd Dr Brian Findlay, has not only ensured that Kettlebaston is cared for but has restored much of its tradition, including reinstating the tabernacle on the high altar.

The Butler years offer a similar picture on perhaps a more restricted scale to the regimes of Father Drew at Throwleigh and Father Beresford at Newborough. In each case a tradition which was built up was entirely apart from the mainstream of the Church of England, and after economic factors meant that the era of one priest per parish came to an end, it was inevitable that dilution should take place. However, it is also fair to say that in none of those three cases was there anything like universal local approval for the religion which was practised in the parish church. Anglo-Catholicism per se did not attract support in the country: it required both explanation and a charismatic priest such as Father Gambier Lowe or Father Nottage to make it successful.

Index of Names and Subjects

Carshalton Tracts 176
Carstairs, Andalusia G. 56
Carter, Revd G. 95
Catford, St Laurence 17
Catholic League 48, 146, 163, 171, 175–7, 179–80, 184
Catholic Priests, Federation of 46
Catholic Reunion, Society for 150
Cavendish, St Mary 54
Caversham, Queen Anne's School 195
Cawthorn, F.T. 210, 213
Chadwick, Enid 141–2, 239
Chambers, Revd G. 232
Chambers, Revd S.C. 146–7
Chandler, Rt Revd A.C. 22, 165
Charlottetown, Cathedral 47
Chase, Revd C.R. 64
Chase, Rt Revd F.H. 188
Chesterblade, Somerset 91
Chevington, All Saints 145, 233
Child, E.C. 104, 106
Child, Gladys M. 104
Child, Mrs M. (née Fielder) 105
Child, Mrs M.M. (née Pain) 105–6, 118
Child, Revd A. 105
Child, Revd E. 105
Child, Revd M. 64, 75, 87–91, 100, 104–132, 234
Child, Revd T. 105
Christchurch, Cambs 134
Christian, E. 163
Church Unity Octave Committee 76
Clapton, All Souls 233

Clarabut, Revd E.A. 80
Clarabut, Revd E.B. 80
Clark, Revd C. 129, 132
Clarke, S. 209
Clerkenwell, Holy Redeemer 22, 234
Clerkenwell, St John 234, 238
Clevedon, All Saints 94
Clevedon, St John 62, 68, 213
Clifden, Lord 77
Clifton, All Saints 132
Clifton, St Paul 188
Coates, Revd A. 225
Cobbold, Revd G.A. 61
Coelian Press 223
Coldham, St Etheldreda 148
Comper, J.S. 152, 153
Comper, Sir J.N. 10, 43, 53, 55, 58, 63, 66, 71, 74, 79, 94, 137, 139, 148–9, 151–3, 191, 225, 232, 234, 239
Compton Beauchamp, St Swithun 93–103, 124–5
Conan Doyle, Dr A. 230
Corbould, Revd W.R. 172
Corringham, St Mary 233
Cottam, Revd S.E. 202–3
Coulson, Revd L. 29
Coussmaker, Revd R. de B. 234
Coveney, St Peter ad Vincula 53, 58, 150
Coward, Noel 134
Cranford, Holy Angels 128–131
Cranford, St Dunstan 100, 121–132
Cranham, Glos 58
Craven, Countess of 96